Power
in
Language

LANGUAGE AND LANGUAGE BEHAVIORS SERIES

Howard Giles

SERIES EDITOR

Department of Communication
University of California, Santa Barbara

This series is unique in its sociopsychological orientation to "language and language behaviors" and their communicative and miscommunicative consequences. Books in the series not only examine how biological, cognitive, emotional, and societal forces shape the use of language, but the ways in which language behaviors can create and continually revise understandings of our bodily states, the situations in which we find ourselves, and our identities within the social groups and events around us. Methodologically and ideologically eclectic, the edited and authored volumes are written to be accessible for advanced students in the social, linguistic, and communication sciences as well as to serve as valuable resources for seasoned researchers in these fields.

Volumes in this series

Volumes previously published by Multilingual Matters in the series Monographs in the Social Psychology of Language and in the series Intercommunication may be obtained through Multilingual at 8A Hill Road, Clevedon, Avon BS21 7 HH, England.

Power
in
Language

Verbal Communication
and Social Influence

SIK HUNG NG
JAMES J. BRADAC

LANGUAGE
AND
LANGUAGE
BEHAVIORS
volume 3

SAGE Publications
International Educational and Professional Publisher
Newbury Park   London   New Delhi

FTW
AEF 2015

For information address:

SAGE Publications, Inc.
2455 Teller Road
Newbury Park, California 91320

SAGE Publications Ltd.
6 Bonhill Street
London EC2A 4PU
United Kingdom

SAGE Publications India Pvt. Ltd.
M-32 Market
Greater Kailash I
New Delhi 110 048 India

Printed in the United States of America

Library of Congress Cataloging-in-Publication Data

Ng, Sik Hung.
   Power in language : verbal communication and social influence /
Sik Huk Ng, James J. Bradac.
      p. cm—(Language and language behaviors series; vol. 3)
   Includes bibliographical references and index.
   ISBN 0-8039-4422-5 (cl)—ISBN 0-8039-4423-2
   1. Oral communication. 2. Power (Social sciences) I. Bradac,
James J. II. Title. III. Series: Language and language behaviors ;
v. 3.
P95.N5 1993
302.2'242—dc20   93-18762

93 94 95 96   10 9 8 7 6 5 4 3 2 1

Sage Production Editor: Astrid Virding

Contents

Acknowledgments

Both authors wish to express their gratitude to Howard Giles for his helpful encouragement throughout the life of this project. His interest was constant, but he never pressured us to finish. Not surprisingly, much of his empirical research and theoretical work was important to our writing throughout the book. On a more personal level, he brought us together by facilitating Ng's crossing the Pacific to spend his sabbatical leave with Bradac, thereby forging a friendship that has since transcended the physical distance.

In our respective home environments there are special people whom we wish to acknowledge separately.

From Sik Hung Ng: Despite suffering from the chill of my preoccupation with the book, Grace and Hallmian lovingly let me get on with the work at home. My former Department of Psychology at Otago University, through the unfailing support of Geoff White and Isabel Campbell, was a steady source of encouragement. I also thank most sincerely Donn Bayard, Marilynn Brewer, Mark Brooke, Janet Holmes, and Mike Platow for their helpful comments on various parts of the book.

From James Bradac: I wish to thank all of my colleagues and assistants in the Department of Communication at the University of California at Santa Barbara for their support over the last three challenging years during which this book was written. Gratitude should also be expressed to several campus administrators who offered unusual aid in the form of special equipment that enabled me to continue working. And a different kind of thank you must be given to Emilda for the different kind of support that she has given selflessly during this difficult period (*support* is a word that greatly understates the case). Thanks to various physicians at the SBMF for sustaining respiration—there is a positive correlatation between breathing and writing. And, as always, thanks to the ps; s, p, f, z, and h; trf and lwm; and swh.

Sik Hung Ng
Department of Psychology
Victoria University of Wellington
New Zealand

James J. Bradac
Department of Communication
University of California, Santa Barbara
United States

CHAPTER ONE

Introduction

Human beings are a clever species of tool makers and tool users. Some of the most remarkable human tools are the specific languages that particular groups of humans have developed and adapted for use in their daily lives. Over the years, the languages have evolved as conventional instruments for communication and, just as important, for influence and control.

Logical people prefer communication to be authentic and transparent. For them, the use of a language should be like using a trolley that faithfully transports the thoughts and feelings of one person to another. If the trolley can be dispensed with and the message not encoded in linguistic form or in any other artificial way, it will be so much the better because then individuals can communicate directly their undistorted thoughts and feelings. This *transportational* view of the use of language for communication, which sees language as a neutral conduit (Reddy, 1979), is not unlike an architect's dream of housing inhabitants of the world in mansions built of glass—transparent and full of light but overexposing and probably nonhuman. The truth of the matter is that the use of a human language such as English does more than neutrally inform hearers or readers. It is inevitably an instrument for enacting, recreating, or subverting power.

Language

The study of language use is not confined to one or even a few academic disciplines. It involves several. Osgood's (1953) comment

1

on language behavior, made almost 40 years ago, is still relevant today and applicable to the study of language use: "In terms of content, study of language behavior runs the gamut from neurophysiology of speech mechanisms and aphasia, through comparative, experimental, developmental, and social psychology, into cultural anthropology and the philosophy of science" (pp. 726-727). Insofar as major developments in the study of language in use are concerned, it is certainly true that they have occurred in pragmatics (Leech, 1983; Levinson, 1983) and sociolinguistics (Fasold, 1984, 1990; Labov, 1966; Trudgill, 1974), two disciplines that are centrally concerned with the subject. Concurrently, developments have also been made in a number of neighboring fields. These include linguistic philosophy (Austin, 1962; Grice, 1975), conversation analysis (Atkinson & Heritage, 1984; Button & Lee, 1987; Sacks, Schegloff, & Jefferson, 1974), ethnography of speaking (Gumperz & Hymes, 1972), discourse analysis (Potter & Wetherell, 1987; van Dijk, 1985), social psychology (Giles & Robinson, 1990), and communication science (Berger & Chaffee, 1987; Knapp & Miller, 1985). The developments are centered mainly on linguistic variables, although nonlinguistic or nonverbal variables, such as kinesic (gaze, posture, and gesture) and proxemic (interpersonal distance, touch, and orientation) features are still very much evident in current research.

In writing about power in language, we are not concerned with language as an idealized Chomskyan structure, but with the situated use of a language and some of the effects this use may have (see Harris, 1983). We assume in our language users only those abilities that any average member of a linguistic community will have acquired by about the age of five. These include the motivation to communicate, the ability for intersubjectivity, the establishment of interactive routines with others, communicative intentionality, stringing of words into purposeful utterances, initiating and sustaining a conversation, and tracking an on-going conversation by the application of metacognitive monitoring (see Haslett, 1984, for a summary). Other abilities are also involved, but as long as the reader bears in mind that we are not referring to infants but to older children and adults, the above list will be sufficient. It goes without saying that literacy will also be assumed when we talk of the impact of written language.

The fact that language provides a culturally conventional tool for power does not mean that words will always succeed or that they will necessarily function more effectively than other tools and resources. For example, in a cultural context in which physical violence is condoned, a dominant person can be a man or a woman of few words. We are simply drawing attention to those parts of everyday life for which the seemingly casual, routine use of language can re-create, enact, or otherwise subvert influence and control. How this works, or fails to work, and why are the concerns of this book.

Power

Power is a widely used concept for the analysis of human social behavior (Ng, 1980, in press). It is the kind of concept that most people think they understand intuitively—until somebody stops and asks them to define it. At the simplest level, one can distinguish between two senses of the concept: *power to* and *power over*. Russell (1938) captured the "power to" meaning very well by defining power as the production of intended effects. We can differentiate these effects into the following. In the positive sense, "power to" is the realization of personal or collective goals. In the negative sense, it is the hindering of other individuals' achievement of goals for the sake of hindering. "Power over," on the other hand, is the relational facet of power. One person has power over another person when the two stand in a relationship of dominance and submission; this may occur in institutional (e.g., the military) or noninstitutional (e.g., a hostage situation) settings, legitimately or illegitimately, between friends or between enemies.

It is a commonly held view that if person A realizes a goal by successfully committing person B to a course of action that B would not otherwise take, then A must also have power over B. Another common view is that if A has power over B, then A must also be able to use B for realizing A's goals. These views are correct to the extent that any instance of "power to" must occur in a social context that comprises inter alia a certain power relation between the persons concerned. However, it is important also to recognize that the positive correlation between "power to" and "power over" may in fact be imperfect. For example, authorities may fail to gain obedience (Milgram, 1974), and "power to" can be instigated by those who initially do not have authority (Gurr, 1970; Mugny, 1982). Situations like these favor keeping the two senses of power conceptually separate. But in most contexts, both senses will pertain: Personal goals are typically achieved in and through relationships. Thus when combining the two senses of power into a single definition, Weber (1947) laid stress on both goal achievement and relational contingencies: Power (*macht*) is the probability that one actor within a social relationship will be in a position to carry out his or her own will despite resistance, regardless of the basis on which this probability rests.

In this volume we are particularly concerned with how language users may, by using language in particular ways, generate influence and control. This concern with "power to" is viable, not so much because power relationships are absent, but because most of them are fluid enough to allow influence and control to be negotiated on the spot. Consider the following incident that happened between two Maori groups in New Zealand.

One Maori group from a tribe in which women had the right to speak in formal ceremonies was visiting another in which women had no such rights. After the hosts had opened the oratory, it was the guests' turn to speak. The speaking turn fell on the guest with the most senior rank, who happened to be an elderly woman chief.

> After a moment's hesitation she began to speak. Immediately there was a protest from the hosts. Calmly ignoring them, the chieftainess continued her speech to the end and then said:
>
> "You Arawa men, you tell me to sit down because I am a woman, yet none of you would be in the world if it wasn't for your mothers. This is where your learning and your grey hairs come from!"
>
> Then, turning her back on them she bent over and flipped up her skirts "in the supreme gesture of contempt." (Salmond, quoted in Coulthard, 1977, p. 48)

Power of Language to Impress and Influence

The use of language in everyday life contributes to the realization of goals—this is "power to." Specifically, we will examine first how language can be used to impress and influence people. What a person says and how he or she says it leave an impression on hearers. Underscoring the relevance of speech to impression formation invokes the old meaning of *personality*, which was derived from the Latin roots meaning "through sound" (see also Scherer, 1979). Our particular interest lies in the power dimension of impression formation: How to measure the power dimension, what processes underlie the formation of a powerful or a powerless impression, and how these processes are related to speech features.

Language provides a conventional resource for influencing people's attitudes and behavior. Influence-attempts may take the form of persuasion, argumentation, or use of threats, promises, requests, demands, orders, and such like. By *conventional*, we wish to underscore the fact that it is customary for humans to use language for enacting these influence attempts. It is conceivable that there may be purely nonlinguistic means for doing these things, but the use of such means would be highly unconventional in our sort of culture.

Aristotle (1909) and other classic scholars (see Kennedy, 1963) recognized a long time ago that facts and logic alone are often insufficient for persuasion. Facts and logic—the prescribed bases of persuasion—must be adapted to the situation, and it is language and language style that will bear the burden of this mission. Contemporary theorists and researchers have recognized that language is the primary instrument of persuasion (Burke, 1966; Gibbons, Busch, & Bradac, 1991; Petty & Cacioppo, 1986), although nonverbal variables are clearly important as well (Burgoon, Birk, & Pfau, 1990).

Situations in which influence attempts are carried out fall into two main categories, depending on whether the direction of the influence attempt is predetermined or relatively free flowing. The prototype of predetermined, unidirectional influence is a monological speech or message directed from the source to the hearer. The monological paradigm has been used in numerous studies of compliance gaining, attitude change, and persuasive communication (Cialdini, 1984; Petty & Cacioppo, 1986; Simons, 1986). It lends itself easily to experimentation, facilitates the inference of causal relationships by predetermining the direction of influence, and simplifies the measurement of outcomes.

Free-flowing multidirectional influence, exemplified by peer group conversations or discussions, applies to the more interactive type of situations. To examine influence in the flow of sequential interaction between individuals is much more difficult than in a monologue. The difficulty is evident in early social psychological studies of social norm formation (Sherif, 1936), leader emergence (Bales, 1950), and group-based polarization (Moscovici & Doise, 1974) in which both past and contemporary researchers have been content with demonstrating influence but have seldom been able to tease out the sequential enactment of influence. As Kelley (1984, 1991) pointed out, the problem here is the lack of conceptual tools that are available in social psychology for dealing with interactional sequence. Nevertheless, some of the conceptual tools are available for coding verbal exchange (e.g., Donohue, Diez, & Hamilton, 1984; Morley & Stephenson, 1977; Stiles, 1978) and analyzing interactional sequence in both the nonverbal (e.g., Duncan & Fiske, 1977) and verbal (e.g., Sacks et al., 1974) domains. We will make use of these tools, especially those developed in conversation analysis (Sacks et al., 1974) and the related fields of sequential analysis and discourse analysis, for examining conversational influence and control.

Power of Language to Depoliticize

In organized social life, regardless of how small (e.g., family) or large (e.g., university department) the organizational unit may be, someone has to tell someone else to obey orders, carry out duties, make sacrifices, do things that the latter would not otherwise do, and the like. The enactment of influence and control, in turn, often produces antithetical side effects. For example, it may trigger resentment and opposition to the influence attempt and lead to interpersonal conflict. What level of trade-off between these antithetical side effects and influence will communicators tolerate? At one extreme, communicators may be totally unconcerned with the side effects; at the other extreme, they may be so concerned that they will abandon their influence attempts. Between the two extremes are varying levels of trade-off, as communicators endeavor to enact influence while preventing side effects or keeping them to a minimum. One way of achieving this is to *depoliticize* the influence message.

Essentially, to depoliticize an influence message is to camouflage it as something else; in doing so, communicators render their influence attempts more palatable to the targets of influence and at the same time lessen their own accountability. For example, a mother who wants her children to stop quarreling may, instead of yelling at them, drop the hint by drawing their attention to the headache from which she is suffering. Dropping a hint, issuing an order in the form of a request, and various other polite forms of communicating an influence message are examples of depoliticization. There are many more, and these need not be polite messages.

The use of language to depoliticize influence messages not only will render them more subtle but may also prevent or reduce resistance from the target. To better capture the distinction between influence per se and depoliticization, one may take note of a parallel distinction made by political scientists Bachrach and Baratz (1962) between decision-making and non-decision-making power:

> Of course power is exercised when A participates in the making of decisions that affect B. But power is also exercised when A devotes his energies to creating or reinforcing social and political values and institutional practices that limit the scope of the political process to public consideration of only those issues which are comparatively innocuous to A. (p. 948)

There are numerous depoliticization strategies, and these can be grouped under three headings: the use of language to *mitigate,* to *mislead,* and to *mask.* The English language has a rich repertoire of linguistic devices that can be put to use for mitigating the harshness of an influence message, masking the reality of influence and control in communication, and misleading people. (The potential for depoliticization is, of course, not confined to English alone, but that is another story altogether.) The linguistic devices for depoliticization are made possible by, among other things, the flexibility of syntax, the potential of semantically loaded words to evoke images, and the availability of cultural conventions that enable communicators to convey or infer meaning indirectly. By one or more of these devices, "power to" is exercised in a depoliticized communication context wherein the fact of influence has been mystified or camouflaged and the exercise of influence has been rendered more palatable. This form of "power to" abounds in rules, regulations, news headlines, the reporting of news about ingroups and out-groups, political propaganda, and even talk among intimate friends. Although we have no objective data on the frequency of depoliticized messages, from daily observations as a native (Bradac) and a foreign (Ng) speaker of English, we are struck by the prevalence of depoliticized messages that we receive from others and—we are only human—send to others.

Orwell (1954) was a forerunner in unmasking many of the devices of depoliticization. More recent studies have stemmed from critical linguistics (Fowler, Hedge, Kress, & Trew, 1979), language therapy (Bandler & Grinder, 1975), discourse analysis (van Dijk, 1987), politeness in speech (Brown & Levinson, 1987), equivocal communication (Bavelas, Black, Chovil, & Mullett (1990), devious communication (Bowers, Elliott, & Desmond, 1977), and many other domains.

Routinization of Language Dominance

Language affects, and is affected by, power relations between groups in society. At one level, the deprivation of power is often associated with psychological deprivation. Mills (1959) argues that members of subordinate groups perceive their situation experientially; most of them, however, cannot relate their personal troubles to public issues, and are unable to define their real interests in terms of the social structure. Relating this insight to language, Mueller (1973) notes that the language of the hard-core poor is a restricted speech code. The categories of restricted speech allow for a grasp of the here and now, but they cannot be used in a reflective way and they do not permit an analysis, hence a transcendence, of the social context. As a result, in using their "natural" language, the poor effectively maintain their own subordination in society as a group. And they may be unaware of this. At least this is one possibility and, it should be noted, a rather controversial one. The idea that restricted (or for that matter elaborated) codes are in some sense bound to whole groups of speakers has been criticized (Robinson, 1979), as has the idea that a restricted performance necessarily reflects impoverished thinking (Labov, 1970).

At another level, powerful groups are better placed than less powerful groups in changing the language and having it accepted for general use. This is most apparent when a country, after conquering or colonizing another country, embarks on imposing its own language on the latter. A similar, although less apparent process takes place within a country or a language community. In either case, the resultant dominant language may extinguish the competing language or language variety. In some subtle ways, it contains features that favor certain ways of thinking but not others, portrays the powerful groups as the norm against which other groups should be evaluated, and trivializes subordinate groups, thus rendering them invisible in the language they know. In short, group dominance is transferred to, and encoded in, the prevailing language variety. Over time, the biased language is no longer marked—it becomes routinized; its use in daily discourse, in turn, helps to reinforce and perpetuate group dominance—it routinizes power relations.

* * *

There are a number of articles, chapters, and books that have crucially informed our thinking about many of the issues pertaining to the discussion of language and power in this volume, for example, Berger (1985); Brown and Levinson (1987); Burgoon (1990); Fairclough (1989); Giles and Street (1985); Giles and Wiemann (1987); Kramarae, Schultz, and O'Barr (1984); Miller (1987); Ng (1990a); Smith (1985); and Wiemann (1985). In a real sense, all of the works that we cite throughout the book have influenced our thinking significantly. But, unlike previous works, our book represents an attempt to take a very broad focus and to integrate the phenomena appearing within this broad scope. Accordingly, we range from the language of newspaper headlines to the language of requests among inmates, from public to private discourse, from macropolitics to micropolitics. We also range from qualitative analyses of naturally occurring speech to quantitative analyses of data collected in language experiments. Thus, for good or for ill, our book is comparatively comprehensive. (We hope that it is reasonably analytical as well.)

It is something of a happy accident that Jaworski's (1993) *The Power of Silence* was published shortly before our *Power in Language,* both works appearing as volumes in the **Language and Language Behaviors Series,** edited by Howard Giles (who no doubt facilitated this positive coincidence). Concepts such as dominance, control, compliance, and resistance are common to both books. But the books depart from each other in that Jaworski examines the ways in which power is denied to social groups through the prevention of discourse, through the silencing of group members, whereas we focus on the ways in which power is achieved through the production of discourse, through verbal activity. In a sense, the two books scrutinize opposite possibilities in the human domain: silence versus speech as instruments of control. We are tempted to say that they represent two sides of the same coin, although it could be argued that they, in fact, represent two different coins. But, apart from essential differences, the books exhibit some similar concerns, for example, when we examine the effects of women's use of the masculine (ostensibly gender neutral) *he* in Chapter 8, we are examining a kind of silencing (although we do not use this term). Furthermore, in the context of our discussion of linguistic devices for depoliticizing influence attempts, one could view depoliticizing acts as strategies for silencing the targets of influence messages, although we do not emphasize this perspective.

In the forthcoming chapters we will examine a large variety of empirical studies, theoretical positions, methodological matters, and substantive issues as these pertain to the use of language for generating influence and control. We will move from the simplest case, that of monological speech and the achievement of power, to the increasingly complex and subtle cases of conversational control and linguistic depoliticization. In a sense, the monologue-power paradigm establishes a baseline at which individual communicators do certain things linguistically to produce the impression that they are relatively powerful or powerless and to achieve actual influence. The more complex and subtle cases depart from this baseline in various ways, and these departures are explicated. Of course, to say that the monological speech-power connection is the simplest case is to engage in a kind of linguistic truncation, for the term *simplest* masks a great deal of complexity as the next chapter will reveal.

CHAPTER TWO

Signs of Power I:
Powerful and Powerless Styles

Some people exude power. One would guess that they get their way more often than not, that they are not typically vulnerable, and that their ideas carry a lot of weight. In the United States, President John F. Kennedy appears to have been such a person, and in Britain, Prime Minister Margaret Thatcher appears to have been one as well. Another, and in this case a notorious, example is the Führer of the Third Reich, Adolf Hitler. These individuals, and countless famous others from a variety of countries and cultures, to a large extent achieved or continue to achieve their power—or at least the appearance of their power—on the basis of their communication in interpersonal or public contexts. A significant feature of this power-inducing communication, the feature that we will attend to here, is the speech or language style such people employ. That there is something distinctive about the styles of the three famous people mentioned above has been suggested by various scholars (e.g., Beattie, 1982; Bull & Mayer, 1988; Burke, 1941; Duncan, 1962).

It is not necessary, however, to focus on public figures to examine relationships between language or speech style and impressions of power. In everyday life, we form impressions of speaker power as we encounter persons for the first time, typically in face-to-face contexts but on television as well (as when we see a person interviewed on a news program about a local disaster that he or she witnessed). Most of the research that we will discuss in this chapter has involved first impressions formed of strangers on the basis of their speech or language, often in restricted contexts in which the person forming the impression is a respondent listening to an audio recording or reading a transcript during the course of an experiment. (The heavy reliance on such contexts constitutes an issue that we will discuss in Chapter 3). Producing an initial impression of power has the potential to later give a communicator real power over a message recipient as well as real power to do things such as winning an election.

It will be useful to discuss first the meaning of *impression of power*, the ways in which this concept has been operationalized in the relevant research. What does it mean to say, "She seems like a powerful person?" We will then discuss some of the meanings of *persuasion* and related concepts. We will subsequently examine particular features of language that have been connected to impressions of power and to persuasive effectiveness; specifically, we will scrutinize *powerful* and *powerless* styles, focusing on the effects of these styles and their major components.

Components of Impressions of Power

Various models have been offered that describe dimensions along which individuals evaluate communicators. As a starting point, it is worth mentioning Street and Hopper's (1982) model. The model implies that the basis for evaluation is perception, that is, what the recipient extracts from a given message will determine the judgment that he or she makes of the speaker. If a person perceives a speaker's accent to be Scandinavian even though professional dialectologists claim that the accent is Italian, the perceiver's evaluations are likely to reflect stereotypes about Scandinavians. Kellermann and Sleight (1989) make a related point that *coherence judgments* (evaluations of the degree to which a message makes sense both internally and in a particular context) reflect the knowledge structures that message recipients bring to the processing of a message as opposed to features that are objectively in the message itself (see also Kellermann & Lim, 1989).

It is worth noting, however, that perceptions may be highly veridical, according to some objective standard of features comprising a message (Bradac, Mulac, & House, 1988). One of the interesting questions here is, Under what circumstances will message recipients accurately perceive message content and form, and alternatively, when will such recipients "distort" message features in the direction of their cognitive biases (stereotypes, processing heuristics, etc.) (Cappella & Street, 1989). The suggestion has been made that second guessing, a situation in which persons doubt their initial interpretation of a message and attempt to reinterpret the message, is a process that is conducive to veridicality (Hewes & Graham, 1989).

Having said that there is a connection between perceptions of messages and evaluations of message sources (and the messages themselves), we can now discuss the dimensions along which messages are evaluated. First, we should note that for us an impression of high or low speaker power is a judgment or evaluation more than it is a perception of some state of affairs. It is an inference reflecting values. For many people it is probably the case that power has a positive valence, whereas powerlessness has a valence that is negative. (Particular contexts will overturn this relationship, however, as when people talk of the abuses of power; Lord Acton's hypothesis also comes to mind: Power tends to corrupt, absolute power corrupts absolutely.) Message recipients perceive certain linguistic features (although this perception may be very diffuse and global), and these features generate evaluative inferences regarding the message source's power.

A model offered by Ryan and Giles (1982) is helpful in thinking about the evaluation of high or low communicator power. These theorists begin with a distinction, already familiar in the speech evaluation literature, between status and solidarity. Status can assume high or low values, as can solidarity. The former concept indexes a person's position in a hierarchy, whether this hierarchy be based on wealth, prestige, physical strength, or whatever. The latter concept indexes a person's proximity to, or degree of inclusion in, a salient group, and such a group may be social, political, ethnic, professional, or whatever. Thus we may feel close to, or be perceived as being close to, fellow academics while feeling estranged from right-wing antiintellectuals. The concept of solidarity is clearly linked to questions of in-group and out-group attitudes and behaviors (Tajfel, 1981).

Both status and solidarity are group-related concepts. Ryan and Giles (1982) suggested that one can propose conceptual counterparts that are essentially individualistic: competence and attractiveness for status and solidarity, respectively. Thus a communicator may be perceived as highly competent or effective, quite apart from his or her membership in a group reflecting a particular level of status. Or one can feel attracted to a particular communicator, finding this person likable, friendly, and so forth, again apart from group membership. The plausibility of this individualistic-group distinction is suggested by special, unexpected cases in which, for example, one is impressed by the performance of a person who one believes holds membership in a low-status group or when one is attracted to a particular person who is a member of the opposition (out-group).

Thus we have status and competence on the one hand, and solidarity and attractiveness on the other. Various studies using factor analytic methods have demonstrated that status-competence and solidarity-attractiveness are, in fact, independent evaluative clusters (Bradac & Mulac, 1984b; Mulac, 1975, 1976; Zahn & Hopper, 1985). At least two studies (Bradac & Wisegarver, 1984; Gundersen & Perrill, 1989) have shown that status and competence can be factorially independent, as Ryan and Giles (1982) would suggest, although we are not aware of a similar demonstration for solidarity and attractiveness.

In forming an impression of communicator power in-group-related contexts, people attend to the dimension of status, whereas in individualistic contexts people attend to communicator competence. We think it is reasonable to assert that typically evaluations of solidarity and attractiveness, as indexed by measures of closeness, likability, warmth, and so on, are not associated with judgments of power in the minds of most message recipients.

The claim that impressions of communicator power are correlated with status and competence, but not with solidarity or attractiveness, is consistent with the results of a study by Bradac and Wisegarver (1984). These authors found that evaluations of a communicator's self-control and self-confidence were positively correlated with evaluations of competence but not correlated with judgments of attractiveness. Another study found a high correlation between rating scales measuring perceived communicator power on the one hand and effectiveness on the other—*effectiveness* defined in the study as the likelihood of the communicators fulfilling their intentions, that is, getting their way (Bradac & Mulac, 1984a). A more recent study by Gibbons, Busch, and Bradac (1991) provided some evidence that various scales pertaining to control of others (dominance, influence, ability to lead, etc.) were correlated with a status-control factor primarily and not with a factor measuring sociability.

So, for us, impressions of power will pertain primarily to judgments of communicator status and competence. Are there other plausible components of such impressions? One that seems intuitively plausible and that also has some empirical justification is communicator dynamism. The dynamism component is represented by scales such as aggressive-unaggressive, active-passive, strong-weak, and loud-soft (Mulac, 1976). The language variable labeled *power of style*, discussed below (O'Barr, 1982), has been linked to ratings of dynamism: Communicators using the *high-power style* are perceived to be relatively high on this dimension (Bradac & Mulac, 1984b).

According to the preceding arguments, a maximally powerful communicator is perceived to belong to a highly valued group, to be competent or effective, and to be active and strong. A maximally powerless communicator is perceived to belong to a devalued group (often but not necessarily an out-group), to be incompetent or ineffective, and to be passive and weak (see Bradac & Street, 1989/1990). It is probably clear by now, but let us emphasize the point, that the dimensions of competence, status, and dynamism are potentially independent. A given speaker may be judged as very dynamic and competent, but as belonging to a lower-class group. Some comments about African-American political candidates in the United States seem to reflect this pattern (an all too familiar and even more stereotypical and racist version of this is, "highly dynamic but incompetent and lower class"). Thus, along with Bradac and Street (1989/1990), we consider status, competence, and dynamism to be the three bases, or primary dimensions, of impressions of communicator power.

Persuasion and Related Outcomes

The fact that people can get things done with words is a central concern of this volume. People make requests, issue orders, threaten, cajole, exhort, persuade, and so forth—speech acts designed by speakers to get hearers to do things, for example, close doors, shoot guns, or change opinions. Some things that we want others to do can be accomplished without language, such as moving out of our way (we can physically move them), but such things are confined to an exceedingly narrow realm in which others are the passive objects of our actions, a realm of absolute "power to." The vast majority of our goals are formulated in regard to active others who possess minds and intentionality, and these goals are achieved essentially through language (see Gibbons, Bradac, & Busch, 1992).

Language is the primary instrument for achieving influence. Although nonverbal factors such as physical attractiveness undoubtedly play a significant role in persuasion and compliance gaining (Burgoon et al., 1990), these factors are in the final analysis ancillary, because for person A to understand what person B wants—the very baseline of influence—B's desire or need must be expressed in a propositional, that is, linguistic form: "I want your money" or "I want your vote." Of course, people can also communicate their desires indirectly: "I sure could use some cash" or "I am not a candidate for office at this time"—indeed this may be more common and strategic than the direct expression of wants (see Chapter 5). But indirect expressions are also linguistic and, like any other linguistic expression, may convey unambiguous meanings only if the communicator and message recipient have a normal grasp of linguistic conventions.

In this chapter and the next one we will examine connections between language use and influence, both persuasion and compliance gaining. Persuasion refers to affective or cognitive changes of message recipients, and compliance refers to overt behavioral changes. The two types of changes are closely related in that behavior change can lead to attitude change and vice versa, as several classical theories suggest (e.g., Festinger's, 1957, theory of cognitive dissonance; Brehm's, 1966, reactance theory; and Bem's, 1972, self-perception theory). But persuasion and compliance are by no means identical outcomes, for one outcome can occur in the absence of the other. Actually, the research to be discussed has not typically made a principled distinction between persuasion and compliance, choosing to look at one or the other outcome without explicit justification. This distinction is potentially useful however, because language may affect the two types of outcomes differently; for example, in some situations threats and orders may produce compliance without producing a corresponding affective or cognitive change (Murdock, Bradac & Bowers, 1984).

A reasonable question at this point is, What is the relationship between persuasion or compliance gaining and the components of impressions of power discussed in the preceding section? Generally, we would expect that as ratings of competence, status, and to a lesser extent, dynamism increase, the tendency to be persuaded and to comply will increase as well. Indeed a number of studies have shown that perceived communicator competence and authoritativeness are directly related to attitude change on the part of message recipients (Burgoon, 1989; Burgoon, Jones, & Stewart, 1975). On the other hand, in some situations communicator solidarity or attractiveness will be a more important correlate of persuasion than will perceived competence (Bettinghaus & Cody, 1987, pp. 62-82). In the latter sort of situation, there may be little or no association between impressions of power and persuasive effectiveness. Another way of saying this is that sometimes beliefs about communicator abilities will guide decisions, whereas at other times affective reactions will be especially influential (Bradac, Sandell & Wenner, 1979).

Powerful and Powerless Speech Styles

The question now becomes, What features of language, either spoken or written, affect persuasive outcomes and impressions of communicator status, competence, and dynamism? Perhaps a useful starting point is the variable *powerful* versus *powerless* style, because research on this variable purports to be exclusively focused on language and power. (By contrast, some of the language variables discussed in the next chapter have more scattered foci and diverse histories.) The powerful versus powerless style variable emerged from the empirical work of anthropologist O'Barr and associates (Erickson, Lind, Johnson, & O'Barr, 1978; O'Barr, 1982), although a case could be made that an earlier point of origin was linguist Lakoff's (1973) intuitively derived essay. Lakoff was primarily interested in connections between gender and language, whereas O'Barr focused on more general aspects of social power. We will return to Lakoff and the question of communicator gender in the next chapter.

O'Barr initially recorded and later transcribed verbal communication transpiring over many hours in an American courtroom in North Carolina. Examination of the transcripts revealed a cluster of linguistic features that certain speakers used frequently and that others did not. The speakers drawing from this cluster tended to be uneducated witnesses, i.e., inexpert testifiers, defendants, and so on, people viewed by O'Barr and associates to have one thing in common: low social power. The speakers who avoided using linguistic forms from this cluster tended to be lawyers, judges, expert witnesses, and so forth—individuals with relatively high social power. The low-power forms were these:

1. Hedges: "I *sort of* liked it"
2. Intensifiers: "I *really* liked it"
3. Tag questions or declaratives with rising intonation: "I liked it, *didn't I?*" "I liked it?"
4. Hesitations: "I . . . *uh* . . . liked it."
5. Deictic phrases: "That man *over there* liked it."
6. Polite forms: "*Yes sir*, I liked it."

The nonuse of these forms by ostensibly high-power speakers resulted in speech that was comparatively direct, fluent, and terse.

Issues Regarding High- and Low-Power Styles

Two issues should be raised at this point: (1) Is powerless language the marked form or are both powerless and powerful styles marked as a result of their deviation from some neutral style, dwelling at the midpoint of a powerful-powerless continuum? (2) Is a high- or low-power style an attribute or a trait that speakers exhibit uniformly across contexts or does the use of one style or the other vary as a function of contextual variation?

In regard to the first issue, there is a small amount of relevant data. A study by Bradac and Mulac (1984a), which used brief written messages as experimental stimuli, found that ostensibly powerful messages (that is, messages that did not contain any of the six features described above) were rated to the powerful side of the midpoint of a powerful-powerless seven-point scale, as were messages containing polite forms and intensifiers (which raises another issue, discussed below: Do all of the powerless features identified by O'Barr function identically?). This suggests that the absence of ostensibly powerless features yields messages that are evaluated as relatively powerful, in fact, that the powerful style is marked. In the same study, tag questions, hedges, and hesitations fell on the powerless side of the midpoint, hence these powerless forms also are marked. It should be noted that the Bradac and Mulac study used a completely within-subject design wherein all respondents read and rated all messages. Accordingly, the powerful messages were compared with the powerless ones and may have been perceived as relatively powerful as a function of perceptual contrast effects. The opposite may equally be true, that is, powerless messages may themselves have been rated as relatively powerless owing to perceptual contrast effects. A differently designed study is needed to sort out which one of the message types is marked or if both types are marked.

A more recent study (Gibbons et al., 1991) had respondents read either powerless or powerful messages in a between-subjects design, and among other things, respondents performed a thought-listing task after reading the message (which was a persuasive one arguing in favor of comprehensive examinations for senior undergraduate students). The thoughts listed by the respondents were subsequently assigned to several categories, including positive thoughts about the speaker's language and a parallel negative-thought category. Relevant here is the finding that very few respondents had positive thoughts about the language in the high-power style condition; they attended instead to the quality of the speaker's arguments. On the other hand, in the low-power style condition, many respondents spontaneously offered negative comments about the speaker's language.

So, in a situation in which there was no immediate basis for language comparison (contrary to the previously described within-subject design) respondents apparently paid little attention to the high-power style, whereas they did notice and think about the low-power style. This finding indicates that the low-power style is the marked case or, if we can talk more meaningfully of degrees of markedness, that the low-power style is more strongly marked than the style of high-power. This may be an example of a more general phenomenon: the *negativity effect* (Kanouse & Hanson, 1972; also Peeters, 1971). It has been shown in a large variety of contexts that people weight negative information more heavily than positive information in forming impressions of others or in making decisions (Hamilton & Zanna, 1972; Kahneman and Tversky, 1979; Kellermann, 1984, 1989). For example, observers' evaluations of a person who is presented as articulate *and* sinister are more negative than their average evaluations of an articulate person and a sinister person. Similarly, in making a decision, especially when the decision involves taking risks, individuals assign more weight to potential costs than to potential gains. So, for example, when a person is deciding which one of two cosmetic surgeons to consult, he or she would be less likely to consult the one who is presented as having a 60% *failure* rate than the one having a 40% success rate. In a sense, negative information is more informative than positive information, or at least people act as though it were. And they may be right, not always—that is for sure—but in the sense specified by a group of psychologists in Belgium and Poland: The negativity effect is functional as a counterweight to correct the Pollyanna bias of adopting the attitude that in the absence of relevant information relating to a given environmental reality, a person should proceed to act as if the environmental reality were good rather than bad (Peeters & Czapinski, 1990).

In essence, what we have been proposing above is that to the extent that low-power speech is seen as negative, it attracts special attention and, as a result, will become more strongly marked. The proposal is conditional on the negative evaluation of low-power speech. This is an important condition because low-power speech features may not always be perceived negatively. For example, hedges, intensifiers, and the like are customarily used among friends and (some would argue) by women to maximize conversational participation and foster the joint production of text (Coates, 1988; Holmes, 1986; Tannen, 1984). In this type of context, it may be the case that the absence of the low-power speech features will be perceived negatively and that this absence will become the more strongly marked form—if the negativity markedness argument is generalizable. There is a strong need to investigate the effects of power of style in a variety of informal contexts.

The second issue mentioned above, that pertaining to power of style as an enduring trait on the one hand or a variable behavior affected by context on the other, must be discussed in the absence of directly relevant data. That is, no researchers (to the best of our knowledge) have sampled speakers' language across contexts and subsequently coded the data in terms of the variables identified by O'Barr and associates. Still, there are some points that can be made here. As a place to begin, we should note that the implication of O'Barr's courtroom research is that power of style is a learned attribute—highly educated persons learn to talk in one way, and those with little education learn a different style. This view is compatible with, for example, Bernstein's (1971) notion of a social class basis for *elaborated* and *restricted* codes—there are ways of speaking that are more or less permanently attached to speakers. Historically, dialectologists have taken this position: As a result of geographical and social factors, members of particular groups use particular dialects.

On the other hand, a large variety of phonological, syntactic, and semantic features have been shown to vary within speakers and between contexts. Speakers engage in style shifting as situations change. (Speakers may also shift styles to cause a situational change; see Giles & Hewstone, 1982.) Some shifts in style reflect changes from one communication genre to another, for example, as one moves from the description of an event to the telling of a joke (Hopper & Bell, 1984). Other shifts reflect changes in the speaker's psychological state or mood, for example as one moves from a situation in which one feels certain about how to behave to a situation in which there is a high level of subjective uncertainty (Berger & Calabrese, 1975).

It seems to us that both genre changes and changes in psychological state may result in a particular speaker's moving from the use of a powerful style to a powerless one or vice versa. In regard to the former sort of change, one might point to parent A talking to parent B and subsequently talking to parent B's infant daughter. We would expect parent A to shift in the direction of low lexical diversity and decreased speech rate, increased rising intonation, and increased use of tag questions. This would represent a movement from a genre of adult conversation to the genre labeled *baby talk* or *motherese,* which appears to include some of the powerless speech markers (Snow & Ferguson, 1977). In regard to changes in psychological state, there is some evidence that decreases in speaker uncertainty are associated with lower levels of filled pausing (a form of hesitation; Berger & Calabrese, 1975), higher levels of lexical diversity (Sherblom & Van Rheenen, 1984), and higher ratings of fluency (i.e., low hesitation; Berger, Karol & Jordan, 1989; see also Berger & Bradac, 1982).

One intriguing study that involved recording and transcribing many hours of talk of a counselor and a client in therapy sessions across time found that the patient increased her use of tag questions from early to later sessions (Winefield, Chandler, & Bassett, 1989). This increase was associated with an increase in linguistic forms reflecting self-confidence and positive self-esteem. It should be clear that this outcome is paradoxical from the standpoint of O'Barr's (1982) research and of other studies (Bradac & Mulac, 1984a) that associate tag questions with evaluations of low speaker power. It suggests that in some social contexts an increased use of tags may be a sign of increased social responsiveness (an attempt to gain a response from one's listener) rather than an increase in self-perceived powerlessness (see Chapters 4 and 5 for a further discussion of the various roles of tag questions). But apart from the possibly paradoxical result, this study supports the idea that changes in psychological state can be associated with changes in level of tag question use.

This being said, we do not deny the possibility—even the high likelihood—that some speakers tend to use more of the linguistic indicators of powerlessness whereas other speakers tend to use fewer of these. That is, the use of powerful and powerless speaker styles may be idiolectical to an extent. What we are more skeptical about is Bernstein's (1971) idea that whole groups of speakers, for example, those with little or much education, are strongly inclined to use one style or another across a variety of situations and regardless of changes in psychological state.

Effects of Powerful
and Powerless Styles

A number of studies have examined the communicative consequences attached to the use of high- and low-power styles. It seems reasonable to summarize these in a chronological fashion, because there is a decidedly cumulative aspect to the work in this area.

After conducting the descriptive investigation that led to the establishment of the powerful and powerless style construct (an investigation centering on antecedents of variation in power of style), O'Barr and associates asked a question about the consequences of this variable: Does the low-power style reduce the effectiveness of persons testifying in a courtroom setting? Rather obviously, this question has an important implication if it is answered affirmatively: The testimony of a witness may be discredited to some extent merely on the basis of his or her low-power style rather than on the basis of the substance of the testimony. To the extent that this is true, it would seem to introduce an element of irrationalism into the judicial process that ostensibly depends on rational deliberation for its success (see also Danet, 1990; Nemeth, 1981).

To explore this question Erickson et al. (1978) conducted an experiment to examine the consequences of power of style for both a male and a female when testimony was both heard (via a tape recording) and read (via a transcript) by male and female respondents. (Thus they used a four-variable between-subjects experimental design). Respondents in the study were college students who participated in 1 of the 16 cells of the design, for example, one group of males heard a low-power message delivered by a female, another group of females read a high-power message delivered by a male, and so forth. The testimony was created by the researchers on the basis of actual courtroom transcripts, and this basic testimony was transformed into high- and low-power versions. Both versions were audio recorded by an actor and an actress for use in the audio condition. It is important to keep in mind that the substance or propositional content of the testimony was constant across conditions.

The major finding was this: Both the male and the female testifier were judged as more credible and more attractive by both male and female respondents when they used the high-power style. There were some complex interaction effects for particular dependent measures, but these seem to us to be generally uninformative—certainly much less important than the finding that the high-power style boosts communicator credibility and attractiveness regardless of communicator or respondent gender. Thus an implication of this finding is that witnesses who use a low-power style may be judged less believable than those who use a high-power style, despite the fact that what they say is identical in substance.

A subsequent study by Bradac, Hemphill, and Tardy (1981) created a hypothetical courtroom scenario where one person ("Zander") was cast in the role of plaintiff or defendant and testified in a high- or low-power style (a 2×2 between-subjects design). In this scenario, Zander participated in a barroom fight and either punched (defendant role) or was punched by (plaintiff role) "Johnson." Respondents were college students who participated in one of the four cells of the design; in this case written versions of the testimony were used in all conditions. Perhaps the most interesting result for this study was that higher blameworthiness was attributed to Zander when he used the high-power style, regardless of his defendant or plaintiff status. That is, he was seen as having been more responsible for the barroom altercation, as having contributed more to its occurrence, when he avoided tag questions, hedges, hesitation forms, polite forms, intensifiers, and deictic phrases. Power of style did not affect respondents' ratings of Zander's masculinity-femininity. It is worth noting that a pilot study conducted showed that the high-power style led to more positive evaluations of Zander's competence and attractiveness, a result paralleling the finding of Erickson et al. (1978).

A follow-up study was conducted in which respondents read testimony of both the defendant (Johnson or Zander) and the plaintiff (Zander or Johnson). In half of the cases the defendant used the high-power style and the plaintiff, the low-power style; in the other half, the role-style combination was reversed. Order of plaintiff-defendant testimony was counterbalanced. A major negative finding was that the high-power style/high blameworthiness connection was not replicated. But a strong effect emerged for respondent judgments of communicator internality (a measure of the extent to which respondents judged the communicator to be the kind of person who believed that he controlled what happened to him): The high-power style yielded ratings of higher internality. Again, a pilot study showed that both Zander and Johnson were rated as more competent and attractive when using the high-power style.

A third study examined the effect of high- and low-power styles in a different type of communication situation: a crisis-intervention context involving a counselor and a client (Bradac & Mulac, 1984b). The scenario given to respondents was that a mildly depressed student had phoned into a counselor seeking advice. The respondents were told that they would hear an audio tape recording of this interaction. An actor and an actress played both the counselor and client roles, yielding two combinations: male counselor/female client and female counselor/male client. Each of these combinations was intersected with four combinations for power of style: high-power counselor with high-power client, high-power counselor with low-power client, low-power counselor with low-power client, and low-power counselor with high-power client.

The authors speculated that use of the high-power style by the counselor might have a negative effect for respondent judgments of competence, because the counselor might appear less open, more controlling, less empathic, and so on. But the results showed otherwise: The use of the high-power style by both client and counselor, regardless of gender, produced higher ratings for status-competence (collapsed in one factor), attractiveness, and dynamism. The high-power style produced especially high ratings for both counselor and client when the interactant used the low-power style, which appears to represent a perceptual contrast effect. Finally, there was some evidence that the counselor was perceived to have more empathy when he or she used the high-power style.

In one study, Carli (1990) asked male and female university students to listen to an audio tape of identical persuasive messages presented by a man or by a woman, half of which contained the low-power features of hedges, tag questions, and disclaimers.

A strong effect of language style was obtained, and this was consistently unfavorable to the low-power style across measures of speaker competence, confidence, intelligence, powerfulness, and knowledgeability.

Thus, across the studies described so far, there are some highly consistent results. The high-power style produced higher ratings of communicator competence, status, dynamism, and attractiveness. The outcome for attractiveness, typically measured by items pertaining to warmth, friendliness, likability, and so forth, is the most surprising in some ways. It suggests that people are attracted to powerful others, that they do *not* want to admire them from afar or keep their distance from them. A phrase used in the United States during the 1970s comes to mind: Power is sexy. Alternatively, what might be unattractive about the low-power style is that the communicator using this style seems to be low in self-control, which is a stigmatizing trait in many Western cultures (Stern & Manifold, 1977). There is a hint of support for this idea in Bradac and Wisegarver's (1984) finding that low lexical diversity (discussed in the next chapter) led to respondent judgments of low control of communicator behavior.

Another consistent finding is that the positive effects for use of the high-power style or, conversely, the negative effects for use of the low-power style appear to be independent of communicator gender. (It is probably worth mentioning that the use of *positive* and *negative* in the previous sentence reflects a bias, suggesting that communicators want to appear competent, high in status, and so on; in some contexts this will not be the case.) Both male and female communicators receive higher ratings of competence, status, dynamism, and attractiveness when they use the high-power style. Also, one of the studies (Bradac et al., 1981) found no connection between power of style and ratings of communicator gender. The evidence is less consistent for respondent gender. Although a majority of studies have found no interaction between power of style and respondent gender (Hosman, 1989), a few have found weak effects (e.g., Bradac & Mulac, 1984a), and one study obtained a strong interaction effect, indicating that high- and low-power styles produced dissimilar judgments of status and competence for female respondents but not for males (Wiley & Eskilson, 1985).

Most of the research on the powerful versus powerless style variable has examined the outcome of impression formation exclusively, not attending to the effect of stylistic differences on message recipients' attitudes toward recommendations contained in the message. The studies by Carli (1990) and Gibbons et al. (1991), discussed briefly above, are exceptions in this regard.

In the first study reported by Carli (1990), pairs of respondents discussed a topic on which they disagreed and afterward indicated their opinions on the topic. The postdiscussion opinion of each respondent was compared with his or her initial opinion obtained some six weeks earlier. A change of opinion in the direction of the discussion partner was taken as indicative of the partner's persuasiveness. It was found that women who used more hedges, tag questions, and disclaimers were *more* persuasive with men. There were no other significant results: language style had no effect on how persuasive women were with other women, or men with either men or women. As the author pointed out, the results of this experiment could have been confounded to the extent that speakers who used the low-power style were also more pleasant or friendly than those who used the high-power style. To control for this possibility, a second experiment was carried out using an audio tape of identical persuasive messages that either contained or did not contain the low-power features. This was the experiment that we referred to earlier in this section. The results pertaining to speaker persuasiveness confirmed the significant finding of the first experiment, namely, female speakers were more persuasive with male listeners when their messages were worded in the low- rather than in the high-power style. In addition, the reverse was found for female respondents listening to female speakers—they were less persuaded by low- than by high-power female speakers.

Gibbons et al. (1991) constructed a message arguing in favor of undergraduate comprehensive examinations for seniors, which was presumably belief discrepant for the students who were respondents in the study. Powerful and powerless versions of the message were produced, as were versions exhibiting strong and weak arguments. Thus there were four types of messages: powerful—strong, powerful—weak, powerless—strong, and powerless—weak. (A third variable, high versus low *personal relevance*, was also created. It is not discussed here, because it yielded main effects only, i.e., did not interact with power of style or argument strength.)

Respondents were asked to evaluate the proposition regarding comprehensive examinations after reading one of the four message versions; this was a measure of persuasion (Petty & Cacioppo, 1986). Perhaps surprisingly, the results indicated that argument strength was the sole determinant of persuasion, that power of style had no effect on this outcome. On the other hand, power of style had a very strong effect on respondents' impressions of communicator competence, whereas argument strength had a substantially weaker impact on this dimension of impression formation. It appears that for this topic (examinations), one that respondents were quite familiar with and had considerable knowledge about, the powerless style did not suggest negative things about the soundness of the position advocated by the communicator, even though respondents noted this style and used it to make negative attributions regarding source competence. Strong arguments alone led respondents to evaluate the position relatively favorably.

Obviously, it would be premature to conclude that power of style does not affect persuasion (especially in light of Carli's finding mentioned above). Perhaps this stylistic variable would have an effect in the case of a persuasive message on a topic that message recipients had little knowledge about, and for which attitudes were not well established. In such a case, power of style may be used as a basis for making inferences about the soundness of the communicator's position, because message recipients may have insufficient knowledge to evaluate substantive claims.

Components of the Low-Power Style: Untangling the Knot

Does each of the features of the powerless style function identically in producing judgments of low communicator competence, status, and so forth? That is, for example, are tag questions equivalent to intensifiers in reducing evaluations? This question has been a topic of research since Bradac et al. (1981) suggested that various elements of the low-power style are potentially independent at both the level of message production and the level of message effects. For example, under conditions of high negative arousal a given speaker may be highly disfluent or hesitant and also extremely impolite. This would be a case in which two of the elements of the low-power style do not covary positively, as the initial work by O'Barr and associates suggests they should. At the level of message effects, it is rather easy to imagine contexts in which polite forms will be seen as indicating high rather than low competence—at a formal dinner attended by the presidents of several nations, for example.

In an initial study exploring the potentially dissimilar effects of the various components of the low-power style, Wright and Hosman (1983) examined the relationships among hedges (high versus low usage), intensifiers (high versus low), communicator gender, and respondent gender. The questions were, Would hedges produce respondent ratings of defendant credibility, attractiveness, and blameworthiness that differed from ratings produced by intensifiers? Or would both language features serve to reduce ratings on these variables to the same extent? And would one or both variables interact with defendant gender and/or respondent gender?

Accordingly, a $2 \times 2 \times 2 \times 2$ design was used. Male and female respondents read and subsequently evaluated transcripts of testimony scripted by the experimenters to represent one of the eight combinations of hedges, intensifiers, and gender. Results indicated that high and low levels of intensification did not differ on the variables measured (at the level of main effects). On the other hand, a high level of hedging reduced ratings of credibility and attractiveness but did not reduce ratings of defendant blameworthiness. There was also an interaction effect of speaker gender and intensification; a female speaker was judged to be more attractive than a male when a high level of intensification was used; at a low level of intensification, male and female speakers did not differ. And there was a speaker gender × hedges interaction effect: A male speaker was judged to be more credible than a female speaker when a high level of hedging was exhibited; when few hedges were used, male and female speakers did not differ. There were no effects for respondent gender.

In a subsequent study, Bradac and Mulac (1984a) examined the separate effects of hedges, hesitations, tag questions, polite forms, deictic phrases, and intensifiers, using brief messages each containing three instances of one of the subcomponents of powerlessness. The powerless messages were compared with the effects of brief messages that were ostensibly powerful, containing none of the above forms. Eight different "powerful" messages were created, as were eight different messages for each of the sub-components of "powerlessness" (8 x 7 = 56 total messages). Each respondent read and evaluated 28 messages (4 messages representing each of the seven types in a completely within-subjects design). For each respondent, half of the messages were attributed to "Susan Vivianson" and half were attributed to "John Jackson" to examine the influences of communicator gender on respondent judgments. The context described to respondents was that the communicator was interviewing for a job.

Respondents rated the powerful messages as most effective and most powerful, as expected. Also rated as relatively powerful and effective were messages exhibiting high levels of politeness and intensification. Deictic phrases were rated as neutral, just about at the midpoint of the seven-point scales measuring power and effectiveness. Hedges and tag questions were perceived to be relatively ineffective and low in power. The lowest ratings for power end effectiveness were given to hesitation forms. This pattern held for both male and female communicators, that is, gender of speaker did not affect ratings either as a main effect or in interaction with other variables.

In a related study, another group of respondents evaluated all 56 messages along a bipolar scale running from "will create desired impression" to "will not create desired impression." Half of the respondents were told that the communicator (again ostensibly interviewing for a job) wanted to appear authoritative because he or she believed that the position being sought required this sort of demeanor, and half of the respondents were told that the communicator wanted to appear sociable. The questions were (1) Would power of style interact with communicator intention to create an impression? (2) Would communicator gender interact with both power of style and intention?

The results indicated that power of style and perceived communicator intention did indeed yield an interaction effect but that, once again, communicator gender had no apparent consequence. However, the nature of the interaction effect suggested only slight differences between the two intentions for the seven message types. Specifically, for the authoritative intention, the ostensibly powerful messages and the polite messages did not differ, both types being rated highest in likelihood of achieving the desired impression. These were followed by intensifiers (likely to achieve impression), deictic phrases (neutral), hedges (unlikely), tags (unlikely), and hesitations (least likely). For the sociable intention, the highest likelihood ratings were given to polite messages, the next highest to both ostensibly powerful messages and messages containing intensifiers, and the next highest to messages containing hedges (slightly above the neutral point). Messages exhibiting deictic phrases and tag questions resulted in the same relatively low rating of likelihood of achieving the impression of sociability, and messages displaying hesitations resulted in the lowest ratings.

Generally, use of hesitation forms and tag questions was judged as unlikely to achieve the desired impression for both the authoritative and sociable intentions, whereas use of intensifiers, polite forms, and ostensibly powerful forms was judged as likely to achieve the desired goal. This pattern for likelihood ratings corresponds to the pattern obtained in the first study for ratings of effectiveness and power, suggesting a relatively stable hierarchy of power levels. Only hedges and deictic phrases fluctuated across studies, and this fluctuation was slight. It is especially important to note that both polite forms and intensifiers were judged to be relatively powerful, which deviates from what would be predicted on the basis of O'Barr's research.

Hosman and Wright (1987) conducted a study on the combined effects of hedges and hesitation on judgments of communicator authoritativeness and attractiveness in a hypothetical courtroom context. Messages exhibiting high and low levels of hedging and hesitation were manipulated in a two-variable design, and respondent gender was added as a third variable. For ratings of authoritativeness, the highest ratings were given to messages that contained no hedges or hesitation forms; the lowest ratings were given to messages that contained both forms and to those containing many hedges but no hesitations. The latter result suggests that hedges may have especially negative consequences for judgments of authoritativeness.

For ratings of attractiveness, once again the highest ratings occurred for the messages without hesitations or hedges. However, in this case the lowest ratings were produced by messages high in hesitations but low in hedges. Rated somewhat more positively were messages exhibiting no hesitations but high levels of hedging. The latter results suggest that hesitations have especially negative consequences for judgments of attractiveness. However this claim is qualified by the surprising result that the second most positive condition was the high hesitation/high hedge combination. For some reason, when hesitations occurred in the context of hedges, they became considerably less stigmatizing. Hosman and Wright (1987) speculated that there is something more familiar or less enigmatic about a message containing both features as opposed to a message containing many hesitations but no hedges and that this greater familiarity heightened attractiveness ratings.

Thus hedges and hesitations produced variable results, depending on whether attractiveness or authoritativeness judgments were involved. But for both types of judgments, the absence of both features produced the highest ratings, which suggests that communicators might be advised to avoid using them generally (assuming the intention of appearing authoritative and attractive). Finally, Hosman and Wright (1987) found no effect of respondent gender, which is generally the case for studies of power of style as suggested above (but see Wiley & Eskilson, 1985).

The most ambitious studies attempting to examine the separate effects of the various components of power of style were conducted by Hosman (1989). Both of these were very complex in design. Accordingly, we will focus on what is most germane to this discussion: the combined effects of high and low levels of hesitation, hedging, and intensification on authoritativeness judgments when the various combinations were compared with a prototypically powerless message, that is, a message containing all of the features of powerlessness described earlier. Thus there were nine messages representing the intensifier, hedge, and hesitation combinations (high, high, high; high, high, low; etc.) and the ratings of each of these combinations were compared with ratings of the powerless prototype. A clear pattern emerged across both studies: Only messages exhibiting low levels of each of the three language features and messages exhibiting high intensification but low hedging and hesitation differed from the prototypically powerless messages. The one exception to this pattern occurred in one of the two studies in which a low-intensifier, low-hesitation but high-hedge message also differed from the powerless prototype, an anomalous finding that may be due to chance.

This is a suggestive pattern. It indicates that the presence of either hedges or hesitations is sufficient to depress ratings of authoritativeness, although as shown in the Wright and Hosman (1983) study hedges may be especially potent depressants. Furthermore, high intensification does not by itself reduce authoritativeness judgments; only when high intensification occurs in the context of high hedging or high hesitation is authoritativeness diminished. This is consistent with the pattern obtained by Bradac and Mulac (1984a) described above.

Another study of the potentially independent effects of the various features of the powerless style was undertaken by Vinson and Johnson (1989). These researchers thought that the powerless style might produce more negative reactions when presented in writing than when presented orally. Respondents were asked to either read or hear versions of a message that exhibited high or low levels of hedging and hesitation. Results demonstrated that both hedging and hesitation produced strong main effects on communicator credibility, and as expected, these effects were negative. For the credibility variable, oral versus written presentation did not interact with power of style. An award-for-damages measure produced an interaction that indicated higher damage amounts when powerless testimony was delivered orally. There was also some evidence that respondents perceived more hedges in the written message but more hesitations in the oral presentation. A regression analysis showed that across measures perceived hesitations accounted for more variance than did perceived hedges.

A recent study of the subcomponents of powerless style was conducted by Hosman and Siltanen (1991). In an initial experiment, these authors compared the independent effects of an ostensibly powerful message with those of a message containing intensifiers, one containing hedges, one containing hesitations, and one containing tag questions. The dependent variables examined were authoritativeness, sociability, control of others, and control of self. The latter two variables are novel in this line of research. Control of others refers to the extent to which the communicator is perceived to be influential, dominant, a leader, and so on. Control of self refers to perceptions of the extent to which the communicator is confident, self-assured, and so forth. For authoritativeness, control of others, and control of self, a rather stable pattern emerged: The ostensibly powerful message and the intensifier message produced the highest ratings; the hesitation and tag question messages produced the lowest ratings; and the hedge message fell between these extremes, although it did not differ significantly from hesitations in the cases of authoritativeness and control of others. For sociability ratings, only the powerful message and the tag question message differed significantly, the latter message receiving the lowest rating.

The second experiment by Hosman and Siltanen (1991) compared the effects of messages exhibiting high or low levels of intensification, high or low levels of hedging, and high or low levels of hesitation, which yielded eight message versions ($2 \times 2 \times 2$). Main effects were obtained for hedging and hesitation, with high levels of these variables producing low ratings of authoritativeness, control of others, and control of self. Intensification did not produce significant effects in this experiment.

The results of the two experiments suggest to the researchers that the connection between evaluative judgments (e.g., authoritativeness) and power of style may be mediated by perceptions of the extent to which communicators are in control of their own and others' behavior. As the researchers indicate, this suggestion needs to be tested with a causal modeling procedure.

Thus across the several studies that have attempted to untangle the knot of the power of style construct, a few tentative generalizations emerge. It appears that frequent hedges and hesitations in a message are likely to produce impressions of low communicator power. The presence of one of these forms may be sufficient to depress ratings of authoritativeness, effectiveness, and status, although the presence of both forms may depress ratings even further. The presence of tag questions also seems likely to depress such ratings. On the other hand, a high level of intensification is not likely to affect impressions of power negatively, and it may even enhance these impressions, a result that is consistent with studies of language intensity (e.g., Burgoon et al., 1975; Burgoon, Birk, & Hall, 1991). Use of particular forms—for example, hedges—may produce variable effects, depending on communicator gender and medium of presentation, although relatively little research has been done on contextual qualifiers of the effects of these forms.

The studies of Bradac and Mulac (1984a) suggest that polite forms do not necessarily serve to reduce impressions of power and may even enhance them. It seem likely that the effects of politeness will vary greatly, depending on factors such as perceptions of communicator role and situational demands. Politeness is a complex concept, which will be discussed in more detail in Chapters 5 and 6.

Hedges, hesitations, and tag questions seem to be the clearest indicators of low power. They also seem to imply high communication uncertainty, tentativeness, and perhaps a lack of commitment to ideas or propositions expressed. It is plausible to suggest that judgments of certainty and power are positively correlated and that communicator actions that affect one type of judgment will affect the other as well. Exploration of the language of uncertainty is likely to pay high dividends to theorists and researchers interested in the language-power connection. On the face of it, politeness does not seem to be clearly connected to perceived uncertainty; a different kind of perception or attribution may undergird the relationship between politeness and impressions of power, for example, an attribution regarding personality as opposed to cognitive state: "He appears to be a deferential person." So, perhaps there is a style of tentativeness and a style of deference, and perhaps these styles are largely independent.

* * *

Impressions of communicators can be affected by language. Specifically, the use of a powerless style can reduce judgments of status, competence, and dynamism. At this point there is little evidence that the use of this style can diminish persuasive effectiveness or the likelihood of gaining compliance. But we have offered many qualifiers of these claims. Regarding the last claim, for example, very little research has examined the effect of power of style on persuasion. We will see in the next chapter that other language variables linked to power have been shown to affect persuasive outcomes with some consistency. We have also suggested that the negative effects of the powerless style are probably mainly attributable to a communicator's use of hedges and hesitations. Polite forms, intensifiers, and even tag questions have a more ambiguous status. Their effects seem likely to be highly dependent on the context in which they occur. Of course, this is not to say that context has no effect on reactions to hedges and hesitations. We speculate, for example, that adults expect a high level of hesitation from children and that hesitations therefore go relatively unnoticed in many situations in which children are speaking. On the other hand, high levels of hedging and hesitation produced by adults are probably often noticeable and when noticed probably often lead to stigmatization.

Politeness is an especially interesting form. Polite language may be seen as deferential and indicative of low status in some situations but as effective and indicative of high status in others. For example, if polite linguistic features co-occur with a speaker's use of a valued dialect or language, such features may reinforce an impression of gentility, diplomacy, and such. On the other hand, polite language may reinforce an impression of servility when it is coupled with a speaker's use of nonstandard or stigmatized forms. Similarly, particular contextual features may interact with politeness to affect judgments of power. For example, communicators' membership in a devalued out-group versus membership in a valued in-group may affect the extent to which politeness is viewed as powerless or powerful, respectively. More generally, it may be the case that politeness will not reduce status ratings when polite forms are seen as being instrumental for speakers, that is, as increasing the likelihood of achieving their goals. The connections among politeness, nonstandardness of dialect, valued language forms, and impressions of power are the topics covered in the next chapter.

CHAPTER THREE

Signs of Power II:
More Variables, More Issues

In the preceding chapter, it was shown that virtually all of the research on power of style has focused on the powerless, or low-power, style. That is, research on the powerful, or high-power, style has been framed not on its own terms but, rather, always with reference to powerlessness. Within this research tradition, the powerful style is invariably thought of as the *nonuse* of low-power features such as hesitations and tag questions. This way of thinking about the powerful style has led to research that merely compares the presence of low-power language features with their absence. The research findings, although impressive, do not tell us what particular language variables are positively related to perception of high power. In this chapter, we discuss research that does examine this positive aspect.

To begin this discussion, let us note that in the United States the stereotype of the used-car salesman is well known. Essential features of this stereotype are maleness and a rapid rate of speech. Optional features include speech markers of ethnicity associated with lower-middle-class status. (An accent associated with the British upper-middle class would definitely not fit the stereotype.) An implication of the stereotype is, Don't trust this man. On the other hand, such a person may be viewed as an effective and competent strategist.

Other speech or language variables, in addition to rate of speech, also generate inferences about effectiveness and trustworthiness in message recipients, and we will discuss some of these variables in this chapter. Thus herein we go beyond the powerful and powerless styles to suggest the wide range of linguistic features that can, on the one hand, foster impressions of status, intelligence, and dynamism, and on the other hand, also affect persuasive effectiveness. Specifically, we will discuss accent and dialect (as these are associated with perceptions of standardness and nonstandardness), lexical diversity, speech rate, and language intensity. Following this brief survey, we will raise two important issues on language and power, focusing on the elusive role of gender and the ubiquity of experimentation as a research method. Finally, we will discuss the need for theoretical explanations in this area, and we will suggest some explanatory possibilities.

Other Language Variables

As suggested in the previous chapter, perhaps there is a style of tentativeness and a style of deference. These were the styles examined in the 1970s by O'Barr (1982) and Lakoff (1973) and later by other investigators who explored powerful and powerless speech (e.g., Bradac et al., 1981). But before this work, other research was conducted that has clear and important implications for the problem being pursued in this chapter. Furthermore, other relatively independent streams of investigation that were undertaken concurrently (i.e., in the 1970s and 1980s) are potentially pertinent.

Nonstandardness and Status Ratings

One of the oldest and perhaps most basic topics examined in the general area of sociolinguistics is the connection between language and social or economic status (Haslett, 1990). Some studies pursuing this question examined (and others continue to examine) objective indicators of status and their relationships to objective phonologic or syntactic features (Labov, 1970, 1972). Other studies, which are more pertinent here, have examined connections between linguistic features and perceptions or judgments of status (Giles & Coupland, 1991, chap. 2; Giles & Powesland, 1975). Some of these features reflect dialect differences that emerge from membership in different social groups varying in socioeconomic status, e.g., black vernacular English versus standard American English (historically, the dialect of the white middle-class in the United States). Given that two social groups are perceived to differ along the status dimension and that a particular dialect is associated with each group, it is not surprising that each dialect will carry different status connotations. Thus phonologic features of black English have been shown to produce judgments of lower speaker status than those of standard American English (Buck, 1968). Standard American accent has been shown to produce judgments of higher speaker status than does Mexican-American accent (Bradac & Wisegarver, 1984; Carranza, 1982).

The model here is rather clear: Accent (or other linguistic features) → perception of speaker group membership → judgment of group status → judgment of speaker status. The model becomes more complex and more interesting when other nonlinguistic variables are added to it, for example, communication context. Thus there is reason to believe that prior beliefs about speaker status combine additively with linguistic information, acquired from exposure to the speaker's message to produce a weighted judgment of status (Bradac & Wisegarver, 1984; Giles & Sassoon, 1983; Ryan & Bulik, 1982). According to this additive mechanism of information integration, a speaker with a Mexican-American accent who is believed to be a graduate of a prestigious university may be given an overall status rating that is equivalent to that given to a speaker of standard American English who is believed to have graduated from high school. One might guess, in the absence of research data, that language would completely override contextual information regarding status or vice versa, but such appears not to be the case.

Standardness or nonstandardness of speech, or more generally regionalism, may be a factor in persuasion. In an early study of southern versus standard (northern) American accents on judgments of speaker credibility in a persuasive context, Houck and Bowers (1969) found a relationship between the regional nature of the persuasive topic and accent. Specifically, a speaker employing a northern accent was judged more credible than was the same speaker employing a southern accent when he attempted to persuade northern college-student listeners in regard to a topic unrelated to regional norms. On the other hand, a southern accent was more credible when the topic was clearly related to a southern issue. The first outcome might be attributed to *identification* between the northern students and the northern speaker guise, whereas the second outcome might reflect a general belief that expertise results from direct as opposed to vicarious experience.

A later study further suggests that hearers' identification with speakers can mediate their perceptions of dialect or accent and the extent to which they are persuaded by speakers' messages. Giles (1973) exposed respondents to a message arguing against capital punishment after assessing their attitudes toward this topic. The message was presented in one of five versions: typescript, standard received pronunciation (RP) accent, and three regional accents. Research had shown (and continues to show) that RP accent is accorded higher prestige than are accents of a regional character. Respondents themselves used regional accents in their own speech. Results indicated that accent prestige (with RP at the top) was directly related to perceived argument quality. On the other hand, respondents' change of opinion in the direction advocated by the speaker occurred only in the case of the regional accented guises. This suggests that argumentative superiority was attributed stereotypically to the RP speaker. But when it came to actual feelings about capital punishment, quality of argument was not as important as perception of the speaker as a member of an in-group or out-group via accent.

At one level, the findings of the Giles's (1973) study are at odds with results of the Gibbons et al. (1991) study described in Chapter 2. In the former case, perceived argument strength and persuasion were inversely related, whereas in the latter case, they were directly related. There are several differences between the studies that may represent moderator variables operating to produce the opposing outcomes. For example, perhaps for topics that are highly familiar to individuals strong arguments will impel opinion change, whereas for less familiar topics, perceived speaker similarity will carry most of the weight, even to the point of overriding arguments judged to be strong. A familiar domain may allow people to focus on expertise, and unfamiliar territory may encourage them to place special value on similarity.

Lexical Diversity

Apart from dialect or accent differences, there are other language variables not clearly linked to membership in particular social groups that provide status information. One such variable that has been examined intensively is lexical diversity or vocabulary richness. There is good reason to believe that a speaker's manifest vocabulary range at any point in time is influenced by situational factors, such as factors that produce high or low speaker anxiety. One hypothesis with some support is that increased anxiety serves to reduce a speaker's level of diversity, presumably because words of high habit strength will be elicited by heightened drive and thus overused (Howeler, 1972). And no doubt there is variation in lexical diversity that is attached to individual speakers idiolectically, regardless of fluctuations in anxiety level—some people repeat words and phrases a lot, whereas others do not. On the other hand, evidence for a connection between diversity level and social group membership is scanty and questionable (Sankoff & Lessard, 1975).

Despite the probably weak objective link between social group membership and speaker lexical diversity level, there is evidence of a strong subjective link, that is, naive respondents perceive high diversity to indicate membership in high-status groups, high speaker economic status, and so on (Bradac, 1990; Bradac, Bowers, & Courtright, 1980). Thus, given the following two passages, the former ought to produce higher status ratings than the latter:

> I tried to explain my reasons for leaving, but he seemed too angry to hear what I was saying so I left the building and the next morning began looking for work elsewhere. The job search has continued since that day. I guess one should be more open to diverse employment possibilities than I have been.

> I tried to explain to him how I had reasons for resigning, but he seemed just too angry to hear what I said to him. So, I just left the building and the next day I began looking for other jobs. The job search has continued since that day. I guess I need to be more open to other job possibilities than I have been.

The effects of lexical diversity on judgments of speaker status (and on other types of judgments also) are influenced by different contextual variables. For example, a high-diversity message is likely to produce especially high ratings of status in an informal communication context, and a low-diversity message is likely to produce especially low status ratings in a context that is formal (Bradac, Konsky, & Davies, 1976). A high-diversity message that follows a message low in diversity is likely to produce higher status ratings than will its counterpart that follows a message that is also highly diverse, an outcome representing a perceptual contrast effect (Bradac, Davies, & Courtright, 1977). Finally (although other examples could be given), a speaker who shifts from a high level of diversity to another speaker's lower level will be rated higher in status than will a speaker who diverges from another's lower level by increasing his or her diversity level (Bradac et al., 1988).

In addition to affecting judgments of status, lexical diversity also affects judgments of intellectual competence and perceived communicator control of his or her own behavior (Bradac & Wisegarver, 1984). Specifically, as diversity level increases, judgments of competence and control will increase also. Thus, like accent and dialect, lexical diversity generates inferences about social class, and like politeness, diversity generates inferences regarding personality attributes as well: She is competent and in control. It is also the case that diversity level is linked to judgments of speaker state, just as hesitations and hedges are. There is evidence that diversity level is inversely related to judgments of speaker anxiety (Bradac et al., 1976). There is also some evidence indicating a connection between lexical diversity and persuasive effectiveness. Bradac, Courtright, and Bowers (1980) found that a high-diversity message produced more positive attitudes toward a proposed tuition increase than did its low-diversity counterpart. The effect for lexical diversity was substantially stronger than the effects for two other language variables (verbal immediacy and language intensity, which will be defined later).

So, one might describe lexical diversity as an attributionally rich feature of language in that it provides information—potentially incorrect information, it should be noted—about communicator affiliations, traits, and states. Interestingly, as may be the case with the power of style variable noted in Chapter 2, there is one bit of evidence suggesting that low diversity is the marked case. Bradac, Desmond, and Murdock (1977) created messages representing three levels of diversity: 0.72, 0.82, and 0.92. These values represent average type/token ratios (number of novel words per number of total words) for N 25-word segments of discourse (N is number of segments in a message). There is some evidence that 0.82 is an average type/token ratio for the speech of college students, whereas 0.72 and 0.92 are two standard deviations below and above average, respectively. Respondents who rated speakers exhibiting one of the three diversity levels were much more negative toward the 0.72 message than toward the 0.82 and the 0.92 messages; on the other hand, the 0.82 and 0.92 messages did not differ in their effects. This again may reflect the pervasive negativity effect (Kellermann, 1989; see also Chapter 2). A low level of diversity may violate a *valued norm* of linguistic expression in the same way that use of a broad nonstandard accent does (Ball, Giles, Byrne, & Berechree, 1984).

Speech Rate

Another language variable that has been shown to affect impressions of power, specifically intellectual competence, is speech rate. Whereas accent and dialect are clearly associated with both objective and perceived group affiliations, rate is not; rather it is a variable associated primarily with individual differences (some people speak very rapidly) and with situational variation (anxiety-provoking situations tend to elicit a relatively rapid rate from many speakers). The effects of rate on attributions of speaker competence have been rather consistent across studies. Increased rate is directly and linearly related to competence judgments (Brown, 1980) or directly related up to a point, where a plateau is reached and further increases have no effect (Street, Brady, & Putman, 1983). There is also evidence that an increased rate of speech facilitates persuasive effectiveness, probably because it functions as a credibility cue (Miller, Maruyama, Beaber, & Valone, 1976).

There are some contextual qualifiers of the competence-enhancing effects of rapid speech rate, although not very much research on contextual variables has been conducted. One study suggests that the positive effects of a rapid rate are diminished in the case of elderly speakers, while the negative effects of a slow rate are intensified (Stewart & Ryan, 1982). When the communication situation is a formal one, a slow rate of speech seems especially likely to be downgraded (Street & Brady, 1982), except when the communicator is talking to a naive audience on a highly technical topic, in which case the slow rate can be discounted via an attribution of situational causation (Brown, Giles, & Thackerar, 1985). There is some evidence that rapid speech may be evaluated especially positively and slow speech especially negatively by respondents whose own speech rate is usually rapid (Street et al., 1983). Thus hearers with habitually high speech rates would assign maximally low ratings of intellectual competence to speakers talking slowly about a simple topic in a formal situation. In such a situation (and in others) a slow rate may signal uncertainty about the self-audience relationship, an inadequate grasp of ideas, ideational disfluency, and so on. In this case it would seem to parallel hesitation and hedging, and indeed rate may be correlated with these two variables in many instances of speech production.

Language Intensity

In everyday language people say, "She comes on really strong on that topic" or "He is extremely firm on that issue." Without realizing it, they may be referring to the intensity of the speaker's language. In an early paper on the topic, Bowers (1963) defined intensity as "the quality of language which indicates the degree to which the speaker's attitude toward a concept deviates from neutrality" (p. 345). Thus a speaker can be weakly positive toward a concept, approaching neutrality, or extremely positive; the same logic holds for negative views that a speaker might have. In more technical terms, language intensity is independent of attitudinal valence. In many Western cultures, words such as *very, definitely,* and *decidedly* heighten message recipients' perceptions of a speaker's intensity of feeling or commitment as will words such as *despise* and *loathe* (or *love* and *adore*). In one study, Bowers (1964) found that speakers who used sex or death metaphors were likely to be perceived as highly intense.

The important question for us is, What consequences do high- or low-intensity language have for judgments of communicator competence, status, or dynamism or for persuasive effectiveness? There is no simple answer to this question. It appears that language intensity interacts with a variety of contextual factors and that its effects are accordingly complex. For example, communicators who are perceived initially to be high in competence or status may enhance their persuasiveness by using highly intense language (Miller & Basehart, 1969). On the other hand, communicators viewed as incompetent or low in status would be advised to use language that is low in intensity. Viewing competence as a dependent variable—as a variable affected by high- or low-intensity language—it appears that highly intense language may have negative effects if the communicator's message is attitudinally discrepant from the audience's standpoint (Mehrley & McCroskey, 1970; McEwen & Greenberg, 1970).

Another contextual variable that interacts with intensity in important ways is communicator gender. A study conducted in 1975 by Burgoon, Jones, and Stewart led Bradac, Bowers, and Courtright (1979) to offer the following generalization: "Language intensity and 'maleness' interact in the production of attitude change in such a way that intensity . . . enhances the effect of male but inhibits the effect of female sources" (p. 261). In other words males may enhance their persuasiveness by using high-intensity language, whereas females may do likewise by using language of low intensity. Bradac, Bowers and Courtright (1979) suggested that their generalization regarding gender "is almost certainly bound to a particular set of transitory social circumstances in a way that [our] other generalizations are not" (p. 261). Interestingly, the transitory social circumstances apparently are still with us, because a recent study by Burgoon, Birk, and Hall (1991) replicated the 1975 finding. Specifically, a message produced by a male physician using high-intensity language was more effective than was a comparable message used by a female counterpart. There appears to be something about the male role that "allows" men to use strong words and phrases; on the other hand, the female role apparently favors neutral or even weak expressive forms. We will have more to say about connections between language and gender below.

It appears then, that accent, dialect, lexical diversity, speech rate, and language intensity can all affect impressions of power and persuasive effectiveness just as surely as powerful and power-less speech styles can. Perhaps the ultimately powerless speaker exhibits nonstandard accent or dialect, high hesitancy, many hedges, much repetition, and a slow rate of speech. It does not stretch the imagination at all to think of these characteristics as clustering together, especially in situations when the speaker's nonstandard-ness is highly salient—situations producing high objective self-awareness (Duvall & Wicklund, 1973) or, from another standpoint, situations that threaten group identity (Hogg, 1985). A high level of politeness may also fit into this cluster and in the context of non-standardness, high hesitancy, and so forth may indeed reinforce the impression of low power, despite the positive relationship be-tween polite forms and power impressions uncovered in previous research that examined the effect of these forms in isolation.

Issues in Studying the Signs of Power

Power and Gender

As suggested in the previous chapter by the reference to Lakoff (1973, 1975), much of the research on language and power has invoked the concept of gender for a variety of reasons. The essence of Lakoff's claim is that women in American society (and in others) have been socialized into a low-power role and that a part of this role entails using a style of speech labeled the *feminine register*. The language features representing this register are very similar to the features representing the low-power style (O'Barr, 1982). Although the evidence of an objective connection between femaleness and the use of tag questions, hedges, and hesitations is weak and variable (Bradac, Mulac, & Thompson, n.d.; Smith, 1985), there is some evidence that the use of some forms in some situations can distinguish male and female speakers (e.g., Carli, 1990).

The research of Mulac and associates has consistently shown that discourse, both written and oral, produced by males is rated by naive respondents as high in dynamism, whereas discourse produced by females is rated high in esthetic quality. Furthermore, there is some evidence, albeit less robust, that female language is rated more positively on the dimension of sociointellectual status. This pattern has been labeled the *gender-linked language effect* (see, e.g., Mulac, 1976; Mulac & Lundell, 1982, 1986). Although there is variation across studies (Mulac, Lundell, & Bradac, 1986), some features have been statistically associated with maleness and with high dynamism ratings in two or more independent investigations, for example, commission of grammatical errors. Other features have been associated with femaleness and high ratings of esthetic quality and socioeconomic status, for example, use of adverbs at the beginning of a sentence.

Thus there is some reason to believe that males and females (in the United States, at least) differ to some extent in their use of language, although in ways differing from the style suggested by Lakoff (1973, 1975), and that particular male and female forms affect impressions of power. It seems likely, however, that situational factors such as communicator role are stronger influences on language production than is language per se (Crosby & Nyquist, 1977). For example, a male placed in the role of low authority in an ambiguous situation may exhibit many hesitations and hedges. Also, it is not clear that differences in male-female language behavior are connected to differences in actual or self-perceived power; an alternative possibility is that men and women inhabit (and grow up in) different cultures (Maltz & Borker, 1982; Mulac & Gibbons, 1992). For example, it has been suggested that men learn to view social behavior in terms of the abstract value of justice, whereas women learn to emphasize values of nurturance and concern for individuals (Gilligan, 1982). This distinction is not related in any simple way to differences in power.

However, even though objective linguistic differences appear to be small and their relationship to objective differences in power unclear, there appear to be widely shared, strong beliefs or stereotypes about how men and women talk (Mulac et al., 1986; Tannen, 1986): Women are more tentative, less direct, and more highly involved in conversation, for example. An interesting question is, If objective, behavioral differences between genders are slight and variable, what explains the strong beliefs about gender-linked linguistic differences? It could be that there is an overarching belief that men are in some sense powerful and this belief generalizes to the more particular domain of language, even in the absence of confirming data. Or, perhaps in the past, differences in language behavior were relatively great; accurate beliefs were formed on the basis of these past differences; the differences diminished across generations as gender-based behavioral codes were liberalized, but the beliefs persisted despite behavioral changes and thus became inaccurate—the tenacity of some social beliefs even when confronted with potentially disconfirming data has been noted (Brown, 1965).

Hence many people think that women talk less powerfully than men do, but the best evidence indicates that women (in the United States) are lower on the dynamism dimension of perceived power only. On the dimensions of status and intellectual competence, there may actually be a weak tendency for female language to produce higher ratings than does male language; in this sense, females may use a relatively powerful register. But this register differs from that derived intuitively by Lakoff (1973, 1975).

Limitations of Experimentation on Impressions of Power

Most of the studies exploring connections among impressions of power, persuasive effectiveness, and the use of specific forms of language have employed experimental techniques. The general advantages and disadvantages of experimentation are well known (Cook & Campbell, 1979), so there is no need to discuss these here. Rather, it may be useful to discuss particular advantages and disadvantages apparent in work on language and power.

One advantage was broadly hinted at in Chapter 2: Untangling the knot of the individual effects of the subcomponents of power would be impossible without the controlled comparisons allowed by experiments. And the apparently inconsequential or, at most, slight roles played by both respondent and communicator gender in the production of impressions of power triggered by language have been discoverable through the use of orthogonally manipulated variables. Similarly, orthogonal manipulation in factorial designs has enabled researchers to investigate the potentially qualifying effects of contextual variables, for example, communicator intention to inform a naive audience about a technical topic.

Turning to disadvantages, in real-life contexts power always carries consequences for agents and objects, archers and targets, message senders and message recipients. In almost all of the experiments cited thus far, the consequences for respondents listening to or reading messages varying in language style have been low or nonexistent. That is, for a given respondent rating a given audio-taped message source as highly competent, very little would change in that respondent's life were she or he to change the rating to low competence. But that same respondent might behave very differently depending on whether a judgment of high or low competence were to be made of a physician in a medical context or a candidate for political office.

It is not clear just how the variable personal consequence, or personal relevance, would affect reactions to high- or low-power language. It might be the case that message recipients would attend primarily to message substance, not style, in the case of a communicator talking about something with clear consequences. Conversely, in the case of a situation with low relevance or consequence, language variables associated with power might serve as a peripheral cue that would drive attitude toward the communicator and the message (Petty & Cacioppo, 1986). However, a study that examined the joint effects of personal relevance and power of style did not find the interactive relationship between the two variables just described (i.e., differences in power of style becoming salient under low relevance but not high relevance), rather the two variables independently affected judgments of communicator competence (Gibbons et al., 1991).

In principle, it is possible to incorporate personal consequences in experiments, to attach consequences to messages, but virtually all of the studies of language and power have failed to do so. This is an important gap.

Another gap of some import emerges from the fact that all of the experiments on language and impressions of power have cast respondents in a passive role as processors of audio-taped or written monologues; we do not know how individuals react to differences in power of style in interactive situations. It seems possible, even likely, that a rapid rate of speech directed at one's self by an interactional partner may function differently, may have a different force, than would the same rate overheard when directed at a third party. Or hesitations produced by an interactional partner may affect one's own attempts to gain the floor, to interrupt, and so forth, and therefore, one may respond to these differently than to hesitations produced by a speaker delivering a monologue (see Chapter 4). Interactants have different responsibilities than do readers or hearers processing monologues and these responsibilities may affect message evaluation (Street, 1985).

All of the experiments on language and power have exposed respondents to monologues on a single occasion; they have been one-shot studies. What effect might repeated exposure to low- or high-power messages produced by a single communicator on multiple occasions have on evaluations of this communicator? Perhaps message recipients would come to expect low-power language, for example, by the nth occasion, and accordingly, on this occasion its use would not constitute a violation of linguistic expectations (Burgoon & Miller, 1985); thus, the magnitude of recipients' negativity might be reduced. From another perspective, extremity of reactions to low-power language might diminish as a result of recipients' habituation to it (Linz, Donnerstein, & Penrod, 1984). For habituated respondents the use of low-power linguistic forms would be less informative and less arousing than for those who are not habituated (Bradac & Street, 1989/1990).

All of this is speculative in the absence of research exploring the effects of multiple messages over time. Experiments can examine this sort of multiplicity. The limitation or disadvantage of one-shot experiments is, once again, a practical one, not one that is necessary in principle.

The Need for Explanations

The empirical regularities aside, the question remains, Why do people respond as they do to high- and low-power language? Why do certain forms produce ratings of high intellectual competence, while others produce ratings of high dynamism? Why are certain forms more persuasive than others?

The general possibilities have been discussed by Bradac and Street (1989/1990), and these might be labeled the *inherent-natural* connection between language and power on the one hand and the *associative-conventional* connection on the other. That is, in regard to the former, perhaps some forms (e.g., high volume or loudness and perhaps a rapid rate) are directly or inherently tied to a judgment of high dynamism by virtue of their producing high arousal in message recipients. But in the case of various syntactic and lexical forms it seems likely that a judgment of high or low intellectual competence is rooted in learned conventional associations between the form and the judgment. Message recipients have learned that thoughtful people talk in a certain way. As suggested above, this learning may assume the form of acquiring stereotypical, inaccurate beliefs in some cases, whereas in other cases it may lead to accurate knowledge: People who use certain dialects really do have low social power in the society at large.

But there is another kind or level of explanation that can fill out the picture, a more molecular one that is empirically tractable, although very little of this work has been done in fact. One can explore the cognitive basis of connections between language forms and judgments. For example, what cognitions mediate the perception of a high number of speaker hedges and the evaluation that the speaker is low in competence? Or what do respondents think about when they hear an extremely rapid speaker (Giles, Henwood, Coupland, Harriman, & Coupland, 1992). In a sense, cognitions that mediate perceptions and evaluations of competence, status, and dynamism explain these evaluations: She rated him as competent because she believes that his rapid speech indicates considerable mental agility.

In some cases, evaluations will reflect tacit knowledge structures or schemata that can only be discovered indirectly. For example, one might discover that when a nonstandard accent is used by a speaker, judgments of low status will tend to occur and that these judgments will tend to be associated with beliefs that the speaker is low in control (perhaps measured with a Likert-type scale). Furthermore, one might find (e.g., via partial correlation analysis) that when the beliefs about control are removed, the effects of accent on status judgments are eliminated, but removing the effects of status judgments does not diminish the effects of accents on beliefs about control. Such a pattern might suggest that beliefs about control establish the basis for negative status evaluations of nonstandard accent. Respondents may have little or no awareness of this mediating effect of control-related beliefs.

On the other hand, in some cases one can probe directly thoughts that individuals have while listening to speakers exhibiting high- or low-power language. A retrospective thought listing task can be used following a speech (Giles et al., 1992) as can a task that asks respondents to indicate what they are thinking immediately following interruptions made at points throughout the speech (Hawkins, Pingree, Fitzpatrick, Thompson, & Bauman, 1991). As mentioned in Chapter 2, Gibbons et al. (1991) found that respondents indicated that they thought about low-power language in a message but not about high-power language. This pattern can be assimilated to the more general negativity effect, which may exist because there is social, even biological, survival value in attending to negative information. Thus an explanation for the effects of power of style is that there is some kind of survival value in attending to hedges, hesitations, and so on. Perhaps a variety of negatively deviant language forms function in this way (Bradac, Desmond, & Murdock, 1977).

This a partial and tentative explanation, to be sure, but it does invite the interesting question, What may be the special value in noticing and thinking about the low-power forms (and other negative forms)? Burling (1986) has discussed the survival value of complex language, or language that is lexically and syntactically diverse or in a positive and powerful form. The essence of his hypothesis is that leaders need more complex language than nonleaders to maintain their position in the hierarchy, so those with innate tendencies to speak complexly will gravitate to positions of leadership; leaders have more children than others do, thus complex language is retained in human evolution. This hypothesis is only plausible to the extent that there is a genetic basis for linguistic complexity (there is no evidence for this, although there is evidence of a genetic component in some language pathologies).

Perhaps the very leaders who use complex language are especially attentive to forms that reduce force and precision such as hedges and hesitations. Thus attentiveness to low-power language has been retained and selected across the millennia. It should be clear that all of this is exceedingly speculative, with only the slightest shred of supporting data. Still, the idea that we may have a biological tendency to orient ourselves to signs of power or signs of powerlessness is hardly a radical one. Of course, this tendency will manifest itself variously across cultures, situations, and language users.

More Explanatory Possibilities

Several theories exist that offer additional perspectives on a communicator's use of language, message recipient's perceptions of communicator power, and persuasive effectiveness. These theories were not necessarily designed to inform us about language and power, but they offer pertinent insights nevertheless. We will discuss each of these rather briefly to give a sense of the range of possibilities.

Uncertainty reduction theory, originally formulated by Berger and Calabrese (1975), suggests that a primary social drive in humans is the reduction of uncertainty about other humans. Humans want to be able to predict how others will behave and what they will think in many situations. There is, of course, an upper limit on this desire: Complete predictability leads to boredom (Berger & Bradac, 1982). The theory predicts, for example, that as the nonverbal affiliative expressiveness of a communicator increases, the uncertainty of the message recipient will decrease. Verbal behaviors can also produce increases or decreases in uncertainty. This suggests an idea that is important for us: Power of style, speech rate, lexical diversity, and so on can affect impressions of communicator power, which in turn can affect a message recipient's uncertainty level. Indeed, it seems reasonable to suggest that a communicator's level of perceived power will be an especially important variable in the uncertainty reduction process. For example, if we judge a person as quite powerful, we may be more highly motivated to reduce uncertainty than if we make a judgment of low power. Such a person may carry high reward or punishment potential (Berger, 1979). This point is also consistent with Sunnafrank's (1986) predicted outcome value theory. (There are areas of disagreement between the theories of predicted outcome value and uncertainty reduction, but these need not concern us here.)

Another thing that communicators can do to increase or decrease hearer uncertainty is to violate or fulfill, respectively, the expectations that hearers have for their behavior. The concept of expectations is central to a number of theories, but here we will focus on a theory that is especially relevant in this context: language expectancy theory (Burgoon & Miller, 1985; Burgoon, 1990). This theory postulates that hearers have expectations about the kind of language that communicators will and should use—expectations about word choice, syntax, pronunciation, and such. Thus, for example, hearers may expect that a speaker will use a rich vocabulary and polished English, and for them this may constitute a positive expectation. If this speaker in fact uses much repetition and poor grammar, hearers' expectations will be violated, and this will be a negative violation. Negative violations typically will result in reduced persuasive effectiveness and judgments of low communicator competence. On the other hand, if hearers expect a poor linguistic performance and the speaker dazzles them verbally, this will be a positive violation and it should have positive communicative consequences.

This theory suggests that hearers expect powerful individuals to use powerful language: In many contexts, if such people use powerless forms, the result will constitute a negative expectancy violation. Conversely, the use of powerful language by an ostensibly powerless person should constitute a positive violation in many situations. The predictions of language expectancy theory regarding powerful and powerless language need to be tested directly. There is some evidence that is indirectly supportive: Bradac, Davies, & Courtright (1977) found that if one speaker used a high-diversity style and a second speaker used a low-diversity style, reactions to the second person were especially negative. Presumably, the first speaker established a general linguistic expectation that the second speaker violated in a negative way.

In their discussion of powerful and powerless styles of talk, Bradac and Street (1989/1990) offer a model postulating two general cognitive processes, namely, "perceptual processes which transform actual message behaviors into their perceptual counterparts" and "interpretive processes which produce affective reactions to the perceived behaviors, associating them with personal attributes which are inferred about a speaker" (p. 209). The first process suggests that message recipients may add or delete and thereby distort information from speakers, for example, perceiving low-power forms in discourse when objectively such forms are not apparent. Central to the second process is the construct *range of salience,* which has four components. First, there is weighting, which "indicates that particular language behaviors are weighted in terms of the degree to which they are indicative of power" (p. 209). The second component is shape, which suggests that as the values of a language variable change, judgments of power will change or covary also, but this covariance can assume different forms—linear, quadratic, and so forth—depending on a variety of factors. The third component is width, which indicates "how narrow or wide the range of salience is" (p. 211). For some language variables, only extreme values will be noticed, whereas for others even small departures from an average level will be salient. The fourth component is placement, which "refers to where the behavior is judged to fall within the range of salience—is it closer to one boundary or the other?" (p. 211). Placement influences the extent to which an evaluation is positive or negative on a given dimension (e.g., competence and status). In most communication situations, the four components will operate simultaneously to affect impressions of power and effectiveness of persuasive attempts.

The two theories that remain to be discussed provide a bridge to the next chapter in that they focus on interaction or conversation rather than on monological speech: communication accommodation theory (Coupland & Giles, 1988) and a theory of message relevance in the production of persuasive effects (Sanders, 1989). The former theory has a long history and is well developed, whereas the latter is new and ripe for exploration. Communication accommodation theory assumes that interactants mutually adjust the style and content of their talk on a given occasion. For example, if one person is speaking French and another English, the former can shift to the latter's language or vice versa, perhaps to be polite, to be mutually intelligible, or to express mutual approval. There are many types of communication adjustments that are possible, but two of the most important are convergence (as in the previous example) and divergence, which occurs when one speaker moves away from the other's language or dialect. For example, when an initial speaker uses English and a second speaker who is capable of speaking English, uses French, the second speaker is engaging in divergent behavior. Such behavior may signal disapproval, enhance linguistic distinctiveness, and as a result, may be viewed as impolite. Generally, assuming no contrary information regarding communication intentions, convergence will be viewed as an act that increases solidarity and divergence will be viewed as having an opposite effect.

The connections among divergence, convergence, or more generally, communicator adjustments, and impressions of power, persuasive effectiveness, and so on are extremely complex. In situations in which perceptions of high communicator solidarity will be viewed favorably, convergence will often be associated with persuasiveness. This would typically be the case when both interactants are members of the same in-group. Conversely, in situations of the sort described above, divergence will most likely detract from persuasive success. On the other hand, in situations in which communicator status (as opposed to solidarity) is especially salient, when one speaker diverges from another by moving in the direction of a prestigious style or language, such divergence may enhance persuasiveness. But, as an illustration of the complexity, there is some evidence that one speaker's convergence to another speaker's lower level of lexical diversity can enhance judgments of the first speaker's status, at least when such judgments are made by third parties observing the interaction (Bradac et al., 1988).

Sanders (1989) has offered a theory (perhaps a prototheory) of "message effects via induced changes in the social meaning of a response" (p. 165). The key idea is that persuasion can occur independently of what message recipients believe regarding the persuader's position on a topic. In some situations, probably most typically situations with a strong social-interpersonal component, individuals will respond to a communicator's persuasive recommendation because the response is fitting, coherent, and socially appropriate and not because it makes sense in terms of what the message recipient believes about the world. In Sanders's (1989) words,

in unscripted face-to-face interactions, the effect of a given message on what the partner subsequently says and does is at least in part a consequence of the way that the message limits what can be subsequently contributed relevantly, coherently, to the discursive construction being produced, given structural relations and meaning relations that have already developed among messages produced in the interaction. (p. 166)

Thus a skilled communicator may induce a message recipient to comply to a request for a campaign contribution by making compliance socially fitting with what has transpired in the interaction before the request was made. This compliance may subsequently affect the complier's beliefs about the world (Bem, 1972), but this is a secondary effect. Many linguistic devices exist that facilitate the coherence of interactions (e.g., back references and forecasting), and it seems likely that many powerful communicators have internalized these devices thoroughly.

* * *

The above discussion has reinforced the claim that evaluations of communicators are affected by the kinds of language used as messages are transmitted. Or, more accurately, such evaluations are affected by message recipients' perceptions of language features (Street & Hopper, 1982). In some cases, message recipients should be rather accurate in their perceptions of language, whereas in others, various kinds of distortions may occur that reflect perceptual and cognitive biases (Bradac & Street, 1989/1990). Research in the future might well profit from the further examination of factors associated with accurate perceptions of power-related language features on one hand and inaccurate perceptions on the other. For example, might a low fear of judgmental invalidity and a high need for cognitive structure lead message recipients expecting to hear a low-status speaker to perceive the speaker's accent as nonstandard when, in fact, it is standard (Kruglanski & Freund, 1983; Williams, Whitehead, & Miller, 1972)?

More particularly, a variety of specific language features have been shown to affect judgments of communicators and the persuasiveness of their messages, including accent or dialect, lexical diversity, speech rate, and language intensity. Contextual factors may intensify or attenuate the effects of these features. For example, a slow speech rate may be discounted in the case of a speaker discoursing on a technical topic or perhaps in the case of an adult talking to a child or to a frail elderly person. A low level of lexical diversity may be reacted to especially negatively in formal communication (Bradac et al., 1976).

Researchers could probably continue to document with some profit the effects of particular linguistic forms on impressions of power and persuasive effectiveness, but perhaps more profitable will be studies that examine systematically the impact of contextual features on these impressions, going well beyond the global variables examined in the past such as formality-informality. Researchers might, for example, take a hint from conversation analysts and move to a more molecular level of context, perhaps attempting to uncover conversational places where particular forms, say obscenities, function in one way and other places where they function in another way. For example, an informal (perhaps totally incorrect) observation is that certain types of obscenities occurring at the beginning of a conversational turn function as a kind of speaker transition device and, accordingly, may not be stigmatized even if used frequently ("Shit, I thought that he didn't like me."). On the other hand, obscenities occurring within clauses ("I thought that . . . shit . . . he didn't like me") may be evaluated negatively.

Another line of research, which lays even greater stress on the conversational functions of particular language forms, examines how conversationalists make use of various language forms as linguistic resources for controlling a conversation. A fast speech rate, for example, may facilitate a speaker's controlling a conversation by successfully interrupting a current turn of talk. This does not mean that the monological forms of language identified here and in Chapter 2 will provide the answer for conversational influence and control. Surely, some of them will remain relevant, but because conversational influence is enacted interactionally between two or more individuals and sequentially across time, the relevant language forms must be understood in an interactional and sequential framework that will also incorporate, for reasons that will be made clear in the next chapter, a host of other linguistic resources.

CHAPTER FOUR

Conversational Influence and Control

Everyday conversation is arguably the most pervasive and common of all social interactions among human beings. Perhaps because everyday conversation is so common and ordinary, participants in a conversation tend to take it for granted and do not fully realize or acknowledge the extensive range of personal achievements and failures that are routinely enacted in and through conversation. Yet conversation is inextricably involved in everyday life and can, at times, make or break relationships between individuals, the conduct of their business, and their self-esteem.

In a conversation, participants exchange utterances as well as coordinate the meaning, timing, and sequence of their speech behavior. The exchange and coordination processes between individuals, more than the production and comprehension of speech by individuals, characterize the interactional nature of conversational activities. Coordination processes, in particular, are crucial to the understanding of conversation as a form of social interaction (Clark, 1985; Nofsinger, 1991).

The prototypical form of conversation, in the sense defined by Sacks, Schegloff, & Jefferson (1974), is a speech-exchange system in which the length and order of speaking turns have not been preassigned but require coordination on an utterance-by-utterance basis. Examples are gossip, verbal insult, arguing, intimate talk among family members, and such like. This form of conversation is the "basic form of speech-exchange system, with other forms . . . representing a variety of transformations of the conversation turn-taking system" (Sacks et al., 1974,

p. 730). Other forms of conversation in which speaking turns are to some extent preassigned but still require coordination include ceremonies, interviews, debates, tutorials, and negotiations.

Conversational influence and control, the theme of this chapter, are outwardly most apparent in influence attempts that flow from a speaker in a powerful role to an addressee in a less powerful role. This may occur in a conversation of the type specified by Sacks et al. (1974) and also in other speech-exchange settings in which speaking turns are more or less preassigned. A prime example, taken from the latter type of setting, is teacher-to-pupil communication in the classroom. In the routine course of a lesson, the teacher is institutionally much better placed than pupils to exercise conversational control: The teacher asks a question, presents it to the class as a whole for open bidding, selects a particular pupil as the next speaker, focuses (via the question) the pupil's reply on the topic in question, and afterward evaluates the given reply (Sinclair & Coulthard, 1975). In this conversational sequence, the teacher remains in control of the structure of the talk exchange (who speaks and for how long), its content (topic and focus), and the evaluation of the content. Similarly, dominant television interviewers can also exercise control over all three domains (Owsley & Scotton, 1984).

There are of course conversational settings in which the scope of control by a single participant is less extensive and the direction of conversational influence is more mutual than that in classroom conversation. In these relatively nonhierarchical settings, conversational influence is much harder to track. Nevertheless, they are also prime situations for research on conversational influence, especially in relation to the emergence of leadership and to mutual influence among peers (Hollander, 1985). Throughout this chapter, we will refer to both hierarchically structured (based on social roles such as teachers and pupils, interviewers and interviewees) and unstructured conversations to explicate, in the former, how hierarchical dominance is enacted or resisted during the course of the conversation and, in the latter, how conversational influence emerges.

To examine conversational influence in hierarchically structured and unstructured situations, we will want to underscore the interactional features that distinguish conversational influence from powerful monological speech that has already been discussed in Chapters 2 and 3. Goffman (1959) used the notion of *working consensus* to describe how conversationalists project a definition of the situation on one another and achieve an agreement as to whose claims concerning what issues will be temporarily honored in the flow of the conversation. Given a working consensus, together with an understanding of what is going on (i.e., a frame; Goffman, 1974), conversationalists orient to and engage in conversational moves. In the course of the conversation, they collaborate cooperatively (e.g., trying to make themselves understood) but also contend competitively (e.g., stealing a conversational turn) with each other. They also play along collusively (McDermott & Tylbor, 1983). It is in these kinds of interactional settings that the present discussion of conversational influence will be anchored. The interactional focus will enable us to discuss not only conversational influence that arises from one speaker bludgeoning others into submission, but also—perhaps more important—conversational influence that is achieved with the complicity of those who submit (Edelsky & Adams, 1990; Swann, 1988).

Conversational interaction may be likened to driving an automobile through busy streets: in both activities, participants are required to work out a coordination of their actions through the joint application of relevant shared conventions. The requirement of interpersonal coordination is in addition to the requirement of individual linguistic competence, just as in the case of driving a car, coordination among motorists is needed over and above individual physical driving skills. A physically skilled driver who is ignorant of or unwilling to play by the traffic conventions of a country would have a difficult time trying to drive in that country. Likewise, a linguistically competent person, who is "capable of any of all grammatical utterances, but not knowing which to use, not knowing when to talk and when to stop, would be a cultural monstrosity" (Hymes, 1967, p. 16).

The problem of traffic coordination is "solved" by means of the convention of road codes. Road codes regulate driving conduct such as car speed, maneuvering, and showing courtesy for other road users; in addition, they also standardize the meaning of road signs, traffic lights, and car signals. For a system of road codes to be a usable convention, however, it must be *common* knowledge among motorists (see Lewis, 1969). When this condition is met, the joint application of road codes by motorists will solve the problem of traffic coordination.

Like their motorist counterparts, conversationalists also have to work out a coordination of their conversational behaviors. The successful coordination of conversational interaction is in one sense easier and in another more difficult than traffic coordination. It is easier in that even very young children are able success-fully to coordinate the meaning, timing, and sequence of their conversational behaviors. It is more difficult in that there is no exact equivalent of a copy of the road codes for conversation—most of the social conventions governing conversation are tacit and open to exploitation by dominant, ascendant participants.

For present purposes, we discuss conversational influence under the domains of conversational roles, turn taking, and topic flow. A conversation begins when participants successfully engage each other in their respective speaker and hearer roles. These roles circulate in the course of the conversation as conversationalists take turns at talking. As the conversation unfolds, what is being talked about becomes the current focal topic that will in due course develop into or be replaced by another topic. Role engage-ment, turn taking, and topic flow are integral to conversation although turn taking, because of its central importance to the exchange and coordination of conversational actions, has been the single most well developed area of conversation research. Conver-sational interaction proceeds simultaneously in all three domains, collaboratively at times but also contentiously or even competi-tively at others. In this chapter, we show how conversational roles, turn taking, and topic flow will give rise, respectively, to the power of casting, speakership, and topic control.

Casting

Casting is one of several strategies for engaging participants in their respective conversational roles; the others are mirroring and negotiation (Pearce, 1976). Pearce (1976) explained casting by means of a script-acting analogy. An actor wanting to play a favorite part in a script must find a stage and a group of people to fill the other roles. The actor offers them particular roles and engages them to enact the assigned roles on his or her own terms. Likewise, speakers may cast, by direct or indirect means, their hearers into particular conversational roles. Mirroring is the opposite of casting.

> When coordinating by mirroring, persons communicate by seeking to discover what the other person wants them to do and eliciting feedback to see if they are doing well. Mirroring has a dependent, acquiescent tone and may perhaps best be detected by observing chameleon-like changes as the person moves between various relationships and situations. (Pearce, 1976, p. 25)

In negotiation, there is more *mutual* compromise than in either casting or mirroring. The negotiation procedure may involve, for example, speakers talking explicitly about the episodes that are or may be enacted. Alternatively, at the beginning of enacting an episode, a speaker may invite others to take up complementary roles; this makes the latter feel they are being included in the interaction from the outset. Or the episode can be made attractive to the other individuals, on the understanding that the latter will then reciprocate.

Of the three strategies, casting provides the most direct means of controlling a conversation. Consider the following conversational excerpt taken from Pearce (1976, p. 28).

1. TOM: Hey, did you hear what happened downtown today?
2. DICK: Tell me.
3. TOM: No, I was asking you.
4. DICK: Oh, well, there was a demonstration at the post office . . .

At the beginning Tom tried to cast Dick in a news-teller role by means of an indirect request encoded in the form of a question (1). Dick understood the request not as a genuine request for information but, rather, as a preannouncement used by Tom for telling him what had happened in town. So Dick mirrored himself in the listener role and communicated his intention at the first available speaking turn (2) by saying, "Tell me." In doing so, Dick missed what Austin (1962) has called the illocutionary point of Tom's utterance, and miscoordinated his own conversational role. Note that Dick's miscoordination was a joint result of his mirroring and Tom's ambiguous casting. In the next immediate move (3), Tom tried to realign the conversational roles by explicitly casting Dick into the information-giver role, a role that Dick promptly remirrored himself into. The episodic coordination of conversational roles is reminiscent of the kinesic movements of two dancing partners who, after discovering a wrong footing, collaborate to repair the wrong and then move on with the tempo and rhythm of the music. It should be obvious by now that role casting, and the coordination of conversational roles more generally, cannot be reduced to turn taking even though role casting is enacted over a sequence of turns.

In the stretch of conversation between Tom and Dick, casting and mirroring proceed on a complementary basis. In other conversations, a caster may find no obliging mirrorer, or may be unwilling to switch to a negotiating mode. When this occurs, there will be moments of tension as conversationalists persist in their competition for the control of conversational roles, for example, during combative political interviews (Danet, 1980) and courtroom proceedings (Atkinson & Drew, 1979).

Hearer Roles

To carry out the analysis of the power of casting a step further, it will be useful to develop first a model that differentiates more precisely the various conversational roles. At one level, there are hearer and speaker roles. At another, finer level, there are various hearer roles and various speaker roles. Note that the present focus has been on conversational roles as enacted by conversationalists, and not on social roles in the more general sociological sense (see Hilbert, 1981). Clark and Carlson (1982) distinguished three hearer roles: addressee, participant, and overhearer. The addressee role should be obvious. Participant is a role assigned to a hearer whom the speaker intends to take part on a supportive basis in the conversational act that is directed at the addressee. The overhearer may be an eavesdropper from whom the speaker wants to conceal the message (see Chapter 6) or an audience that the speaker wants to address indirectly. Only the overhearer role will be of immediate concern here.

To illustrate the various hearer roles with an adapted example from Clark and Carlson (1982), let us suppose that Ann and Charles have just discussed, in a private corner of a department store, how absurd deer-stalker caps look. Later, at the checkout counter, Ann addresses the store manager, in front of Charles and with other customers overhearing, "What a handsome deer-stalker cap you are wearing!" In doing so, Ann casts the store manager in the addressee role, Charles in the role of a participant, and the customers who are nearby in the overhearer role. By means of this differentiated model of hearer roles, we can better grasp the social psychological significance of Ann's act of casting: She and Charles are coordinating a sarcastic remark based on a common ground that is closed to both the target (the addressee) and the overhearers.

Casting a hearer into an addressee role is an important step toward engaging a particular hearer in a direct interactional relationship. The addressee so engaged may then be subjected to a round of persuasive talk, an earful of complaints, a stream of verbal abuse, or whatever. Casting a hearer into an addressee role is not always easily achieved, as teachers in charge of a class of naughty pupils will testify. The target pupil whom the teacher wants to reprimand can avoid the addressee role by looking or moving away. Or her classmates may come to her rescue by engaging her in conversation, thus shutting the teacher out. An experienced teacher might ask the class to stand, tell all to sit down except the target pupil, and only then begin to address her. The pupil is caught, as it were, by being cast into the addressee role.

In other situations, speakers may want to avoid a direct interactional relationship with their hearers for strategic reasons. To accomplish this, speakers may cast hearers into the role of overhearers. Thus two men may exchange a homosexual joke, meant to pour ridicule on a gay man who is nearby, by casting the latter in an overhearer role. In doing so, they constitute the latter as the subject of a sexist discourse without having to confront him directly. Clark and Carlson's (1982) differentiated model of hearers represents a conceptual advance over speech act and Gricean analyses (see Chapter 5), which are all premised on a single hearer or a homogeneous group of hearers. A similar but more detailed

model can be found in Bell (1984). But clearly, further development of a theoretical nature is needed to explain the interaction
more fully. For example, how do speakers and addressees coordinate their talk to prevent overhearers from knowing their real
message (e.g., Clark & Schaefer, 1987; see also Chapter 7)?

Speaker Roles

Apart from casting hearers into particular hearer roles, a speaker
can just as subtly self-cast into one or more of several speaker
roles. Goffman (1981) distinguished three speaker roles, called
interactional footings, that can be enacted by the speaker adopting
the corresponding talk-production format. The *animator* is the
person who is presently saying (animating) the words. The words
being uttered are composed by the *author* and express the viewpoint or attitude of the *principal*.

It is possible for a speaker to separate the roles and enact only
the animator role. Acting only as an animator has implications for
conversational influence. By quoting from or attributing an upcoming utterance to another source such as the Bible or the people
of the world, the animator generates two strategic advantages. It
allows the animator to pit a third party (the quoted source) against
the addressee. It also absolves the speaker of personal responsibility should the quoted message provoke a negative reaction from
the addressee. A speaker who succeeds in making his or her
animator role accepted by the addressee will be well placed to
maximize the strategic advantages for conversational influence.
The manner in which this is achieved can be illustrated by referring to the behavior of television news interviewers.

The common ground on which television news interviews proceed contains the common expectation that questions and answers
are preallocated, respectively, to the interviewer and the interviewee. Citing the work of Heritage (1985) and Greatbatch (1988),
Clayman (1988) proposed that the preallocation, which limits the
interviewer's role to that of asking questions, is bound up with the
expectation that the interviewer should display journalistic neutrality. On the surface, neutrality may appear to exclude the making of
evaluative or controversial statements. Yet more often than not,
interviewers do formulate evaluative or controversial statements.

Thus Clayman (1988) found that in a corpus of 10 interviews (drawn from four television networks for a total of 3 hours), an overwhelming 97% of interviewers' turns included precisely these nonneutral statements. Interviewers formulated evaluative statements by one or more of three procedures.

- Embedding statements within a question: "Mister Forbes, would you agree that this kind of huge growth in companies where billion dollar corporations are absorbing other billion dollar corporations tends to decrease, not eliminate, but decrease competition?" (Clayman, 1988, p. 476).
- Softening or mitigating the force of the evaluative statement (see Chapter 5).
- Attributing statements to a third party by shifting to the animator role (see below).

Clayman (1988) cited the following type of interview excerpts to illustrate the animating procedure. This extract is from a discussion about violence among blacks in South Africa. *IR* is the interviewer; *IE*, the Reverend Boesak; and *the ambassador*, the South African ambassador to the United States, who was a co-interviewee.

IR: Reverend Boesak let me pick up a point
1 → the ambassador made. What assurances can you give us that talks
         between moderates in that country will take place when it seems
         that any black leader who is willing to talk to the government is
         branded
2 → as the ambassador said a collaborator and is then punished.
3 → IE:The ambassador has it wrong. It's not the people . . . (p. 483)

IR begins by self-casting into the animator role (at arrow 1) and attributing the upcoming assessment to the co-interviewee, the ambassador. Later, IR renews the animator role and attributes key words (*collaborator* and *punished*) to the ambassador again (at arrow 2). IE, at his speaking turn, accepts IR's animator role while at the same time rebuts the animated assessment and directs his rebuttal at the ambassador and not at IR (at arrow 3). By taking up IR's self-cast role, IE collaborates with IR in coordinating their expected roles as the interview unfolds. This in turn allows IR successfully to animate an evaluative statement while displaying neutrality.

Note that in adopting the animator role, the speaker simultaneously invokes a third party. The third party may be outside the immediate conversation (e.g., the silent majority), or it may be a hearer in the conversation (e.g., a co-interviewee who has finished speaking). In the excerpt above, IR casts the co-interviewee as a participant, formulates the gist of the latter's earlier response, and animates it to solicit a contrasting response from the addressee. The combination of speaker self-casting and hearer casting enables IR "to generate and manage an informal debate between IEs without collaborating with either side" (Clayman, 1988, p. 483).

Another illustration of the strategic use of animation comes from research on gossip dispute. Gossip disputes are serious conversational interactions. At stake are the honor and interpersonal relationships of the accuser, the alleged gossiper, and others who are implicated in the gossip. Such disputes also provide opportunities for learning verbal self-defense and conflict-resolution skills (Eder, 1990). Research by Goodwin (1980a) shows, among other things, the effectiveness of the animator role adopted by the accuser when confronting the alleged gossiper. Instead of making a direct accusation, the young women in Goodwin's study animated a previous episode of gossip in the form of "He-said-she said." The animated talk cushioned the speaker from a direct confrontation with the alleged gossiper; in the cultural context in which the young women usually expressed their interpersonal conflict indirectly in the form of gossip, the animated talk also engaged a third party to help work out the conflict that had given rise to the gossip in the first place.

Thus far, we have been focusing on the animator role of the speaker. The animator role can be combined with the author and principal roles. Speakers who are in a position of authority tend to speak in the combined roles; for example, a judge will announce his or her ruling only in the combined role: "I hereby sentence you to . . . ." Similarly, a speaker who makes a strong bid for authority will self-cast in the combined role. This is exemplified by Jesus: "It is written, but verily I say unto you . . . ."

Speakership

Conversationalists are in a position to exercise the power of casting only if they have gained a speaking turn. In this sense, speakership is the power behind casting. Apart from this, speakership also provides speakers with the opportunity of controlling the immediate and upcoming conduct of the conversation as well as persuading and making an impression on others. This does not mean that the opportunity afforded by speakership will automatically yield success, because success will eventually depend on stylistic variables (Giles, Mulac, Bradac, & Johnson, 1987; Scotton, 1988), message-related variables (Bradac, 1989; Vinokur & Burnstein, 1978), and other variables. It is also true that sometimes it is even more advantageous to pass speakership to someone else than to be engaged in speaking, either because one does not want to go on record, disclose privileged information, or expose one's ignorance on a subject. This being said, the fact remains that speakership makes available the opportunity to exercise the sort of control mentioned above. A person who is unable to get a speaking turn or who is unwilling to take one will be deprived of such an opportunity. There are also longer-term implications associated with the lack of speaking turns. For example, in areas of employment and promotion, other things being equal the quiet person is less likely than the more talkative person to retain employment for a longer period or to gain promotion (Richmond, 1984).

In this section, we first summarize a framework for explicating turn taking and discuss the devices for gaining speakership. In doing so, we will also illustrate how speakership enables the exercise of control over the immediate and upcoming conduct of the conversation. The illustration at this point will be brief—a fuller discussion will be given in the section "Topic Control," later in this chapter. Finally, we review evidence to show the effect of speakership on leader emergence.

Turn Taking

Turn taking is organized by a *turn-construction* and a *turn-allocation* component (Sacks et al., 1974). The former embodies the content of the current speaking turn until a *transitional-relevance place* is reached, at which place the next speakership is allocated. Speakership is allocated in one of two ways: Either the current speaker selects the next speaker or a listener self-selects as the next speaker. In both cases, speaker transfer is effected. When neither option occurs, the current speaker may, but need not, continue. If current speaker does continue, the above turn-allocation procedure "reapplies at the next transition-relevance place, and recursively at each transition-relevance place, until transfer is effected" (Sacks et al., 1974, p. 704). By following the above tacit rules of turn allocation, speakers coordinate their speaking turns sequentially on an utterance-by-utterance basis. The ensuing conversation, according to Sacks et al.'s (1974) approach, exhibits a locally managed social organization characterized by several grossly apparent facts. Chief among the facts are

- Speaker change recurs.
- Overwhelmingly, one party talks at a time.
- Occurrences of simultaneous speech are common but brief.
- Transitions from one turn to the next with no gap and no overlap are also common.
- Repair mechanisms exist for dealing with turn-taking errors and violations (e.g., one of the parties in simultaneous speech may stop prematurely, thus repairing the trouble).

Sacks et al.'s (1974) model of turn taking is designed for spontaneous conversation that, by its very nature, has neither preassigned roles nor regulation by referees and yet can preserve the orderliness of one party talking at a time while speaker transfer recurs. In other speech-exchange systems (e.g., debate) turn taking is easier to explain, because both the order and length of speaking turns are predetermined to some extent. By tackling the more basic (and more difficult to explain) form of conversation, Sacks et al.'s (1974) model lays claim to the discovery of turn-taking organization that is simultaneously "context-free and capable of extraordinary context-sensitivity" (Sacks et al., 1974, p. 699).

The emphasis on rules adopted by Sacks et al. (1974) sets their approach apart from stochastic modeling and from the signaling approach (see reviews by Clarke, 1983; Edmondson, 1981; Wilson,

Wiemann, & Zimmerman, 1984). More generally, the relatively new discipline of conversation analysis inspired by the work of Sacks and associates is aimed at dealing with details of social action "rigorously, empirically, and formally" (Schegloff & Sacks, 1974). Its adherence to observational methods, concern with fine-grained concrete details of social action, and disavowal of abstract theorization distinguished it from the then predominant practices in sociology (e.g., Parsons, 1951). Beginning from a small break-away group within sociology, conversation analysts have since increased in number while still maintaining the original distinctiveness of their intellectual stance. The past 15 or so years have witnessed the increasing influence of conversation analysis (see Atkinson & Heritage, 1984; Zimmerman, 1988) and its proliferation into the neighboring disciplines of the ethnography of speaking (e.g., Moerman, 1988), discourse analysis (e.g., Coulthard, 1977; Potter & Wetherell, 1987), and social psychology (e.g., Clark, 1985; Roger & Bull, 1989; Tracy, 1985).

"Rulely" Speakers

Sacks et al. (1974) described various ways in which the current-speaker-selects-next rule and the self-selection rule operate to bring about speakership transfer. The former rule operates, first of all, by the devices of adjacency pairs and addressing and variants thereof. An adjacency pair, of which question-answer is a prime example, consists of two utterances that are produced by different speakers and are tied together in close sequence such that the first part (e.g., question) always precedes the second part (the answer).

A special variant of the question-type first part can by itself accomplish speaker transfer, provided that it echoes *retrospectively* a prior utterance. For example, the question can be repetitions of parts of a prior utterance with a "question" intonation, a "wh" question (where? who? what?), or a repair. Any one of these special question types will select the relevant *prior* speaker as next speaker. On the other hand, first parts of the pair that introduce something new do not by themselves select a particular next speaker—it is also necessary to couple the first part with addressing. The most explicit form of addressing is calling the name of the addressee. This may be augmented or substituted by various turn signals that cue the selected speaker. Duncan and Fiske (1977) have identified several such cues, and these are expressed by the current speaker in what is said (syntax and sociocentric sequences), how something is said (intonational contour and drawling), and kinesic movements (gaze, hand gestures, and posturing).

Sacks et al. (1974) discussed two other devices for enacting the current-speaker-selects-next rule: tag questions and social identities. Tag questions (e.g., "Ya know?" and "Don't you agree?") have multiple conversational functions (see Chapters 2 and 5). When a tag question is used specifically at the end of a turn unit (i.e., at a transition-relevance place) to select the next speaker, it gives the current speaker the flexibility of constructing any one of a variety of turn units that are not necessarily bound to the form of an adjacency pair. The tag question itself will serve as the first part of the pair.

Sacks et al. (1974) illustrated the device of social identities with the following example. In a conversation involving two couples, an invitation made by a speaker to go the movies will be heard to select as next speaker a member of the other couple, excluding own spouse. The device, which remains undeveloped in Sacks et al. (1974), has implications for conversational shift from *interpersonal* to *intergroup* talk. A similar shift was illustrated earlier in this chapter by the episode in which Ann and Charles coordinated a sarcastic remark directed at the store manager.

Any one or more of the devices that enable the current speaker to select the next speaker may be exploited for controlling the transfer of speakership. The control may be directed, first, toward restricting talk to a subgroup of conversationalists. This can be accomplished by reciprocating the current-speaker-selects-next rule: Speaker A appoints B as the next speaker, who in turn appoints A, and so forth. The $A_1B_1A_2$ sequence, in which two group members alternate turns—and this may or may not be motivated by the desire to monopolize talk—is in fact the most common pattern of speaker transfer in four-member groups (Parker, 1988). Even in six-member groups where there are more people who can potentially displace A in the A_2 slot, the $A_1B_1A_2$ sequence still far exceeds any other sequence (Stasser & Taylor, 1991). In both four- and six-member groups, the $A_1B_1A_2$ sequence has more than a 50% chance of extending to the $A_1B_1A_2B_2$ sequence, which is remarkably high, considering that there are up to four potential intruders who may compete with B for the B$_2$ slot. The picture that emerges from studies above and elsewhere (e.g., Clarke, 1983; Bakeman & Gottman, 1986) is that group interaction is organized around clusters of *dyadic* talk with varying dyadic membership as the interaction proceeds.

Second, the control of speakership transfer may be directed at escaping from a troublesome turn. For example, a person facing a law suit might, when being questioned by a persistent journalist at a press conference, pass the turn to his or her lawyer by addressing the latter with a tag question. Essentially, speakers realize the monopoly and escape functions by casting hearers into particular roles. Both functions reflect the power of casting (see above) that is inherent in speakership and enacted by means of devices for exploiting the current-speaker-selects-next rule.

Self-selection, the second rule governing the transfer of speakership, operates when a hearer succeeds in starting first at the earliest transition-relevance place. Starting first usually means starting fast, before others, and at the right time. It imposes considerable time pressure on the coordination of speakership and requires attentive listening to ongoing utterances. Gesticulating signals (e.g., hand raising) are particularly useful for starting first because, by their nonverbal nature, they can be enacted before the transition-relevance place without disrupting the talk that is being carried out in the verbal channel. The successful first starter gets the turn, sometimes with the aid of linguistic markers of turn entry such as appositionals (e.g., *well* and *but*).

"Unrulely" Speakers

Sacks et al. (1974) also called attention to the fact that a second starter may gain speakership despite starting late and overlapping with the first starter. One device used by the successful second starter is to raise a problem of understanding the prior utterance. This device also functions as a first part of the pair and, by tying with a prior utterance, selects the corresponding prior speaker as next speaker. Sacks et al. (1974) illustrated the device (indicated in bold type) by means of the following excerpt:

R: Hey::,the place looks different.
F: Yea::hh.
K: Ya have to see all ou[r new—]
D: [**It does?**]
R: Oh yeah. (p. 720)

The above excerpt shows clearly that the second starter, D, *interrupts* the first starter, K. This kind of behavior occurs frequently in conversation even though its functions are open to different interpretations (see below). Later, under the topic of repair mechanisms, Sacks et al. (1974) mentioned but did not discuss interruptions. This is presumably due to the apparent unruly nature of interruptions, which do not fit easily with Sacks et al.'s rule-based model. The latter assumes that the rules of turn taking are applicable equally to all participants in a conversation. Clearly, this is a narrow assumption because participants are rarely equal in their ability and motivation to play by the rules. Even if they all follow the conventions, this in itself requires explanation and should not be mistaken for the absence of power play in conversations (see also Searle, 1986). The same criticism applies to other rule-based models of conversation such as Grice's (1975).

Leader Emergence

The relationship between turn-allocation devices on the one hand, and conversational influence on the other has been a recurrent theme in the research literature. One line of research looks at speakership as an expression of dominance factors that exist before or outside of the immediate conversation, such as personality (e.g., Roger, 1989), gender (e.g., Zimmerman & West, 1975), and official rank (see Shaw, 1971). Scholars in this research tradition would begin with a given dominance factor that may be either explicit or implied by a status characteristic such as gender and then proceed to examine how dominance is reproduced in, and affects, conversational interaction.

Another tradition of research, which complements the first, begins with interaction and examines how interaction may play a relatively autonomous part in generating influence and establishing a new power hierarchy, not because the social context is void, but because the social context is sufficiently fluid to allow this to happen. This line of research, more so than the first, is congenial to the theme of the present volume, which lays stress on the use of language for creating influence and control. The research can be traced at least as far back as the pioneering work of Bales (1950) on interaction process analysis. Since then, research in this tradition has shown that the group member who talks the most is most likely to emerge as leader of the group (see Hollander, 1985; Mullen, Salas, & Driskell, 1989). The finding suggests that talk may be viewed as a conversational resource for achieving a high rank in the group. Such a view is also evident to varying degrees in a number of other works, including Austin's (1962) speech act theory (how to *do* things with words), the discourse analytic framework of Labov and Fanshel (1977), and research that treats conversational events as resources (e.g., Edelsky & Adams, 1990; Wiemann, 1985).

The resource view of talk raises a number of interesting questions. To begin with, what mechanisms in the immediate conversation give rise to the amount of talk? One probable answer to this question is speakership. Brooke and Ng (1986) collected speech samples from six mixed-sex conversational groups made up of previously unacquainted students. Before the conversation, group members watched an overseas television documentary on the legality and practice of commercial surrogacy (*The Baby Makers*). The program portrays the views of childless couples, surrogacy agencies, and the legal profession. Respondents were then asked to talk among themselves about whether or not New Zealand should legislate on commercial surrogacy and to reach some broad, but not necessarily unanimous, group decisions. At the end of the group conversation, members of the group filled out a social evaluation questionnaire designed to measure members' impressions of each other (see below). Afterward, the critical measure of conversational influence was taken by asking each member to rank-order all group members in terms of how influential the rater thought they had been in determining the final group decision(s).

The influence rankings within a group were analyzed to yield a Kendall coefficient of concordance that would indicate the degree of consensus on the influence hierarchy that might have emerged after the conversation. The use of a consensual influence hierarchy to index conversational influence was deemed to be more rigorous than simply aggregating the influence ranks and more realistic than the conventional procedure of asking passive observers to do the ranking (e.g., Erickson et al., 1978; Mazur & Cataldo, 1989). The coefficients were significant in all groups. On this basis, the two top-ranking members of each group were pooled to form the high-influence condition and the remaining two or three members were assigned to the low-influence condition.

It was found that group members who had gained more speaking turns or spoken more were accorded a higher influence ranking than others who had fewer turns or spoke less. The average turn size did not differ significantly among group members who were later accorded high or low ranks, suggesting that the volume of talk was determined by the number of turns. Swann (1988) reported a similar result, showing the primacy of speakership over words in her study of classroom talk in which boys, as a social category, dominated the talk more than girls did. Because the amount of talk is generated by the successful gaining of turns, it would appear that speakership is responsible for the amount of talk and, for this reason, may play a critical part in the emergence of leaders.

Brooke and Ng (1986) also measured the frequencies of intensifiers, high terminal intonation, polite forms, tag questions, and hedges, which are some of the low-power language forms that were discussed in Chapter 2. None of these language variables differentiated significantly the high- from the low-influence discussants. The overall results showed that leader emergence need not be defined negatively with reference to the infrequent use of low-power language but positively with reference to words and to turns in particular.

It is not possible to tell from the studies by Brooke and Ng (1986) and Swann (1988) what specific type of speakership was responsible for high accorded influence. Of interest here is the comparison between speakership obtained by rightful means (i.e., in conformity to Sacks et al.'s, 1974, turn-allocation rules) and those obtained by interruptions. Using the same general procedure as in Brooke and Ng (1986), Ng, Bell, and Brooke (in press) replicated the earlier study's result regarding the effect of overall turns on accorded influence. In addition, they attempted to compare the effect of turns gained by rightful means with the effect due to turns gained by successful interruptions on influence ranking. They identified turns gained by interruptions on the basis of a behavior sequence in which the interrupter prevented the first speaker from completing while the interrupter completed his or her own utterance. Coding was carried out with the help of Roger, Bull, and Smith's (1988) classification of successful interruptions but no distinction was made between single and complex interruptions.

Note that Ng et al. (in press) used a purely behavioral definition of successful interruptions that does not depend on any particular motive that may underlie the interruption. The motive may be to cut the first speaker off, to make a point urgently, or as Coates (1988) argued, to collaborate with the first speaker in developing a joint topic by showing enthusiasm and togetherness. The behavioral definition adopted by Ng et al. (in press) was independent of these conceivable motives and other factors such as conversational style (Tannen, 1984).

To compare the effects of speakership obtained by rightful means with speakership obtained by interruption, the authors regressed influence rankings on the two predictor variables in the following manner. When the two predictor variables were entered individually as the only predictor of influence ranking, a significant result was obtained in each case. When both variables were entered simultaneously, interruption turns remained highly significant whereas noninterruption turns became insignificant. The results showed that not only were interruption turns a positive correlate of influence but they were actually a stronger correlate than noninterruption turns. Both findings invite further discussion.

The positive correlation between interruption turns and influence may, at first sight, appear to be counterintuitive. The word *interruption* typically evokes images of rude, disruptive behavior and for this reason may have deterred readers from appreciating the positive function of interruption in enacting conversational influence. In fact, the data in Ng et al.'s (in press) study showed no negative correlation between interruption turns and attractiveness. Perhaps a new look that highlights the positive roles of interruptions is in order. Other authors have suggested that interruption turns may function to support a currently developing topic and to express enthusiasm with the current speaker (Coates, 1988). Conversationalists who are eager to encourage the current speaker to continue talking may try to do so by butting in rather than waiting until the latter dries out, without intending that the current speaker should stop prematurely (Tannen, 1984).

On the basis of prosodic features known to surround interruptions generally (see French & Local, 1983; Roger, 1989), Ng et al. (in press) offered the following explanation of the superiority of interruption turns over noninterruption turns in predicting influence. Successful interrupters generally increased their speech rate and vocal amplitude more than the person being interrupted; for unsuccessful interrupters, the reverse occurred. Prosodic features that were associated with successful interruptions might have made these turn transitions highly salient to participants, and hence speakership, when gained by interruption, would be marked and more easily recalled when participants were later asked to rank each other on relative influence.

Scherer (1979) reported that passive listeners associated perceived speaker influence with loudness (in the United States) and with rapid speech (in Germany). Using these two paraverbal features as dependent variables, Roger (1989) tested for differences between (British) interrupters and interruptees as well as changes from before to during an interruption. The most robust finding was that both the interrupter and the interruptee talked faster and louder during than before the interruption, regardless of whether the interruption was successful or not. The authors carried out statistical tests for successful and unsuccessful interruptions separately and did not report any direct comparison between successful and unsuccessful interruptions. Nonetheless, their results indicate an interesting pattern: *interrupters* talked faster and louder than interruptees in successful interruptions, whereas *interruptees* talked faster and louder than interrupters in unsuccessful interruptions. It appeared that interrupter and interruptee were engaged in a sort of paraverbal duel, and the relative dominance of one over the other was linked to their later success at interrupting or at resisting the interruption.

More research on interruption is needed to focus on the interplay between interrupting and resistance to interruption. It may be possible that high influence is accorded to conversationalists who succeed at both interrupting and resisting interruption. In other words, completing a speakership against interruption may be just as important as gaining the speakership by interruption. The mechanisms by which interruption is enacted, and resisted, would make interesting study and this can be carried out at both the paraverbal level (Duncan & Fiske, 1977; Roger, 1989) and the verbal level. One class of verbal behavior for enacting interruption may be *referring*, that is, the pointing out of the connection or coherence between one utterance and another. An example of referring, given by Sacks et al. (1974), is the raising of a problem of understanding the prior utterance. This is essentially a speech act that seeks clarification of the prior utterance, and there is some evidence showing that it occurs more frequently in same-sex than in cross-sex interruptions (Dindia, 1987). A different example of referring, which occurs more frequently in cross-sex than in same-sex interruptions, is speech that claims agreement with or under-standing of the first speaker's idea (Dindia, 1987). A second class of verbal behavior for enacting interruption is to point out that the first speaker is missing the point: "No! We are not talking about Israelis and Palestinians. We are talking about Iraqi atrocities in Kuwait." Both classes of behavior are closely related to topic control (see next section) and may turn out to be a significant ingredient of successful interruption in future research. The sort of verbal behavior responsible for maintaining speakership against interruption may again be topic related, for example, a speech that develops the current topic as opposed to one that overworks or strays off a topic.

Topic Control

Once a conversation has started, what is being talked about usually is coherent with or bears some relevance to what has been talked about before (Crow, 1983). As the conversation unfolds, what is being talked about also changes, gradually at times and abruptly at other times (Palmer, 1989). In most conversations, especially those that are informal and rambling, topic change occurs naturally when a current topic is exhausted or when some other topics spring to mind. Topic change and its counterpart topic maintenance are part and parcel of the normal flow of conversational activity. Beyond that, they also provide resources that can be harnessed for conversational influence. This type of conversational influence will be called topic control. Although topic control is a poorly understood subject because little research has been carried out on topic generally, it is an important facet of conversational influence. Topic control can generate conversational influence in two distinct but interrelated ways: topic maintenance and topic change.

Topic Maintenance

A speaker who has successfully initiated a topic can maintain and develop it within the duration of the current speakership. There are also interpersonal variables that would motivate later speakers to adhere to the ongoing topic. By adhering to the topic, later speakers pay respect to the first speaker who has initiated the topic and preserve for the latter the autonomy to extend or terminate the topic. In this way, later speakers express their goodwill of safeguarding the first speaker's positive and negative face wants (Brown & Levinson, 1987) as well as cementing an amicable interpersonal relationship. Cooperative topic adherence by later speakers would be more frequent when the status differential favors the first speaker. In addition to interpersonal and status variables, there are devices that are available to first speakers for maintaining a desired topic. These devices will be needed especially when the interpersonal and status variables are unfavorable to the first speaker.

One group of devices for maintaining a topic allows the speaker to safeguard the current speakership against interruptions (see above) and extend it by minimizing turn-yielding cues (see Duncan & Fiske, 1977). Because no speaker can retain speakership forever, the question arises as to how to maintain the topic after the end of a speaking turn. Various devices are available for achieving this; it is these that will be discussed below, beginning with adjacency pairs.

Adjacency pairs are commonly used by speakers to direct the addressee's response to a desired topic. The first part of the pair constrains the content of the second part to the extent that some complementary second actions but not others are "specially relevant for next turn" (Sacks et al., 1974, p. 717). Within the constraint set by the first part of the pair, alternative complementary second actions are available. For example, in response to a question, the next speaker may give a positive answer or one of a number of negative answers (think here of evasive politicians). At times, a silence also counts as a relevant answer. Similarly, the next speaker may agree or disagree with an assessment, accept or refuse an invitation, and so forth. The final choice of a second action is not random, but shows a *preference organization* in favor of agreements, acceptance, and other positive responses over negative responses (see below). Preferred actions are usually performed directly and with little delay. Dispreferred actions, by contrast, are usually delayed, expressed indirectly, prefaced, and accompanied by an account (Heritage, 1988). Positive responses are not always preferred to negative responses, however; much depends on the face wants mentioned above. Thus when a prior speaker has given a self-depreciatory assessment, it is disagreement and not agreement that will be enacted in the preferred action mode.

Because responses to the first parts of adjacency pairs are freer than the question-answer stereotype would suggest (see also Levinson, 1983), the adjacency pair device does not always succeed in directing subsequent turns to a desired topic. The problem of directionality becomes more complex with increasing number of turns. The complexity is reflected in studies on conversational routine (Coulmas, 1981), side sequence (Jefferson, 1972), five-part sequence in classroom discourse (Sinclair & Coulthard, 1975), action planning (Hobbs & Evans, 1980), and sequential analysis (Bakeman & Gottman, 1986; Clarke, 1983). These studies, although relevant to conversational sequence generally, do not generate significant new insight into the maintenance of a topic over a sequence of speaking turns.

Topic Change

Before discussing other topic maintenance devices, we will at this point change the topic (!) to a discussion of topic change. Afterward, the interplay between topic maintenance and topic change will be addressed.

As noted, speakers who change an ongoing topic are posting a potential threat to the face of the speaker who has initiated the topic that is currently on the floor. They may also threaten their own face by giving others the impression of being inconsiderate and inattentive. To enact topic change while minimizing the threat to others' face and to own face, speakers make use of preacts that function as topic-bounding devices. These devices, which Crow (1983) aptly called *transition* markers, include "One more thing," "Incidentally," and "You know what?"

Another group of devices, known as topic-*shading* devices (Crow, 1983), are based on the speaker's claim that what he or she is about to say has some linkage with the ongoing topic. Tracy (1985) summarized four strategies for claiming linkage. These are based, first, on schematic or script knowledge shared by speakers; second, on a particular message idea already expressed by the first speaker; and third, on a metaissue of which both the ongoing topic and the new topic are parts. The fourth device is to claim that there is a mental link between the new and the ongoing topic, as in, "I know exactly what you mean" or "That reminds me of," when in fact the linkage may not exist. These devices can also be used to renew a topic that had been on the floor before but has since been superseded. In addition to enabling speakers to address face wants while they change the topic, topic-shading devices also enable them to reduce the perceived uncertainty of the direction in which the conversation is heading. Uncertainty reduction is important from the point of view of participants because they like to be able to predict future events (Berger & Bradac, 1982).

Although topic change is potentially face threatening and uncertainty arousing, and for these reasons is constrained in its enactment, it can also be directed toward other more task-oriented goals, such as relieving the first speaker of further troubles talk (Coupland, Henwood, Coupland, & Giles, in press; Jefferson & Lee, 1981), advancing the interactional agenda (Sigman, 1983), and encouraging a shy speaker to be involved more actively in the conversation.

Labov and Fanshel's (1977) therapeutic discourse model provides an interactional framework for understanding the interplay between topic maintenance and topic change. Their basic premise, consistent with speech act analysis (Austin, 1962; see Chapter 5), is that conversational sequence is not found between utterances but between the actions that are being performed through talk. To construct the sequence of actions, the authors first relate "what is said" to "what is done." The way in which the two are related, called the mode of interaction, varies in terms of the degree of indirection and reflects the extent to which speakers use discourse rules of interpretation and production. The actions, also called *verbal interactions* in recognition of their interactional nature, are grouped under four domains or sets. The first set relates to the regulation of turn taking—to initiate, continue, or end a unit of speech. These verbal interactions are best understood in light of conversation analysis, discussed in the preceding section.

The authors derived three other sets of verbal interactions—representations, requests, and challenges—from a microscopic analysis of a 15-minute stretch of the conversation between a client and her therapist during a therapeutic session. Within each set, the interactions are linked over two, sometimes more, speaking turns. Thus speaker A may represent some state of affairs by first asserting and then giving an evaluation or interpretation of the assertion. In response, speaker B may agree with, deny, or support the assertion.

In the domain of requests, speaker A may ask B to do any number of things (e.g., to act, inform, attend, and approve) and B may respond by complying with, putting off, or refusing the request. If B complies, A in turn may acknowledge the action. If B puts off the request, A may reinstate, direct, mitigate, or retreat from the request. If B refuses, A may respond in various ways, depending on whether or not B has supplied an account of the refusal. In the absence of an account, A may withdraw from the interaction. When an account has been given, A may reject or accept the account, or renew the request.

In making or renewing the request, A may do so in either a mitigated or aggravated way. Likewise, challenges can be made in either a mitigated (e.g., in the form of questioning) or aggravated (e.g., by insulting) form. In response to the challenge, B may defend himself or herself, admit the challenge, or break off the interaction. The response may then lead A to retreat from, mitigate, or aggravate the challenge, and so forth. Labov and Fanshel's (1977) discourse analytic framework places speech acts in the context of interactional acts between conversationalists. The interactional linkages that they have attempted to identify in the domains of representation, request, and challenge are more complex than those represented by adjacency pairs in conversation analysis. In a similar vein, Edmondson (1981) attempted to add an interactional dimension to speech acts and argued that the investigation of interactional structure should be concentrated on exchange linkages and exchange structure.

In their analysis of therapeutic discourse, Labov and Fanshel (1977) assigned special importance to *challenges,* defined as "any reference (either by direct assertion or more indirect reference) to a situation, which if true, would lower the status of the other person" (p. 64). They observed that challenges were pervasive: Requests often turned out to have a hidden agenda of making challenges; even in the more purely ideational domain of representations, a speaker might make a statement about events that were known to be disputable (D-events), thereby implying an immediate challenge or paving the way for a later challenge.

Using Labov and Fanshel's (1977) model, but also her own research, Blum-Kulka (1983) analyzed the ways in which political interviewers used challenges to pursue their evasive politician interviewees and bring them back on topic. In recent time, television political interviews have acquired a dramatic flavor as interviewers become more investigative and eager to open up controversial (D-events) topics (Heritage, 1985). Often, political interviewers aim at extracting explicit, quotable answers from their interviewees. Realizing their goal may on the surface appear to be a simple matter of directing the interview sequence by posting questions in a particular order. However, that presumes optimal cooperation from (political) interviewees who may in fact give vague answers, dodge the question, or stray off to a new topic altogether. To succeed at pinning down evasive interviewees, interviewers have to do more than ask questions; they often use challenges to enforce explicitness and to negotiate a higher level of cooperation than the initial level offered by interviewees.

Blum-Kulka's (1983) data consist of 20 hours of interviews that took place on Israeli television between 1980 and 1982. Typically, the opening moves by interviewers were D-events, encoded in the form of challenges, Socratic in nature (paving the way for future discussion on the topic introduced), and sometimes containing a hidden agenda. In their responding moves, interviewees seldom cooperated fully—they tended to evade questions. To enforce explicitness, interviewers reformulated in an emphatic or aggravated manner the challenge contained in the initiating move. This is illustrated in the following question sequence (Blum-Kulka, 1983):

> Mishal: Mr. Gur . . . you have repeatedly stated that you consider
>   yourself qualified to become prime minister. Tonight you
>   have talked about objective qualifications for the job. What
>   makes a person qualified to become prime minister?
>   [G's answer]
> Mishal: Let's be more practical. If . . . will you present your candidacy?
>   [G's answer]
> Mishal: Do you see yourself as one of the candidates? (pp. 139-140)

Blum-Kulka (1983) summarized the interviewers' reformulations as follows.

> The reformulations seem in effect to be saying "We understand what
> you mean, i.e. what you have conversationally implied—and the
> audience is probably aware of the implication too, but our norms
> require that you should state your propositions instead of implying
> them (which would be acceptable under normal conditions), so say
> it. If you do, we'll move on to a different topic; possibly also have
> you quoted in the news; if you don't, we'll continue to challenge
> you." (p. 146)

In a way, interviewers are trying to remind their interviewees of their obligation to the Gricean maxims of quality, quantity, relevance, and manner (see Chapter 5). They do not always succeed, though. As a matter of fact, interviewees often succeed admirably in suspending the interviewers' topic and implementing their own. Consider Gur's reply in the following excerpt (Blum-Kulka, 1983):

> Mishal: . . . Are you satisfied with the current leadership of the
>   Labour Party?

Gur: There are several things which in my opinion need improvement. But we shouldn't ignore the fact that towards the last elections we grew as a party and drew to us many forces. . . . I think that the coming period will be crucial for the leadership of the party. In my estimate the year and a half (till the next election) will suffice for our leadership to pull the party together and move it forward. (p. 143)

The interviewer's initiating move implied criticism of the present state of the Labor party and called for a strong defense. Gur, in his opening representation ("There are several things which in my opinion need improvement"), gave the impression that he was going to comply with the expectation set up in the initiating move. The remainder of his move, however, was framed in terms of the party's past ("grew" and "drew") and future ("coming period") not its present. In this way, he shifted the topical focus away from the touchy area of the present to relatively innocuous issues; afterward, he danced around, as it were, the bait set down in the interviewer's topic. At the same time, he countered the interviewer's implied criticism by portraying the party as one that had a track record of achievements and would continue to make even greater progress in the future. While doing all this, he used referential objects ("party" and "leadership") already contained in the interviewer's question as semantic bridges to create the impression of both semantic and ideational coherence.

The above interview excerpt also illustrates the complementarity between conversational influence analysis, as presented herein, and the analysis of non-decision-making power by political scientists (Bachrach & Baratz, 1962) referred to in Chapter 1. The latter illuminates the strategy used by powerful groups in society to mobilize organizational bias for excluding unsafe topics from reaching the public forum. The activities of a free press, however, often succeed in opening up closed issues as topics for public debate. The ensuing struggle for topic control is no longer played out in secret, but in interviews that are or will be later broadcast to the public. An adequate analysis of political processes nowadays will certainly include the analysis of topic control in public debates.

* * *

The assignment of conversational roles, turn taking, and conversational sequence are integral parts of highly conventionalized conversational activities that also provide the resources for expressing and generating influence. In this chapter, we have examined these resources in terms of casting, speakership, and topic control. Each of the resources provides a range of devices for enacting influence and these have been discussed in turn.

The resource approach that we have been developing lays stress on speakership both as a conversational resource in its own right and also for the enactment of casting and topic control. Without speakership there will be no conversational influence. Yet given the interactional nature of conversation, the power of casting, speakership, and topic control is contingent on the continued presence of hearers who remain in the conversation either by choice or a result of being kept there by others. The moment hearers physically remove themselves from the conversation, the sting of conversational influence will cease. Exit from the physical setting of the conversation may be the only available counterpower that is left for an individual who is unwilling or unable to engage in a verbal fight. A teenage girl who can bear no longer the insults from her parents may react by shutting herself in her room or, failing that, by running away from home. In most everyday conversation, hearers make psychological exit while remaining in the physical setting of the conversation—by keeping silent when talk is expected, looking away from the speaker, turning the radio on, and so forth. These and various other behaviors will have to be considered in the study of conversational influence from the exit or passive resistance angle, because the categories of casting, speakership, and topic control are primarily about the more dominant conversationalists and do not capture as fully the behavior of those who are less dominant.

CHAPTER FIVE

Mitigation:
Be Indirect and Be Tentative

It is a truism that a competent language user is able to express the same intention in more than one way. A duke who wants the window shut to keep out the cold can express this intention to his butler, Robert, in any one of the following ways.

7. Shut the window!
8. Shut the window, please.
9. Can you shut the window, Robert?
10. It is cold in here, Robert.

There are, of course, still other ways of expressing the duke's intention. Of the listed examples, utterance 7 is an imperative; 8 is a direct request; 9 is an indirect request encoded in the form of a question, to which the butler can logically reply, "Yes, I can, my lord," without moving over to shut the window; and 10 is an even more indirect form of request. Using utterance 8 as the baseline, we can order the remaining utterances in terms of how strongly or weakly they express the force of the duke's intention: utterance 7 strengthens, whereas 9 and 10 weaken the force conveyed in utterance 8. The point of interest is that the butler, being a competent language user as opposed to a logician, will nevertheless discern from the indirect utterance of 9 or 10 the duke's intention.

The above example shows different ways of using speech to perform the act of directing the hearer to close the window. Austin (1962) captured this performative, social function of speech by coining the phase *how to do things with words* for the title of his book. He proposed that when a speaker produces an utterance such as "It is cold in here, Robert" the speaker is performing three acts. There is first of all the act of uttering the words. This act, called the *locutionary act*, requires vocalization efforts; the words, once produced, have a determinate sense and reference independent of the particular situation. The second act (the *illocutionary act*) is the act of making an assertion, a request, a directive, a promise, a judgment, and so forth that is being performed *in* uttering a sentence by virtue of the illocutionary force associated with the sentence. To the extent that the force associated with the elocutionary act is in accord with conventional procedure, the act itself is also determinate at least in principle (see Levinson, 1983; also Bach & Harnish, 1979, for an alternative view). The *perlocutionary act*, the third act, is the act of producing effects on the audience by uttering the sentence. Perlocutionary effects are specific to the particular situation and are not achieved invariably by the same utterance or just by making an utterance. Austin (1962) summed up the three acts as follows:

> Thus we distinguish the locutionary act (and within it the phonetic, the phatic, and the rhetic acts) which has a *meaning*; the illocutionary act which has a certain *force* in saying something; the perlocutionary act which is *the achieving of* certain *effects* by saying something. (p. 120; emphasis in the original)

The notion of illocutionary act was one of the earliest attempts to focus on "what is done" in speech. It is also by far the most central part of speech act analysis and, for this reason, has now become synonymous with the term *speech act* (Searle, 1969).

Utterances 7 to 10, given above, illustrate how the force of a speech act (or more precisely, the force of the illocutionary point of a speech act—see below) can be strengthened or weakened. Both kinds of modifications, which are common in the use of language in everyday life, have been the subject of extensive analysis in the speech act literature (e.g., Edmondson, 1981; Labov & Fanshel, 1977; Lakoff, 1974; Searle, 1976). They are not easily ordered without taking into account the social or discoursal context in which they occur. For example, adult males who rarely use *please* would, when they do use it, make their speech acts sound preemptory. In such a context, *please* has the effect of increasing the force of the speech act rather than decreasing it. Intonation is also crucial: With the appropriate intonation *please* could sound mitigating or sarcastic.

The four examples given above are not meant to convey a precise scale of force. Indeed, there is likely to be disagreement, even among native speakers of the same language variety, as to the relative ordering of the utterances in terms of forcefulness (see, e.g., Preston, 1989). There is little systematic research examining how the average language user, as opposed to the linguistic expert, actually interprets the relative *forcefulness* of the different ways of expressing a directive, even though there have been studies of children's *understanding* of mitigation (e.g., Bennett, 1990) and numerous others comparing direct and indirect speech acts within the *politeness* framework (e.g., Brown & Levinson, 1987; Holtgraves, 1986). Much of what will be discussed below is confined to analyses made by linguists and is clearly in need of substantiation by research that involves ordinary language users in natural settings. That said, we believe the contrast between strengthening and weakening the force of a speech act has theoretical merit that will be borne out, perhaps in a more complex form, by empirical research.

Some speech acts are affectively neutral, but more often than not, they are negative or positive. For example, directives (e.g., orders, demands, and requests) are mostly negative in that they are face threatening (Brown & Levinson, 1987) or unwelcome to the hearer (Fraser, 1980). Reproaches are also negative communicative acts (Cody & McLaughlin, 1985). Praise and compliments, on the other hand, are usually affectively positive. The negative-positive effect distinction, like the strong-weak modification distinction, is in reality a continuum and should be thought of as such, even though in the interest of simplicity, both distinctions will be treated here as simple dichotomies.

Holmes's (1984a) schematic classification suggests that affect (negative or positive) and force modification (weakening or strengthening) may be combined to yield four broad categories. One of these categories, which consists of the weakening of the illocutionary point of affectively negative speech acts, coincides with mitigation. To mitigate is to signal to the addressee that the speaker's intention behind an unwelcome communication has been softened (i.e., reduced in force, scope, etc.). In terms of speech act theory, mitigation is the attenuation of the strength with which the illocutionary point (i.e., intention or purpose) of an unwelcome speech act is communicated. By attenuating or softening the force of the illocutionary point of a speech act that is intended to oblige the addressee to respond in a particular way, mitigation renders the influence attempt less confrontational. There is evidence to show that the use of mitigating devices can defuse or attenuate interpersonal conflict (Labov & Fanshel, 1977). In this sense, mitigation functions as a strategy of depoliticization.

Note that mitigation is not a type of speech act. Rather, it is an attempt at reducing the harshness or hostility of the force of a speech act—"to soften the effects of an order, ease the blow of bad news, make a criticism more palatable, and the like" (Fraser, 1980, p. 342). How, then, do speakers mitigate the force of their communication? Euphemisms, such as *annoyed* for *insulted,* are common mitigating devices and these have been discussed extensively (e.g., Lutz, 1989). In an important paper on the subject, Fraser (1980) mentioned six mitigation strategies and devices: the use of indirectness in performing a speech act as well as the use of distancing techniques, disclaimers, parenthetical verbs, tag questions, and hedges. These overlap greatly with the prosodic, syntactic, lexical, and discoursal mitigating devices discussed by Holmes (1984a). Various other devices can also be discerned from Brown and Levinson's (1987) work on politeness, a subject that is closely related to, but separate from, mitigation (see below and Chapter 6).

Two of the principal features of the diverse mitigating devices are indirectness and tentativeness, which may appear either singly or jointly. Indirectness and tentativeness are basic to human communication and have been the subject of both philosophical and empirical analyses in the contexts of indirect speech acts and politeness. Together they cover all the major devices proposed by Fraser (1980) and Holmes (1984a), with the exception of Fraser's distancing strategy. The latter strategy, also discussed by Holmes (1984a) under syntactical devices and by Brown and Levinson (1987) under impersonalizing devices, seems to be less directly related to mitigation and more to masking. For this reason, distancing will be discussed in Chapter 7 under the topic of masking.

Be Indirect

Utterances 9 and 10 illustrate how the force of a speech act can be mitigated by indirectness. The duke does not directly tell the butler to close the window; instead he leaves it up to the butler to infer what is required of him from question 9 or from hint 10. By means of one or the other indirect speech act, the duke performs a potentially unwelcome act without offering explicit direction. The literature on indirect speech acts offers a way of understanding how this may work by analyzing the rules that enable the speaker to convey meaning indirectly and the addressee to infer the indirect speaker's meaning—in contrast to the sentence's literal meaning (Searle, 1975; also Austin, 1962; Grice, 1975). The production and comprehension of indirect speech acts can be thought of in terms of a two-stage process comprising a trigger and an inference stage, in that order (see Brown & Levinson, 1987). The speaker makes use of one or more triggers to signal to the addressee that some inference about what is really meant must be made from what is actually said. The addressee, in turn, infers the indirect meaning. In the interest of presentation, the inference process that underlies single utterances and dialogues will be discussed before the trigger process.

Inference of Indirect Meaning

Single Utterances

The utterance *Shut the window!* takes the linguistic form of an imperative. The meaning that is intrinsic to the imperative grammatical mood is to signal to hearers that the speaker is giving an order. The imperative mood restricts the meaning potential to the literal sentence meaning (propositional content) of the utterance. As a result, an imperative that is directed at an addressee in a face-to-face situation has the same directness as an order that is constructed in the more elaborate declarative grammatical mood: "I order you to shut the window." The two utterances mean what they say, literally.

By contrast, the indirect utterance *Can you shut the window?* takes the interrogative grammatical mood and conveys more than one meaning. The message intrinsic to the interrogative mood is to indicate that the speaker is asking a question, which is the literal meaning or direct illocutionary point of the utterance. However, the direct illocutionary point cannot be the only or indeed the "real" meaning, because the butler is obviously capable of shutting the window and the duke already knows this. The duke would have been insincere if he had intended his utterance to count only as a question for information that he already possesses. In terms of speech act theory, the direct illocutionary point is said to have failed the *felicity conditions,* and for this reason is defective. The butler, alerted by the failure of the message to meet felicity conditions but still believing that the duke has a relevant point to make, will seek another (nonliteral) meaning for the utterance. He would therefore ignore the direct illocutionary point and attempt to infer an indirect illocutionary point.

Seen in this way, an indirect speech act actually enables the speaker to perform a direct illocutionary act, which carries the direct illocutionary point, and also an indirect illocutionary act, which conveys the indirect illocutionary point. By means of an indirect speech act, a speaker conveys his or her intention via the indirect illocutionary act that occurs *concurrently* with the direct illocutionary act. As a result of the concurrence of two acts (the number may be even greater because more than one indirect illocutionary act may be involved), the actual illocutionary point is nonspecific or indeterminate. Indeterminacy may backfire on the speaker if and when the addressee misses the point or deliberately takes up the direct instead of the indirect illocutionary point. (For this reason, speakers may prefer directness to indirectness. The question of how to mitigate when directness is used will be discussed under "Be Tentative," below.) On the other hand, however, a speaker can exploit the indeterminacy strategically for negotiating compliance from the addressee (see Edmondson, 1981) or, as will be shown later under the topic of indirectness in longer segments of discourse, for backtracking when the addressee objects to the indirectly conveyed intention.

At this juncture, it should be noted that although the interrogative mood is an intrinsic marker for questions, in practice it has been commonly used by native English speakers for making *requests*. An indirect request that has been routinized through regular usage is known as a *conventional* indirect speech act, for example, "Hello. Is Sybil there?" said by a telephone caller (see Ervin-Tripp, 1976). Particular interlocutors may have their own communal conventionalized indirect speech acts that appear opaque to outsiders. The process of conventionalization is not confined to indirect speech acts that are constructed in the interrogative mood. Thus the implicit request encoded in the utterance *It is cold in here, Robert,* which is phrased in the declarative mood, may be highly conventional between the duke and his butler, even though outsiders will be slow to catch the point if at all. Similarly, lovers, diplomats, and gang members may each have their own corpus of conventionalized indirect speech acts for in-group communication. It is, therefore, useful to think of conventional indirect acts as specific to particular linguistic communities. This implies that some indirect speech acts are more universally conventional than others. This point has some bearing on the inferential sequence and will be discussed later.

Dialogues: Grice's Cooperative Principle

The above discussion of the inference process relates to a single indirect speech act. We now turn to dialogues. When considering indirectness in dialogues, we find Grice's (1975) framework more useful than conversation analysis (see Chapter 4; also Levinson, 1983, for a different opinion). Some cooperation is necessary if any communication is to proceed at all. Grice (1975) summed up this cooperation in the form of a cooperative principle and four associated maxims of conversation. Conversationalists, according to Grice, generally expect each other to obey the principle (see below for exceptions): "Make your conversational contribution such as required, at the stage at which it occurs, by the accepted purpose

or direction of the talk exchange in which you are engaged"
(p. 45). The principle embodies four maxims: The first three relate
to the content and the fourth to the manner of the talk exchange:

- *Quantity:* Say only what is required, no more, no less.
- *Quality:* Be nonspurious, be sincere, speak the truth.
- *Relation (Relevance):* Be relevant, to the point.
- *Manner:* Be perspicuous, avoid ambiguity and obscurity.

The maxims bear a close resemblance to the felicity conditions
proposed by Austin (1962) and are arguably more general (see
Brown & Levinson, 1987) and easier to understand than the latter.

To illustrate how the maxims are invoked during talk exchanges,
Grice gives examples such as the following:

> A: Smith doesn't seem to have a girlfriend these days.
> 11.B: He has been paying a lot of visits to New York recently.

The literal sentence meaning of B's speech act in 11 upsets the
maxim of relevance. If this literal meaning is all that is intended
by B, then B would have been noncooperative. But this would
contradict the shared assumption of cooperation. To preserve this
assumption, A is forced to engage in more mental work and may,
for instance, infer that Smith has a girlfriend in New York. By
upholding the cooperative principle, interlocutors infer meaning
beyond the literal meaning when the latter appears to fail one or
more of the Gricean maxims. The inference enables them to maintain the belief that what the speaker says somehow makes sense
and that the speaker is really sincere, being relevant, and so forth.
Grice calls this kind of inference *conversational implicature,* or more
precisely, particularized conversational implicature. The qualifier
particularized indicates that the particular context of the utterance,
in addition to the content of the utterance and the cooperative
principle, is crucial for an utterance to implicate some other indirect proposition. (The term *implicate* is used rather than *imply*
because the inference process does not necessarily follow the rules
of formal logic.)

We have noted earlier that cooperation is generally, but not
always, expected. Hearers who have reasons to suspect that the

speaker is telling a lie will no longer expect the latter to follow the cooperative principle, despite the extra efforts that the speaker may be making to appear to be cooperative. Similarly, in many joking situations the speaker and hearers have to collaborate by temporarily suspending the principle to make the joke funny. To know when and when not to apply the principle is an important part of a person's communicative competence. That said, it remains true that hearers in a wide range of situations behave as if they were following the principle (see, e.g., Levinson, 1983). In fact, hearers tend to overattribute cooperativeness to speakers who are seen as a source of authoritative communication. For example, when children are asked the same question repeatedly in a Piagetian-type clinical interview, they take for granted that all the questions must be relevant and consequently respond by changing their answers from one question to the next, often from a correct to a wrong answer (Siegal, 1990). Similarly, when working on judgmental tasks, respondents take into account not only base-rate information but also any other information given by the experimenter, however irrelevant the latter information may be in the statistical sense (Kahneman, Slovic, & Tversky, 1982; Krosnick, Li, & Lehman, 1990).

Inferential Sequence

The above discussion of the inference process has been couched in the formal perspective of a grammarian-cum-logician without regard to how ordinary language users actually carry out their inference. This formal perspective, which is a legacy of both the Cartesian variant of the myth of literal meaning and linguistic philosophers' preoccupation with the cadavers of written languages (see Rommetveit, 1983), has influenced some of the earliest empirical research on the inference process (e.g., Clark & Lucy, 1975). Essentially, it proposes three sequential steps. First, the addressee comprehends the literal meaning of an utterance from its grammatical mood, propositional content, and other linguistic markers. Then he or she checks the literal meaning against the particular communication context and in light of what he or she knows about the speaker. Finally, if the addressee considers the literal meaning to be inappropriate, incomplete, or defective in any way, she or he will proceed to construe indirect meaning(s). The tools for implementing the final step are supposedly based on Gricean maxims, Austinian felicity conditions, or some other similar rules (e.g., *conversational postulates* by Gordon & Lakoff, 1971; *contextual implication* by Sperber & Wilson, 1982).

The inference sequence outlined above is fraught with difficulties. An obvious difficulty relates to the second step: In the context of metaphor comprehension, for example, no "defective" literal meaning is needed to trigger a search for alternative nonliteral meanings (Keysar, 1989; see also Chapter 6). More important to our current concern, there are good reasons for thinking that ordinary language users routinely bypass the first step in most everyday communication contexts that involve indirectness. Even though indirect speech acts are constructed in a grammatical mood reserved for some other form of expression (that is, in a noncanonical sentence form, see Dore, 1977) and their propositional content bears no immediate logical connection with the indirect illocutionary point, they do not necessarily require hearers to engage in menu-type, elaborate computations. Should every occurrence of an indirect speech act require a full menu of computations starting from the very first step, this would make nonsense of the acknowledged fact that language users constantly adapt their language by common convention for facilitating, not slowing down, the conveyance of intentions from one person to another. Recall the earlier discussion of the conventionalization of indirect speech acts. It would be most improbable that an addressee would go through all the preparatory steps when confronted with an indirect speech act that has been conventionalized for the situation in which the act occurs. This is shown by communication misunderstandings for which the addressee automatically latches on to the indirect meaning even though it is the *literal* meaning that is intended by the speaker. Ervin-Tripp (1976) collected samples of misunderstandings such as the following one in which a professor telephones a room-permits office to obtain some information:

Do you have a room for 20 on Monday nights?
Just a minute. . . . Yes I do. Give me your name, department, and course number, please.

The hearer's interpretation is directive. Speakers who anticipate misunderstanding have to disclaim the interpretation at the outset, for example: "I don't want to book a room right now, but do you have a room for 20 on Monday nights?"

Gibbs (1979) asked respondents in two experiments to read stories, one line at a time, that ended in an indirect request (e.g., "Must you open the window," meaning "Please leave the window closed"), a literal use of the same sentence, or a direct request (e.g., "Do not open the window"). After each story, respondents made a paraphrase judgment of that story's last line. The length of time that respondents took to make paraphrase judgments since the presentation of the last line of the story was measured. If respondents compute the literal meaning of an indirect request before paraphrasing its indirect meaning, then indirect requests should require a longer period of time to paraphrase than either literal uses of the same sentences or direct requests. The results showed that the response times did not differ significantly across the three conditions, suggesting that respondents had bypassed the literal-meaning step.

Further experiments (Gibbs, 1982, 1983) were conducted to detect the presence or absence of the literal-meaning step by a different procedure. In this procedure, respondents were asked to derive the indirect meaning and were later tested on the literal meaning. If the literal-meaning step must precede the derivation of the indirect meaning, then this prior experience with the literal meaning would have facilitated the later responses to the literal paraphrase sentences compared with respondents who had not been asked to derive the indirect meaning. However, no facilitation effect was found, suggesting again that respondents had by-passed the literal-meaning step when deriving the indirect meaning. Gibbs (1984) concluded that the experimental evidence on the whole failed to support the sequential model that claims that individuals must first analyze the literal meaning of a sentence as part of the process of computing the indirect meaning.

It appears, then, that the inference process does not necessarily begin with the computation of the literal meaning. The anomaly in the model can be traced to the emphasis theorists have placed on the utterance per se, which in turn has led them to start their analysis from the very words of an utterance. This purely academic starting point leads quickly to the analysis of literal meaning and is then taken to be the typical starting point of the inference process used by ordinary language users. Of course, there are communication contexts in everyday life that do require this type of starting point, for example, listening to a lecture in mathematics, building a bomb according to given instructions, preparing a meal by following a menu, and so forth. In these and other referential communications, there is a high premium on the precise communication of technical, complex ideas and little room for nonliteral meaning. The problem arises when other communication contexts that are designed in the indirect mood are also subjected to the same model. In these contexts—as well as many others—language users bring with them expectations, or *frames* (Tannen, 1979), that assist them in narrowing down the range of potential interpretations. Gibbs's (1982, 1983) experiments, reviewed above, bring this problem into sharp focus.

Gibbs's conclusion has been challenged, though. Dascal (1989) pointed out that Gibbs had used highly conventionalized figurative speeches in his experiments and, for this reason, the generalizability of Gibbs's conclusion to less conventionalized forms of indirect speech (e.g., conversational implicatures and novel metaphors) remained to be demonstrated. In his successful defense on this very point, Gibbs (1989) cited evidence from other psycholinguistic experiments relating to novel metaphors, sarcasms, and ironies to corroborate his finding.

Another criticism that Dascal (1989) raised is more problematic, and it casts the inferencing process in new light. The experimental evidence produced or cited by Gibbs relied solely on the length of response time, without any data about what had actually happened in individuals' minds from the moment that a sentence was presented. Dascal (1989) proposed that it is possible that the processing of the literal and indirect meanings "run in *parallel*, and [are] eventually completed almost simultaneously" (p. 254; emphasis added). This parallel-processing model, which contrasts greatly with the sequential nature of the three-step model, is in accord with other results on discourse comprehension reviewed by Kintsch (1988). Its validity in relation to the specific inference of indirect meaning remains to be substantiated. For example, it cannot easily accommodate the results of Gibbs (1982, 1983) reviewed above. In any case, the point to note for present purposes is that ordinary language users usually get to the point of an indirect request very quickly; whether they achieve this by computing the indirect meaning straightaway or by computing both the indirect and direct meanings simultaneously through parallel processing is a separate issue.

The swiftness with which indirect meanings are inferred is not difficult to understand once we shift from the grammarian-cum-logician perspective to a social-psychological one that views human beings as competent language users who, since infancy, have been confronted with social situations in which indirect communication is the norm rather than the exception (see Rommetveit, 1983). For example, young children are expected to ask adults for favors using indirect requests of one sort or another and not to *tell* adults what to do. Indirectness is also culturally valued for the sake of maintaining the addressee's sense of autonomy and independence. Very young children may find this difficult to comply with, because indirect requests require the use of more complex linguistic forms than do direct requests. There are also some quaint forms of indirect speech acts that are particularly baffling to children, for example, "I'll be very happy unless . . ." (Carrell, 1981). Yet by the age of 4 years, children have already mastered the full complexity of the linguistic system of requests (Ervin-Tripp & Gordon, 1986). Around that age, they are known to exploit their repertoire of request strategies in accordance with situational demands and with their social orientations (Goodwin, 1980b; Sachs, 1987). A girl, aged 3, was reported as saying to her mother, "Isn't it true that when you feel hot you want a drink? So I feel hot." (Blum-Kulka, Danet, & Gherson, 1985, p. 113).

Holmes's (1983) study of classroom verbal interaction shows that teachers communicated their directives to pupils by a wide variety of indirect forms. Even very young pupils acquired very quickly a high degree of sociolinguistic competence in interpreting correctly and taking up directives that were expressed in various indirect forms. Holmes (1983) attributed the acquisition of competence first to pupils' recognition of the pervasiveness of the teacher's control over classroom activities and their desire to please the teacher. Second, the teacher frequently exploited the pupils' motivation to please by framing directives in the indirect forms of praise and condemnation. As a result, pupils soon learned that the teacher's every wish was their command. With this orientation, they learned to scan all of their teacher's utterances for potential directive function. At times, they reacted to the perceived indirectness even though it was the literal meaning that the teacher had really intended, resulting in misunderstandings that were remarkably similar to those cited earlier from Ervin-Tripp (1976).

In addition to studies that examine children's understanding of indirect *requests* and *directives*, there are other studies that look at children's understanding of indirect meaning generally. Here again the evidence shows that children are attentive primarily to the utterance context and only secondarily to the utterance per se. Olson and Hildyard (1981) present a typical experiment that shows this. In their experiment, children were read a story wherein a boy who was unhappy with his share of popcorn said to his friend, "You've got more than me." When asked to recall what the boy had said, kindergarten children usually reported the boy's underlying intention ("Give me some of your popcorn.") and not his very words. Attention to the utterance per se, in addition to the utterance context, became marked only among older second grade children (who reported both the intention and the exact words of the boy's utterance). There is also reason to suppose that even the second graders' utterance-oriented attention might have been forced by the experimental task requirement, because children rarely give literal interpretation in natural discourse situations (de Villiers, 1984).

Studies of child development have shown that the literal comprehension strategy of attending to the very words of an utterance and ignoring the context becomes prominent well after the child has mastered the contextual strategy of attending to, and computing the speaker intent from, the context rather than the utterance alone (Ackerman, Szymanski, & Silver, 1990; Beal & Flavell, 1984; Bonitatibus, 1988a). The onset of literacy and formal schooling, which favors analytical referential communication, coincides with and may contribute to the development of the literal comprehension strategy (Bonitatibus, 1988b). It would be a mistake to extrapolate from this sequence of development that once the literal comprehension strategy has been mastered, it will become the fresh starting point of language comprehension in later years. A better view is to regard the two strategies (and maybe others) as parts of children's—and adults'—"pragmatic/sociolinguistic competence" that enable them to adapt their language behavior to communication contexts in their own worlds (Rice, 1984). Unless the communication context is unfamiliar or the form of expressing the indirect speech act is quaint, ordinary language users are competent enough to infer quickly the indirect illocutionary point. They do this by computing the indirect illocutionary point instantaneously or by computing the direct and the indirect illocutionary points simultaneously through parallel processing. This competence enables language users to participate in conversation that often involves rapid exchanges of indirect speech acts.

Production of Indirect Speech Acts

The production of indirect speech acts can be understood in terms of the triggering or signaling process. Generally, speakers trigger their listeners to infer the indirect meaning from their messages by designing messages that fail to fulfill one or more of the Gricean maxims. Grice (1975) distinguished four types of failure:

Opting Out: To indicate plainly one's unwillingness to cooperate (e.g., "I can't say anything more")
Violating: To quietly and unostentatiously fail to fulfill a maxim
Clashing: To resolve a clash between one maxim and another
Flouting: To blatantly fail to fulfill a maxim

Of the four types of failure, clashing and flouting provide listeners with the clearest triggers for focusing on the indirect illocutionary point. Clashing can be illustrated by the following example taken from Grice. Two women, A and B, are planning a holiday in France. B knows that A wants to visit C, but B does not know C's address:

A: Where does C live?
12.B: Somewhere in the south of France.

B's noninformative reply upsets the maxim of quantity. Yet to be more informative would upset the maxim of quality (be truthful). To resolve the clash between the maxims in question, B chooses to sacrifice quantity (presumably a less important maxim than quality). In doing so, B implies that she does not know C's address without openly admitting her ignorance. The example illustrates the twin functions of clashing: speaker B not only mitigates the illocutionary point (the point of expressing her belief of the whereabouts of C) but also masks an unpleasant truth (her ignorance).

Clashing is restricted to situations in which two maxims are at odds with each other. By comparison, flouting is less restricted, as it can work on any one of the maxims to create a trigger that would alert the listener to focus on the indirect illocutionary point. There are various specific triggering devices, and these will be examined first in relatively simple messages and then in longer segments of discourse.

Triggering Devices: Simple Messages

In this part of the discussion we will show how messages that flout the Gricean maxims will trigger indirectness, which in turn will mitigate the negative affect present in the messages. Indirectness based on flouting the maxim of manner is relatively straightforward, which has already been mentioned. It is the flouting of the other three maxims that will be discussed below with materials drawn from Brown and Levinson (1987).

Quantity. Flouting the maxim of quantity is basic to all instances of indirectness, because in being indirect, speakers must say something different from (either more than or less than) what they exactly intend to mean. There are specific ways of flouting quantity that will give rise to indirectness.

A mother who wants to remind her son to wash the car can do so by saying, "Has the car been washed?" This indirect speech act will be heard as meaning "Have you washed the car?" By omitting *you*—the addressee—from her utterance, the mother mitigates her interrogation and paves the way for the addressee to admit his negligence indirectly "No, it hasn't" rather than directly "No, I haven't." An employer who does not want to recommend favorably a long-time employee for a new job may do so by making only scant comments. This way of flouting the maxim of quantity amounts to a no-comment comment where one is clearly called for in the circumstances, and as a result, it implies a criticism of the employee. The most extreme form of no comment is probably silence. Instead of making a verbal reply to a rude remark, a "speaker" can use a well-timed silence to communicate his or her displeasure. Nothing is said, yet something has been said.

Likewise, the reply in utterance 13, called an *understate* (Brown & Levinson, 1987), is implicitly critical.

> A: What do you think of Harry?
> 13.B: Nothing *wrong* with him.

The stress on "wrong" directs attention to the criticism.

Quality. The maxim of quality is flouted when the truthfulness of the propositional content of an utterance is so obviously defective that the listener is forced to do extra mental work in inferring the underlying, unspoken truth. This yields obvious advantages for the speaker when the unspoken truth is offensive and, if stated explicitly, can be used for holding the speaker accountable. Brown and Levinson (1987) listed four ways of flouting the maxim of quality: contradiction, irony, metaphor, and rhetorical question. To illustrate how these can serve to mitigate an affectively negative message, Brown and Levinson provided the following types of implicitly critical messages. In example 14, the speaker uses contradiction to imply a criticism when she is asked during a job interview if she is happy working for her former employer. The remaining examples are self-explanatory.

14. Well, yes and no. (contradiction)
15. John's a real genius. (irony—after John has just done 20 stupid things in a row)
16. Mary's a real fish. (metaphor, implicating coldbloodedness)
17. How many times do I have to tell you . . . ? (rhetorical question—too many times)

Relevance. The most common way of flouting the maxim of relevance is by dropping hints. This is how the duke asks his butler to close the window in sentence 10. Two other devices besides hinting are to give association clues and to presuppose. Brown and Levinson (1987) provided the following types of illustration:

18. How do you think we are for expenses in this time? The marriage at mooLavaaLeyoo came and that was five rupees. (association clues imply that the speaker wants to decline a request for money)
19. At least I don't go around boasting about *my* achievement. (presupposition implies that someone else has been boastful)

Longer Segments of Discourse

The discussion thus far has focused on the use of indirectness for mitigation in relatively short segments of discourse. There is more room for mitigation in longer segments of discourse that occur either within a single or across several speaking turns. Within a single speaking turn, a speaker may generate a long segment of speech that contains a *narrative response* as a mitigating device. Labov and Fanshel (1977), in their analysis of a therapy conversation, identified incidences in which the patient conveyed an aggressive message by the narrative as a whole: The narrative response functioned as a mitigating device "because the aggressive message . . . is never stated directly" (p. 336).

In a sequence of conversation involving several turns at talking, a speaker can carry out the indirect illocutionary act of a mitigated utterance at a particular turn and the direct illocutionary act of the same utterance at another turn. These enactments across speaking turns can be linked with the responses of the other speaker to achieve a strategic effect. Consider the following text, taken from Downes (1984, pp. 307, 324). Arthur is walking with Brenda, a married woman with whom Arthur has been having an affair.

20. Arthur: What's the matter with you tonight?
21. Brenda: I'll tell you what's the matter with me, Arthur. I'm pregnant.
22. Good and proper this time, and it's your fault.

In the first part of the conversation, Arthur puts a question (20) to Brenda, who latches on to its literal meaning and replies with the relevant information: She reveals to Arthur that she is now pregnant (21). The two utterances form an adjacency pair, a common conversational sequence in which the first part of the pair obliges the next speaker to provide the relevant second part (see Chapter 4). At the completion of sentence 21, Brenda could have proceeded to *troubles talk* (Jefferson & Lee, 1981; Coupland et al., in press). She does not. Instead, she immediately accuses Arthur of getting her pregnant: "Good and proper this time, and it's your fault." The accusation is direct and emphatic. How does Arthur respond? The conversation continues:

23. Arthur: *How do you know it's mine?*
24. Brenda: Why, don't you want to take the blame?
25. You are backing out now.
26. Arthur: What blame?
27. There is no blame on me.
28. I just want to know whether it's mine or not.
29. It's not bound to be.

Even a cursory reading of the text from 23 to 29 would leave the reader with the impression that Arthur is trying to deny Brenda's accusation, at first indirectly and then, in utterance 29, more directly. Question 23, the focus of the present discussion, functions not merely as the first part of an adjacency pair but also as an indirect denial of Brenda's accusation. The indirectness offers Arthur two interrelated communicative advantages. It attenuates the force of the denial and allows Arthur to retract from the denial if and when it is necessary to do so. The facility for retraction is provided by the literal meaning of 23, to which Arthur does retreat later, claiming in 28 that he *just* wants to know whether or not the baby is his. Arguably, question 23 may also serve to remind Brenda— again indirectly—of her other sexual relationships. The above excerpt shows that by examining direct and indirect illocutionary acts and how they are strategically positioned in various speaking turns to achieve multiple goals (see also Tracy & Coupland, 1990), one can appreciate better the power of mitigation brought about by indirectness.

Be Tentative

During the height of the Gulf Crisis, President George Bush wrote a letter to President Saddam Hussein explaining his determination to see an Iraqi withdrawal from Kuwait before the January 15, 1991, deadline. The letter never reached President Hussein. The Iraqi foreign minister, Tareq Aziz, read the letter but refused to deliver it to Hussein, claiming that its language was impolite and not proper for messages between heads of state. Bush conceded that his letter was "direct" but maintained that it was not "rude." The controversy over Bush's use of direct language figured prominently in television broadcasts in both the United States and New Zealand. On January 11, 1991, one major New Zealand newspaper, the *Otago Daily Times*, carried the headline "Letter to Hussein direct, not rude."

The ill-fated Bush-to-Hussein letter raises the issue of the relation between mitigation and politeness, which will be discussed in a later section. The letter is also a dramatic example of the choice of the direct mode of expression. One may ponder over the possible reasons behind Bush's choice of directness. The president might have felt that given the superior military might of the U.S.-led alliance and the perceived rightfulness of the mission he was championing, directness would be the diplomatically proper mode of communication on his part—indirectness would have been seen as a sign of weakness and a betrayal of the rightfulness of the alliance's mission. Or the president could have strategically chosen the direct mode of expression, so as to deliberately engineer the rejection of his letter by the Iraqi foreign minister to legitimize military action on Iraq.

Another intriguing possibility is that this communication failure represents a clash between Middle Eastern and American cultures, or between *high-* and *low-context* cultures, respectively (Ting-Toomy, 1985). Cohen (1987) argues that many Arab communicators are highly sensitive to issues of face in personal contexts, more so than their American counterparts. This sensitivity leads to a preference for indirectness in messages about decisions that will affect message recipients. It also leads to a high concern with the social implications of messages, even in contexts that Americans would view as purely informational. Or in Cohen's (1987) words, "whereas Arabs use language for social effect, Americans see it primarily as an instrument for transmitting information" (p. 38). Thus President Bush may have intended to produce a direct and informative message, but its effect may have been to threaten the face of its actual (and, by projection, intended) recipient.

Bush might also have been concerned that a less direct message would have encouraged his addressee to miss the point about the alliance's determination in enforcing the deadline, which was only a few days away. That is, the underlying proposition might be garbled in transmission (a semantic problem) or the intended force of the proposition might be misconstrued (a pragmatic problem).

The potential of indirect, mitigated messages to be misunderstood is greater for powerless than powerful speakers. There is some evidence that an implicit promise will be taken as a promise only when the speaker's power to reward is perceived to be adequate and that an implicit threat will be taken as a threat only when the speaker's punishment power is sufficient (Murdock et al., 1984). That is, the speaker's perceived power to deliver is a clue used by hearers to disambiguate the meaning of implicit messages. This suggests that only speakers who are powerful can in fact allow their power to speak for them, as it were, by using indirectness and thus avoid the pitfalls of explicitness.

Thus there are power-related and social factors that limit the use of indirectness; it is also the case that speakers may prefer directness for clarity of expression or for longer-term strategic goals. Furthermore, there is also cultural variation in the choice and valuation of the direct and indirect modes of expression. German (House & Kasper, 1981) and modern Hebrew (Blum-Kulka et al., 1985) speakers, for example, prefer directness of expression more than English speakers do. Thus there are situations in which indirectness will not be used either because indirect messages are not viable or because they are deemed by speakers to be less effective than direct messages. How, then, do speakers mitigate while being direct?

To understand the means by which speakers combine directness and mitigation, we can take a cue from the speech behavior of speakers who are direct and *polite* in their communication. Brown and Levinson's (1987) work suggests that polite directness can be achieved by adding *redress* to a direct speech act, for example, apologies, accounts, and hedges. By appending redressive elaborations to an explicit message, the speaker seeks to return face to the addressee even as the addressee's face is trampled on by the primary act contained in the message. Relating this idea to mitigation, but bearing in mind that mitigation and politeness are not identical, we propose below that speakers who are direct in their communication can bring about mitigation by being *tentative* in their speech behavior.

In the following, we will discuss specific prosodic and verbal means of realizing tentativeness as a mitigating strategy. Both prosodic and verbal tentativeness can be appended to indirect as well as direct influence-messages. In the latter case, tentativeness functions as a mitigating strategy independently of indirectness. For this reason, speakers who use direct messages can nevertheless mitigate by being tentative.

Prosodic Devices

Holmes (1984a) summarized various prosodic devices for conveying tentativeness. The better known ones are intonation and stress. A fall-rise intonation pattern conveys tentativeness, as in *Put the TV ^{on}*. Low stress serves the same function. Compare telling someone to shut up in a gentle low voice (mitigated) to saying the same with strong or normal stress. High pitch, a third device, indicates tentativeness due in part to the deferential overtones derived from its association with the voice quality of children, especially the voice of girls (Kramarae, 1982). In their analysis of classroom discourse, Brazil, Coulthard, and Johns (1980) noted that pupils often used high rising terminals (HRTs) when answering their teacher's questions. The association between high pitch and tentativeness was very much evident in the authors' interpretation of the function of HRTs:

> We discover that very often the pupils are in fact requesting an evaluative, high key follow-up by ending their answer with high termination. Only when the pupil is confident does he end with mid-termination requesting agreement; while low termination virtually never occurs and when it does is heard as "cheeky" or "sullen." (Brazil et al., 1980, p. 78)

The functions of HRTs, like intonational patterns generally, vary across communication contexts and across linguistic communities and do not necessarily serve to indicate tentativeness. Among young New Zealand English speakers, for example, there is some evidence (Wells & Bayard, 1992) to show that a high terminal pitch contour in declarative contexts functions primarily as a device to continue a narrative, particularly when the high termination is coupled with *and: Then I saw* ^John, *and he was with his* ^friend, *and they went into* ^Wizards. The use of high termination in tandem with *and* as a narrative-continuative device appears to be spreading rapidly among children and teenagers in both New Zealand and Australia. Kylie Mole, the gum-chewing teenage schoolgirl character in the popular Australian television show "Comedy Company," personified the use of the narrative-continuative device in her prolonged, nonstop monologue (see Britain, 1992; Guy & Vonwiller, 1984; Horvath, 1985, for a discussion of other instrumental goals, as well as affective goals, behind HRTs in New Zealand and Australian English).

Reservations

A second way for speakers (and writers) to be tentative is to express reservations of one sort or another. Reservations indicative of tentativeness are either addressee-, speaker-, or other-oriented, and these will be discussed in turn.

A speaker can set his or her message in a tentative mood by expressing reservations about the addressee's *willingness* or *ability* to cooperate. As a result, the primary act being performed by the speaker is understood to be conditional on the addressee's cooperation. A common device for doing this is the tag question, as in "Do me a favor, will you?" Tags that function as mitigators are usually, but not always, associated with rising intonation, depending on tag type and the nature of the accompanying main clause (see Holmes, 1984a). Another means of showing addressee-oriented reservations is to use disclaimers. For example,

If you wouldn't mind . . .
If it's not too much trouble . . .
If you are sure that it's okay . . .
If it's not an inconvenience . . .

The above disclaimers can also be placed at the end of a primary message.

In addition to addressee-oriented reservations, speakers can orient reservations toward themselves. One variety of speaker-oriented reservations is set up by acknowledging doubt about the speaker's warrant for the accompanying illocutionary act. This is commonly indicated by a disclaimer placed at the start of a primary message and cast in the following form: "I hate to do this, but" or "I'm no expert, but." Disclaimers that are placed at the start of a primary message convey reservations about some *forthcoming* act. This prospective use of disclaimers (see Hewitt & Stokes, 1975) requires mental anticipation and should be distinguished from retrospective remedial strategies (e.g., excuses, justifications, and apologies; see Antaki, 1988; McClure, 1991), which are accounts *after* the act. As a result of the anticipatory requirement of disclaimers, disclaimers are more difficult than accounts for children to learn. Bennett (1990) found in his experiment that although 25% of 5-year-olds understood the mitigating function of disclaimers, it was not until 8 years of age that the proportion reached 50%.

A second variety of speaker-oriented reservations consists of expressing doubt about the *validity* of the propositions that are conveyed in the primary message. There are several devices for implementing this. Speakers can, in the first instance, use what Holmes (1984b, 1986) called *modal tags*. The specific function of modal tags may be the mere expression of uncertainty (e.g., "The sky is cloudy tonight. That's the Southern Cross over there, isn't it?"), or it may be the mitigation of influence-messages. For example, suppose that after years of drifting from one place to another with his female companion, Chris now wants to settle down and raise a family with her. "It's time that we should have our own family, isn't it?" he says. Similarly, a modal tag can be used to mitigate an accusation ("That's my money, isn't it"—a girl says to a boy whom she suspects of misappropriating her money) or a criticism ("Some of the mistakes are quite unnecessary, aren't they?").

Parenthetical verbs are another device for showing reservations about the validity of the asserted proposition: *I guess, I suppose, I reckon,* and *I gather.* (The pragmatic effects of *I think* and *I believe,* according to Holmes (1984a), are less certain.) A third type of device consists of personalized epistemic modals, as in *it seems to me.* Some hedges (*sort of, kind of,* etc.) can also convey tentativeness by qualifying the truthfulness of the asserted proposition. Using this device, a witness who wants to stress the tentativeness of her testimony in court may say, "I saw a sort of European-looking person pointing a kind of knife at the victim." Apart from showing tentativeness, these validity qualifiers also suggest that the speaker is not prepared to take full responsibility for the correctness of the asserted proposition (see also the discussion of hedges in Chapter 2).

Apart from addressee- and speaker-oriented reservations, speakers may also express reservation by attributing the content of the message to an *unidentified* source. An example of this other-directed reservation is the all the too familiar phrase "A source close to the White House has indicated that." Serving the same function are *depersonalized sentential adverbs* such as *allegedly* and *reportedly*. These devices, like the validity qualifiers that are used for expressing speaker-oriented reservation, signal tentativeness and serve notice that the speaker cannot be held responsible for the truthfulness or otherwise of the message.

The Yin and Yang of Mitigation

This section deals with the polite and impolite faces of mitigation and with mitigation's self-serving and altruistic motivations. The point of departure here is once again Fraser's (1980) seminal paper, in which he raised the issue of the relationship between mitigation and politeness and discussed the multiple goals of mitigation in terms of their underlying motivations.

Polite and Impolite Mitigation

A high degree of mitigation and politeness often occur together. Consider, as suggested by Fraser (1980), the following request from the moderator at a seminar to one of the participants: "I'd appreciate if you would kindly sit down." The utterance is relatively mitigated and polite. Opposite to this, the utterance "Sit down!" said in the same context would be unmitigated and impolite. Beyond these two combinations of mitigation and politeness, two others are possible in principle. The easier of the two to think of is unmitigated-polite, as in the stock phrase "Sit down, please." Regarding the remaining combination (mitigated-impolite), Fraser (1980) makes the claim, "I find it difficult to construct a case where the speaker is viewed as impolite by having mitigated the force of his utterance" (p. 344). On this basis, he concluded that "mitigation occurs only if the speaker is also being polite," that is, the mitigated-impolite combination does not exist.

However, there is no reason why a mitigated message cannot be expressed in an impolite form because, in principle, mitigating the force of a message does not necessarily affect the politeness or rudeness of the message. For example, the moderator could have said, "I'd appreciate if you would be considerate enough to try and warm the seat with your ****." The speaker has mitigated the force of the illocutionary point—that he or she intends the addressee to sit down—by using an indirect figurative speech and expressing reservations; yet the utterance is rude in using obscene language (****) and implying that the addressee has been inconsiderate.

The impolite side of mitigation is not only conceivable, but may also be instrumental to the success of an influence attempt by, paradoxically, attacking rather than saving the addressee's face. In the example above, where the addressee is behaving reprehensibly, the speaker who wants to counter the behavior may have better success by embedding an attack on the addressee's (positive) face within the mitigated message. The attack links the reprehensible behavior with the loss of face, reminds the addressee of such, and casts the addressee as an outsider; in this way, it activates forces for compliance that are otherwise inaccessible to polite mitigation. (See Austin, 1990, for an analysis of the dark side of politeness; Chapter 6 for a discussion of the use of politeness for gaining or regaining power.)

Mitigation, then, has a polite and an impolite face. Mitigation can be independent of politeness as much as politeness can be independent of mitigation, and for this reason, the two can best be thought of as orthogonal dimensions of interpersonal communication. The relation between mitigation and politeness is also complicated by the fact that the speaker and the addressee may perceive the same direct message differently on the politeness dimension. Thus whereas President Bush was adamant that his letter to President Hussein during the Gulf crisis was proper and not rude, the Iraqi foreign minister regarded it as impolite.

Self-Serving and Altruistic Goals

In general, the goals of mitigation are either speaker- or addressee-oriented. Fraser (1980) calls them self-serving and altruistic motivations of mitigation, respectively. One of the self-serving goals is to lessen the anticipated antithetical reactions that the addressee may have to the speaker because of the speaker's unwelcome speech act. A second type of the self-serving goal is

> to "get off the hook," not for performing the act with its unwelcome effects, but for what doing the act implies about the speaker's beliefs. . . . For example, if the speaker, a physician, were to say, "Difficult as it is to believe, given your life-style, the analysis shows you have a social disease." The speaker is not asking to be excused for providing a diagnosis, but, rather, indicating that the associated implication which would arise from the *fact* of the disease is one which he does not wish to be committed to." (Fraser, 1980, p. 345, emphasis in original)

Cameron, McAlinden, and O'Leary (1988) examined the distribution of the use of tag questions by speakers who occupied either a powerful or a relatively powerless role (e.g., doctor versus client, teacher versus pupil, and television presenter versus audience). It was found that a subset of tag questions that functioned clearly as mitigating devices was used exclusively by *powerful* speakers of both sexes. This raised the intriguing question of why powerful speakers had to mitigate at all. The most probable chain of events, according to the authors, is this: Powerful speakers such as judges (in relation to the accused) and teachers (in relation to pupils) were in an authority position to criticize → they did criticize → and afterward they mitigated their criticisms. The mitigation appearing at the end of the script may very well be motivated by addressee-oriented goals, that is, the speaker may wish to restore the addressee's face wants after these have been trampled on. Yet these altruistic goals are secondary within the overall script.

Altruistic goals, as alluded to in the example above, are primarily oriented toward the welfare of the addressee. Fraser (1980) illustrated this by the example that a bearer of tragic news may reveal the news gently to the addressee to soften the blow of the painful truth on the latter. The self-serving and the altruistic goals may be enacted sequentially over two or more speech acts, as shown in Cameron et al.'s (1988) study or enacted in the same speech act.

* * *

Linguistic features of indirectness and tentativeness have traditionally been discussed in the context of women's speech and treated as expressions of insecurity (e.g., Lakoff, 1973). Although later research has questioned the view that tentativeness is female specific, it continues to focus on indirectness and tentativeness as expressions of powerlessness (e.g., O'Barr & Atkins, 1980; see Chapter 2). The same passive focus is evident in the work of Preisler (1986), who linked tentativeness to speakers' socioemotional roles and contrasted this with the linguistic assertiveness of task-oriented speakers. In this chapter, we adopt a more active stance and highlight ways in which many of the linguistic features of indirectness and tentativeness can serve as an instrument of power by depoliticizing influence attempts.

The extent to which mitigation may enhance the effectiveness of an influence attempt has not been discussed in this chapter. Intuitively, one may expect that mitigation would attenuate rather than accentuate the effectiveness of an influence attempt. This is because, first, mitigation means that the force of an order, a directive, a criticism, and so on has been softened; and second, tentative speakers are generally perceived as less competent, less confident, and less powerful than assertive speakers (see Chapter 2). Perhaps there is an effectiveness cost attached to the implementation of self-serving and altruistic goals of mitigation. Yet, as shown in Chapter 2, the relevant empirical evidence is either equivocal in regard to specific forms such as intensifiers or, in the case of Carli's (1990) studies, actually in favor of mitigation in specific circumstances: *Female* speakers were better able to change *men's* opinions toward their own position when they spoke tentatively than when they spoke assertively.

CHAPTER SIX

Misleading Words

In ancient China, bearers of military bad news risked being executed on delivery of the unwelcome message to their emperor. These pitiable messengers had absolutely no control over what to say or how to say it. But supposing they had, what could they have done to save their lives?

They could have lied. By embarking on this course of communication, they could have chosen between two prototypical forms of lying: either withholding the bad news, or (mis)informing their emperor that the battle had been won, not lost. Ekman (1985) labels these two forms of lying *concealment* and *falsification*, respectively. For various reasons, not the least being that falsification results in particularly vicious consequences, people typically use falsification only when concealment is impossible. Concealment, on the other hand, is not always possible because other individuals may ask questions or reveal the truth. There are, however, other options available to speakers who for various reasons do not want to falsify or conceal outright. It is these other options that will concern us mainly, even though there will be occasions where our discussion (e.g., on deception) will necessarily touch on concealment and falsification.

Metts (1989) proposed a three-point continuum from covert to overt misrepresentation of information. Omission of all relevant information (concealment) serves as one anchor, and explicit contradiction of truthful information (falsification) as the other. The points between concealment and falsification are represented by messages reflecting degrees of *distortion*. In the context of communication between intimate partners, which is the topic of Metts's

(1989) study, distorted communication can be viewed as the manipulation of the details of the situation; one partner actually informs the other of the event but manipulates the facts by "exaggeration, minimization and equivocation" (p. 165). It is possible that each of the three listed forms of distortion can be expanded further (e.g., equivocation; see Bavelas et al., 1990) and that other forms also exist. Indeed, given that deception has coexisted with truthfulness in human communication for as long as human civilization itself (Hyman, 1989; Knapp & Comadena, 1979), it would be naive to underestimate the diversity of distorted communications that do not rely on outright concealment or falsification.

In this chapter we discuss some of the ways in which speakers use words to mislead their hearers. To introduce the concept of misleading words, consider the following event. At the 1968 Democratic Party national convention, where delegates were charged with nominating a candidate for president of the United States, there were violent confrontations in the streets of Chicago between the police and individuals protesting the Vietnam War. The situation was highly polarized, with potential voters aligned both with and against the police, both with and against the war. Hubert Humphrey emerged as the nominee, and in his acceptance speech to the audience of delegates, he said, "This must never happen again in the streets of Chicago"—or words to that effect. Given the degree of polarization in the larger audience of voters, this was a strategically ambiguous thing to say. Both hawks and doves, despite their enormous political differences, could agree with this sentiment. The former group could interpret this utterance to mean "Protesters will not be allowed to take over the streets," whereas the latter group could read it as "The police will not be allowed to riot." One can view this sort of strategically ambiguous speech act as an attempt to mislead the audience (or that part of an audience) that would disagree with the speaker's true attitude.

Mislead means to move someone's thinking in a wrong direction; in this context *wrong* means away from the speaker's real intention or feeling. Or, more subtly, speakers may mislead their hearers by failing to reveal their true position and by failing to admit that they even have a position. Or, more subtly still, speakers may mislead their hearers by presenting one model of reality while suppressing alternative models.

The use of misleading words can confer power on speakers, partly because such use potentially reduces speakers' vulnerability. There are situations in which revelation of one's true attitude or opinion can be dangerous and in which nevertheless one must say something—for example, when one is asked a direct question regarding one's political preference and when this preference is antithetical to that of the questioner. The use of misleading words is one form of communication that may enable speakers to wriggle out of such difficult situations. In addition to avoiding costs, the misleader can gain rewards; in this more positive sense, too, the use of misleading words confers power on speakers. For example, a candidate for office may lead particular voters to think that she supports a certain position, thereby gaining their vote, but may never explicitly articulate support for this position, thereby protecting herself against commitment.

Initially, we will talk about devious (Bowers, Elliot, & Desmond, 1977) and equivocal (Bavelas et al., 1990) messages, which constitute a paradigm case of misleading symbolic communication. We will then turn to some related types of messages, e.g., lies, secrets, and evasive messages, invoking a theory of propositional communication offered by Bradac, Friedman, and Giles (1986). Following this, we will view deception more broadly and will examine verbal and nonverbal correlates of deceptive messages for both encoding and decoding. A question here is the extent to which deceivers have control over their verbal and nonverbal behaviors. Another question is the extent to which receivers of potentially misleading messages are aware of the thrust of such messages; the topics of mindless message processing, implicit injunctions, and politeness are pertinent here.

Finally, we will discuss (very selectively) the role of metaphor in communication and cognition, focusing on the ways in which the use of particular metaphors by speakers may prevent hearers from thinking of alternative metaphors. The establishment of the correct metaphor for a segment of reality may occur when speakers are aware of what they are doing—creating a metaphor that is useful for them—but hearers are not. Speakers who subtly control metaphors gain power over the thoughts of others, for in important respects, thoughts are essentially metaphoric.

Devious and Equivocal Messages

Devious Messages

In Chapter 5, we showed how indirectness of speech may be used for mitigating the harshness of such speech acts as criticisms and directives. Indirectness may also be used for other, more devious purposes. These sorts of devious messages are ubiquitous in diplomatic, political, and courtroom discourses. In everyday conversation, too, interlocutors make use of indirectness for encoding devious answers to escape from embarrassing questions such as the following: "Were you convicted of driving under the influence of alcohol last year?" Rather clearly, in some cases a direct yes answer will damage the reputation of the respondent, and a direct no answer (if incorrect) may be perceived as a lie if the true state of affairs is known or later discovered. Both answers are potentially damaging to the question's target. The trick, then, is to somehow satisfy the questioner's demand without responding with a yes or no. How might this be accomplished?

At a general level, according to Bowers et al. (1977), the respondent must exploit the slippage that exists between the pragmatic and semantic dimensions of natural language. He or she must answer in such a way that the questioner is satisfied that the question's demand has been met, even though a literal semantic analysis would fail to show a direct correspondence between the question and the answer. One way of exploiting the slippage is by means of indirectness. For example, in response to the question "Were you convicted of driving under the influence of alcohol last year?" the respondent might say, "I still have my driver's license." The surface meaning of the reply bears no logical connection with the question, yet the reply implicates (see Chapter 5) an answer that will satisfy the questioner that the question's immediate demand has been met. In this case the respondent would hope that the questioner would infer that the answer is no. Such an inference would depend on implicit mediating inferences, for example, persons holding a driver's license have not been convicted of driving under the influence of alcohol, because persons so convicted would have their licenses revoked. Thus a proposition expressed leads to a proposition inferred. The inferred proposition might be incorrect—there may be (typically are) circumstances under which drivers convicted of this offense will be allowed to retain their licenses. But the incorrect inference is made by the questioner—the respondent is not directly responsible for this inference. In this case an expressed proposition leads to an inferred proposition, which leads to another inferred proposition: the inferred answer is no.

More abstractly, proposition A is asserted, which entails proposition B, which in turn entails proposition C. The entailments among propositions are inferential and informal, not logical. They depend on communicators' world knowledge and linguistic knowledge working in concert. The entailed inferences are those that the devious communicator wants his or her hearer to make, but because the literal meaning of the proposition asserted differs from the desired inference, the communicator cannot be blamed for fulfilling his or her intention. The engineering of a hearer's inference combined with a lack of accountability constitutes the essence of deviousness. Devious communicators who are effective have a good intuitive sense of the likely chain of inferences that will occur on the basis of an expressed proposition.

Can a speaker follow specific rules to be devious? Are there guidelines that can be used by hearers who are anxious to detect deviousness? We construe Bowers et al. (1977) as suggesting that these questions about the production and detection of devious messages can be answered affirmatively. For example, they suggest that utterances exhibiting a high ratio of negatives to other forms are suspect: "Please don't think that just because I don't write I am trying to say I don't love you any more" (p. 239). It seems to us that this sentence and others like it are potentially confusing and difficult to process, but are not necessarily devious. There is a difference between confusing hearers and causing them to form a specific inference while avoiding accountability.

More generally, we think that it may be impossible to specify particular guidelines for producing and for detecting devious messages even though, as will be seen below, there are signposts that can be culled from current research on equivocal communication. Any utterance, any group of lexical items, can reflect deviousness. It all depends on a speaker's intention: "I want hearers to infer X but I do not want to be held responsible for their inference; I won't say X; I will say Y instead and they will infer X." It seems to us that the particulars of the X/Y relationship in the previous example are potentially almost infinitely variable. On the other hand, specific message features (e.g., high levels of negation) may be likely to trigger a judgment of deviousness in hearers, regardless of the speaker's real intention. This judgment may be incorrect from the standpoint of the speaker but may nevertheless affect hearers' subsequent responses. This would be an interesting topic for research: What message features are a part of a person's *naive theories* (see Kempton, 1986) of deviousness?

We share Bowers et al.'s (1977) wish to enable hearers to discover deviousness wherever it may occur. What is needed is not only a focus on specific message features but also some procedure for sensitizing hearers to speakers' intentions. Why are some people very capable of correctly perceiving devious intent, but others are not? In the absence of research on this question, we cannot say much, but two things occur to us: (1) Research on this topic might be analogous to work on cues and organismic factors that facilitate the discovery of overt duplicity, or lying (Ekman & Friesen, 1974), and (2) it may be the case that some people are highly aware intuitively of the possibility of slippage between the semantic and pragmatic levels of language, while others are not. In regard to the second point, perhaps it may be possible to train or enhance this sort of linguistic intuition; on the other hand, such intuitions may be relatively impervious to change once they are formed—this is an empirical issue.

Equivocal Messages

Whereas Bowers et al. (1977) were primarily concerned with the devious, misleading aspects of nonstraightforward communication, the more recent experimental research by Bavelas et al. (1990) attempts to highlight the problem-solving function of non-straightforward communication in an avoidance-avoidance communicative conflict situation in which, as we have noted, the respondent must reply to a question and yet the only available unequivocal messages would lead to negative consequences. Bavelas et al. (1990) carried out 19 experiments involving adults and children in both laboratory and naturalistic settings, the results of which "all confirmed that equivocation is the predictable and intriguing consequence of a communicative avoidance-avoidance conflict" (p. 262).

Of special interest to us here is the four-dimensional model that Bavelas et al. (1990) invoked to delineate the production and detection of equivocation. The four dimensions are sender, content, receiver, and context. These four dimensions, which were adapted directly from Haley's (1959) study of schizophrenic communication, overlap with the well-known communication factors in persuasion research (e.g., Hovland, Janis, & Kelley, 1953). The dimensions are considered to be "fundamental" components of communication generally, "in the sense that they are always true: There can be no communication without my saying something to you in a given situation" (Bavelas et al. 1990, p. 33).

Bavelas et al. (1990) illustrated equivocation on each of the four communicative dimensions with the following kinds of examples. The speaker can deny that he or she is personally saying anything by prefacing the message with phrases such as *the management requires me to inform you* or *they say*. In this way, the speaker equivocates on the sender dimension. To equivocate on the content dimension, the speaker can design a self-canceling message by saying, "Well, yes and no. On the one hand I agree, but on the other hand, I don't feel that I can agree." To avoid addressing the receiver while still addressing him or her, the speaker can address no one in particular or address the receiver as a member of a social category: "People like you make me nervous." The fourth dimension, context, was defined rather narrowly (presumably for experimental purposes) as the *immediately* preceding message which in turn must be a *question*, actual or implied (see Chapter 7 for a broader definition of communication context). A typical context is as follows. A student participant in an experiment would be told that another student, who has just given a class presentation that was poorly prepared and poorly delivered, passes her (the participant) a note asking, "How did I do?" The question, "How did I do?" anchors the context so defined. If the participant chose to reply, "You were braver than I would be!" she would be judged as avoiding the question, that is, equivocating on the context dimension.

The dimensions are intercorrelated to varying degrees, most highly between context and content, and least so between context and receiver, across the 12 experiments for which correlational data are available (Bavelas et al., 1990, pp. 317-324). The four-dimensional model has heuristic value for sign posting specific communicative domains in which devious messages may be produced—and detected.

Lying, Evasion, and Related Forms

When we discussed concepts such as intentions and deviousness, we were talking about a part of the more general realm usually labeled *deception*. This realm is inhabited by a variety of objects, including lies, tall tales, fibs, secrets, evasive maneuvers, and fictions (Hopper & Bell, 1984). Generally, deceptive communicators fail to provide message recipients with an accurate picture of their beliefs, or more actively, they provide them with an inaccurate picture. The key idea here is that a true belief is obscured in some way, which at least potentially empowers the obscurer. Given the variety of deceptive acts appearing in everyday communication, is there a way of getting to their essence, of integrating them, thereby rendering them conceptually sensible? One theory suggests an affirmative answer, and we will briefly summarize this theory here.

Theory of Propositional Communication

The baseline for the theory of propositional communication is the idea of truth telling. What does it mean to say that someone intends to tell the truth? Bradac et al.'s (1986) theory has a scope condition that focuses on intended messages, as opposed to messages actually produced. In this sense, the theory is about planning or strategy formulation. (One of the reasons for this focus reflects what we have said above: The analyst cannot infer deception, deviousness, and so on—accurately and beyond doubt—strictly on the basis of objective message features.) Crucial to truth telling is *accuracy:* The speaker intends to produce in hearers an accurate belief regarding the speaker's belief X, when X is the topic at issue. "What do you think of candidate Jones?" "I think he is a philanderer." In this case, the respondent offers a proposition (I think that) about another proposition (he is a philanderer), and both propositions are pertinent to the topic (Candidate Jones). The latter fact suggests another variable that is crucial to truth telling—the intention to produce an utterance that is *relevant:* The speaker believes that a particular utterance Z is relevant to the topic (Jones). Relevance refers to a pragmatic belief about the way in which particular semantic features cohere with, for example, the issue defined by a question.

Two other speaker intentions are important for dealing with truth telling. First, the speaker intends to produce an *utterance* as opposed to withholding an utterance (after all, truth telling is a form of telling, not nontelling). Second, the speaker believes that the utterance is one for which he or she will be *accountable.* In this context, accountability refers to the belief that an utterance can be understood in one way only by any reasonable hearer (the propositions indicated above will be taken literally). Thus truth telling = + accuracy + relevance + utterance + accountability. Each of these four critical intentions are two-valued in the theory; that is, they can assume positive or negative forms, they can be present or absent. If, referring to the current example, the value of the utterance changes from + to −, but the other values do not change, we have a *secret.* A secret is the intention to withhold an utterance that would be accurate, relevant, and understandable in one way only. If the value of accountability changes from + to −, an act that can be called *devious truth telling* emerges. Sometimes speakers want to leak the truth with impunity. If both utterance and accountability assume negative values, we have *devious secret keeping* (probably a rare form). This is the *truth-telling family.* Membership in this family changes as the values of utterance and accountability vary from + to −, while accuracy and relevance remain constant at +.

If the values of accuracy and relevance change from + to −, we jump from the *truth-telling family* to the *falsehood* and *evasion families*, respectively. Falsehood is the intention to produce an utterance that is inaccurate, relevant, and unambiguously interpretable (– accuracy + relevance + utterance + accountability). Using this as the baseline, if the value of accountability changes to –, we have a *devious falsehood* (–++–). This is the form that Bowers et al. (1977) attend to primarily. If the value of the utterance changes to –, we have *falsehood avoidance* (–+–+)—this is the withholding of a relevant utterance that would produce a false belief about a speaker belief. A fourth and almost certainly rare member of the falsehood family is *devious falsehood avoidance* (–+– –).

Evasion occurs when a speaker intends to produce a message that is irrelevant but also unambiguously interpretable (± accuracy – relevance + utterance + accountability). The accuracy of the evasive utterance is not the issue—it may represent accurately one of the speaker's many beliefs about the universe, but not a belief that is relevant. *Evasion avoidance* occurs when the speaker intends to withhold an unambiguously irrelevant remark. When accountability assumes a negative value, the speaker intends *devious evasion*. *Devious evasion avoidance* is the fourth member of the evasion family, occurring when relevance, utterance, and accountability all assume negative values.

Thus changes in accuracy and relevance are responsible for variation across families, whereas changes in utterance and accountability are responsible for variation within families. The three families (truth-telling, falsehood, evasion) with four members apiece define 12 states of speaker intentionality, which underlie communication about beliefs. Even though the theory is decidedly speaker oriented, it may be the case that hearers make inferences about speaker intentions in terms of accuracy, relevance, and so on. It may be the case that particular message features in particular contexts trigger hearer judgments of a speaker's intentional nonutterance, accountability, and so forth. The 12 states may constitute a kind of code for deceptive acts understood by both speakers and hearers. Individuals who can exploit this code with high creativity may empower themselves in many communication contexts.

Of course, to say this is not to condone the use of secrets, devious falsehoods, and such. One position would have it that the goodness or badness of these communicative actions depends on the motives of the communicator (Bradac et al., 1986). But one could argue that the very use of devious falsehoods, for example, regardless of motivation, warps the communication environment in negative ways by departing from an ideal of complete and truthful revelation (Habermas, 1979; Jourard, 1971). Proponents of the first position appear to recognize that sometimes speakers need to use the devices of deviousness to prevent others from gaining power over them, whereas proponents of the second position appear to desire the elimination of power differences altogether.

We should also note that the theory described above is almost certainly an oversimplified sketch of the mental states undergirding propositional communicative acts. It does not attend to cultural variations, and there is reason to believe that lies and secrets may be constituted differently in different cultural groups. For example, in Russia (and in other Russian-speaking countries) there are two rather distinct kinds of lies: one (*lgat*) suggesting "false consciousness" or a rather profound breach of a moral order, and the other (*vrat*) indicating a typically venial act performed for localized, pragmatic reasons (Mondry & Taylor, 1992). This qualitative distinction suggests, minimally, the need for an expansion of the taxonomy offered by Bradac et al. (1986). Perhaps other data would suggest that for some groups particular distinctions offered in the theory would need to be collapsed.

Language of Deception

Quite apart from the idea of an abstract code of deceptiveness, as we suggested above one possibility is that communicators do things verbally or nonverbally to create the impression in others that they are deceptive. Another possibility is that particular verbal or nonverbal cues can serve as objective indicators of deceptive intent. Although we see some problems with the latter possibility as suggested above—particularly that the connection between deceptive intent and specific message features is bound to be a tenuous one—a large body of research has examined this possibility and should be acknowledged here, albeit briefly. In regard to the possibility of objective indicators of deception, perhaps the most prominent explanatory model has invoked the concept of arousal. The basic idea here is that for most people the act of deceiving someone produces some degree of anxiety in the speaker and this anxiety in turn affects both verbal and nonverbal behavior. A refinement of this idea is that the anxiety produced by deception may be different from anxiety produced by other acts and that this difference may have behavioral consequences. This proposition was tested directly by de Turk and Miller (1985). After noting that a number of studies have indicated that a variety of facial, bodily, and vocal behaviors can discriminate between deceivers and truth tellers with some degree of reliability, these researchers described a study examining these behaviors in three different conditions: low arousal nondeception, high arousal deception, and high arousal nondeception. The first two conditions were created by having respondents tell the truth or lie about, respectively, the pleasantness or unpleasantness of slides they were viewing. The third condition, the most novel one, employed truth telling respondents who were exposed to white noise to increase their level of arousal.

A manipulation check indicated that physiological arousal was, as expected, higher in the latter two conditions and lower in the first one. Six behavioral cues distinguished deceivers from both aroused and unaroused nondeceivers (the sign for the deceivers is in parentheses): adaptors (+), hand gestures (+), speech errors (disfluencies; +), pauses (+), response latency (+), and message duration (−). As hypothesized, vocal behaviors (compared with facial and bodily behavior) were especially indicative of deception. A later study by the same researchers (de Turk & Miller, 1990) demonstrated that the same six behavioral cues, when used to train naive respondents, enhanced the trainees' ability to detect deceptive acts. The results were interpreted as providing further evidence of the validity of these cues as indicators of high arousal deception. In a related study, DePaulo, Stone, & Lassiter (1985) provide seemingly contradictory evidence that vocal behaviors are more useful for deception detection than are facial and bodily behaviors when communicator (deceiver) arousal is low. It may be that the contradiction is more apparent than real, however, because the high arousal conditions of de Turk and Miller may not have been equivalent to those of DePaulo et al. Equating levels of arousal across studies is an ongoing problem in this area of research. The problem is compounded by the possibility that the

Yerkes-Dodson law, which specifies an inverted-U function between arousal level and performance (e.g., telling a lie), is affected by task complexity. Relative to complex tasks, simple tasks displace the inflection point of the curve toward higher arousal (Kahneman, 1973). As the task of lying differs in complexity across studies, comparison of arousal levels across studies becomes extremely difficult. Also the former researchers did not employ a low arousal deception condition, presenting another difficulty for the comparison across studies.

But, regardless of these possible differences, it seems reasonable to suggest that when communicators engage in deception their arousal level increases (to a lower or higher level depending on the circumstances) and that hand gestures, speech errors, pauses, and the like will vary accordingly. These behaviors may, in fact, be useful for detecting deception, although almost certainly detection accuracy will depend on having available a baseline of the communicator's nondeceptive activity. It is important to note that the behaviors discussed thus far are exclusively nonverbal—even the vocal behaviors are paralinguistic, not entailing semantic or syntactic features. It seems to us that the connection between deceptive intent and the verbal features of messages will be more tenuous than that between such intent and nonverbal features, because verbal features of messages are more controllable. The devious communicator will often choose words carefully to produce a particular effect. But while he or she utters these carefully chosen words, some nonverbal leakage may occur.

However, it is also possible to talk meaningfully of *verbal* leakage. That is, some stylistic features of messages may reflect low speaker control, particularly in spontaneous discourse in face-to-face interaction (as opposed to planned discourse, e.g., a formal speech). For example, there is some evidence that level of arousal is inversely related to a speaker's level of lexical diversity, that is, the ratio of novel (distinct) to total words in a message (Howler, 1972). Thus one could argue that deceivers will tend to use a high level of repetition in their utterances. Similarly, some evidence suggests that verbal immediacy is inversely related to speaker arousal (Bradac, Bowers, & Courtright, 1979). A low level of immediacy exists when a speaker includes many linguistic devices that serve to distance himself or herself from the content of the message, for example, words that displace an object temporally or spatially when there is no grammatical requirement for this displacement ("there he is" versus "here he is" when both options are appropriate). There is, in fact, some indication that deceptive activity is associated with relatively low verbal immediacy (Kuiken, 1981).

Thus arousal produced by deception may result in utterances that are lexically redundant and low in immediacy. In the case of a given devious communicator, the *planned* message might not include a high level of redundancy and a low level of immediacy, but these levels may be manifest in the *performance* of the plan if arousal and the demand on cognitive processing capacity are high enough to disrupt the conscious suppression of leakage cues. Of course, deviousness may be served sometimes by using high redundancy and low immediacy to *appear* to be highly aroused—once again it seems to us that particular lexical features cannot be used with high certainty to infer devious intent or lack thereof. Skillful deceptive communicators will exploit with high creativity the nearly infinite number of linguistic possibilities available to them.

Related to the arousal-deception connection is the connection between emotion and deception (Ekman, 1985; Zuckerman, DePaulo, & Rosenthal, 1981). Whereas arousal is often viewed as a diffuse state of energy, emotions are relatively more specific—happiness, surprise, and anger. One possibility is that particular emotions (e.g., fear and guilt) are associated with deceptive acts (Friedman & Tucker, 1990). That is, when communicators lie they feel fearful or guilty. Furthermore, the experience of fear or guilt may be linked to specific nonverbal behaviors, particularly facial displays. Thus nonverbal behaviors indicative of fear or guilt occurring with the expression of a belief-related utterance may signal deception.

It is worth emphasizing, however, that fear or guilt may be experienced for a variety of reasons other than deceptive intent. There is another interesting problem with the idea that nonverbal indicators of emotion are linked to deception and are, therefore, useful for detection purposes: In normal interpersonal communication, spontaneously produced emotions may be difficult to decode accurately. That is, the emotion experienced by the speaker and the emotion inferred by a hearer may have low correspondence in some cases. Two intriguing studies by Motley (1991) and Motley and Camden (1988) suggest that some people are quite accurate in judging enhanced emotions when a portrayer is instructed to convey fear, guilt, and so on but are surprisingly unreliable in judging spontaneous emotions. Motley (1991) hypothesized that facial displays of speakers serve to indicate that some (not a particular) emotion is being experienced and that the speaker's verbal message is used by a hearer to infer what the specific emotion is. For example, if the speaker is describing a gruesome accident, his or her facial expression may be taken as indicating disgust.

An implication is that the fear or guilt experienced by a deceiver in a spontaneous communication context may yield a facial display that is ambiguous from the hearer's standpoint. And it is unlikely that the deceiver's verbal message will help to disambiguate this display, because in many situations the message will be about something not typically associated with fear or guilt—persons lie about an almost unbounded number of topics.

Quite apart from the objective connections between arousal or emotion and verbal or nonverbal behavior and between such behavior and accurate or inaccurate detection of deceptive intent, we can ask the question: What behaviors do people *think* are caused by deception? Results of research on this question, summarized by Friedman and Tucker (1990), suggest that the following behaviors are believed by a significant number of persons to indicate deceptive intent: averted gaze, implausibility of utterance, postural shifting, a slow rate of responding, and a rapid rate of speech. Thus a speaker denying guilt who avoids eye contact while speaking rapidly may be perceived as lying, even though the denial is honest. In fact, hearer beliefs about deception cues are likely to interact with a variety of factors in producing judgments of deception, an implication of a model offered by Friedman and Tucker (1990). These theorists suggest that there are input variables that affect speakers (e.g., arousal and emotion), speaker behavior cues that are potentially valid indicators of deception (e.g., speech errors), speaker behavior cues that are potentially invalid indicators (e.g., averted gaze), and hearer or detector variables (e.g., nonverbal sensitivity). This and many earlier models (Ekman, 1985; Greene, O'Hair, Cody, & Yen, 1985; Zuckerman et al., 1981) point to the distinct likelihood that deception will be a complex process, a position with which we agree.

Thus it may be possible for message recipients to detect the deceptive intent of those who would mislead them and thereby message recipients may be empowered. On the other hand, devious message senders may gain power by learning to control those behaviors that indicate or are perceived to indicate deception. Such behaviors constitute a kind of language of deception available to speakers and hearers alike. Typically, deceptive speakers will want to avoid these behaviors to appear truthful. But we can imagine complex situations wherein deceivers will employ these behaviors intentionally while making accurate statements, to *appear* to be lying and thus inviting false accusations that can later be used as a badge of innocence.

Words That Bypass Critical Thought

There are messages that deflect attention and scrutiny while at the same time achieving their desired effect. Such messages convey to hearers specific injunctions or beliefs but remain unexamined and thus beyond criticism. An intriguing possibility is that many of the messages that we are exposed to in everyday life function in this way (Berger & Roloff, 1980), although their effect is probably typically innocuous. (Later on, we will examine innuendo messages that have more serious, incriminating consequences.) That is, many times we do what people say ("close the door") or agree with what they say ("Paris is nice in spring." "Yeah."), without paying much attention to the semantic or syntactic details of their utterances. Were we to attend to the details of the thousands of messages we receive daily, we would have little energy left for anything else.

So it may be the case that many messages are processed relatively mindlessly (Langer, Blank, & Chanowitz, 1978). For example, if John steps in front of Mei-ling in a line of people waiting to buy tickets and explains or apologizes for this action by saying, "because I need to purchase two tickets," Langer et al.'s (1978) results would suggest that Mei-ling may well accept this account even though a moment's thought would indicate that the utterance does not provide a good account for John's intrusion.

There are three issues here. The first issue is, How does John's message result in Mei-ling's compliance? The answer lies partly in the kind of compliance itself: It is a routine, overlearned reaction of little personal relevance to a familiar episode. Another part of the answer has to do with Mei-ling's perception of John's state of need—the probability of compliance is enhanced by the attribution of the need to uncontrollable rather than controllable factors (Folkes, 1985).

Just as compliance can be mindless, so can *non*compliance (Langer, Chanowitz, & Blank, 1985), and this raises the second issue: What kinds of factors would encourage relatively mindless, uncritical processing of a message? Petty and Cacioppo's (1986) elaboration-likelihood model suggests that mindless information processing is more salient when, among other things, personal involvement is low, forewarning of the content of a message is absent, and the person's need for cognition is low. In modern times, according to an interesting observation made by Cialdini (1984), individuals are increasingly exposed to an information-laden environment that is fast-paced and saturated with clever one-liners, 30-second commercials, political plugs, and so forth. These environmental influences divert message processing away from the particular argument of a message to the message form. So when the message form suggests that the message is an offer of an explanation or apology, this may be enough to elicit the well-practiced script of either accepting or refusing the offer in a relatively automatic fashion, thus bypassing critical thought. Elicitation is automatic, especially when the message form is linguistically marked (e.g., by the word *because*). Cialdini (1984) likened this to automatic, fixed-action patterns observed in infrahuman species and labeled the underlying principle primitive consent for an automatic age. In addition to Petty and Cacioppo (1986) and Cialdini (1984), conversation analysis (see Chapter 4) suggests a third kind of factor in terms of adjacency pairs. John's message is the first part of an adjacency pair that has the force of prompting, fairly automatically, a relevant second part (Sanders, 1989).

The third issue, which can be seen as qualifying the first two, has to do with why John's message might succeed in placating Mei-ling. Mei-ling's autonomy or freedom of action (i.e., negative face) is threatened by John's intrusion, which is one definition of rudeness. Typically, communicators prevent or reduce the perception of rudeness by offering polite apologies that signal their acknowledgment of the potentially threatening character of their action and that disclaim responsibility or conscious intent. In the previous example, *because I need to purchase two tickets* may automatically be assimilated by the addressee to the cognitive category polite act, for this is what is expected in this type of situation. Thus situational expectations may bias interpretations of messages, thereby decreasing both effort and accuracy of cognitive processing.

More generally, politeness in speech is a ubiquitous communicative form that causes, among other effects, the reduction of hostility toward communicators or the prevention of same, inattentiveness to actions or messages, and forgetting or minimizing of perceived communicator intentions. There is a large body of research on politeness that we will not attempt to summarize here. On the other hand, aspects of the classic work of Brown and Levinson (1987) at least should be acknowledged and discussed briefly. As noted in Chapter 5, these theorists postulate that human communicators attempt mutually to safeguard positive and negative face wants by using polite redress when their messages are face threatening. According to their theory, the degree of polite redress would be greater when the speaker is less powerful than the hearer, when the social distance between them is larger, and when the magnitude of demand or imposition of the message is stronger.

Brown and Levinson's (1987) theory has been subjected to a number of empirical tests, critical analyses, and extensions (e.g., Baxter, 1984; Brown & Gilman, 1989; Craig, Tracy, & Spisak,1986; Coupland, Grainger, & Coupland, 1988; Tracy, 1990; Wood & Kroger, 1991). It is probably accurate to say that support for the theory has been mixed. On the one hand, the variables of power, social distance, and magnitude of demand have been shown to affect speaker's use of politeness strategies, but on the other hand the nature of this effect seems to differ from the specific predictions. For example, the theory indicates that as distance between a speaker and a hearer decreases, attention to face concerns will decrease as well. But some evidence suggests that the use of polite forms will decrease as intimacy increases, if the speaker demand is a large one (Lim & Bowers, 1991), especially when positive face is threatened; contrarily, the inverse relationship between intimacy and politeness may hold when speaker demands are low. It is also the case that the theory assumes an additive relationship among power, intimacy, and demand magnitude; that is, if power increases by two units and intimacy decreases by the same amount, then tendencies toward politeness will decrease by a factor of four. In fact, it appears that the relationship among the three variables affecting politeness is complexly nonadditive; two- and three-way interaction effects have been obtained in empirical studies (Leichty & Applegate, 1991; Lim & Bowers, 1991).

Thus there is reason to believe that as a speaker's self-perceived power decreases, his or her use of polite forms will increase when the situation involves demands or criticisms made of the hearer. This suggests that in some (perhaps many) contexts polite speech can be seen as an attempt to gain or regain power—a phenomenon that Austin (1990) referred to as the dark side of politeness. And it is probably the case that typically such an attempt is invisible because politeness is an extremely pervasive communication mode—politeness rarely stands out (the notable exception is provided by Uriah Heep in Dickens's *David Copperfield*).

Other messages that bypass thought have more insidious consequences than those examined above. A prime example is innuendo. An innuendo is a statement about a person or something coupled with a qualifier about the statement. The qualifier may be a denial, for example, "P is not a criminal." Here, the denial qualifies the statement that "P is a criminal." Despite the denial, readers of the sentence will be swayed in a negative direction, as if the qualifier *not* has been skipped, discounted, or otherwise disconnected from the statement. Similarly, self-denial of undesirable conduct (e.g., "I'm not a crook") tends to encourage hearers to become suspicious of the conduct, rather than discouraging them from suspicion. The qualifier of an innuendo is not necessarily a *not*; the negation supplied by the qualifier may be a question: "Is P a criminal?" Wegner, Wenzlaff, Kerker, and Beattie (1981) found that the negative effect of an incriminating question was even greater than that of an incriminating denial. They also found, in the context of media commentary on public figures, that the credibility of the source did not affect significantly the innuendo effect.

Innuendo effects occur not only in media commentaries on public figures but apparently also in courtroom trials, letters of recommendation, and interview questions (Kassin, Williams, & Saunders, 1990; Wegner, 1984). Even when hearers have been fore-warned that the assertion they are about to hear is false, they are still susceptible to innuendo effects (Wegner, Coulton, & Wenzlaff, 1985). So, why is it that once a statement has been expressed, attempts to deny, question, or forewarn it are unlikely to succeed? To rephrase the question in terms of the central theme of the present section: Why is it that qualifiers bypass critical thought?

Of the various explanations offered thus far (e.g., Wegner et al., 1981), the most encompassing one proceeds along the following lines. Positive information conveyed through the statement is understood first and is then cognitively reprocessed in light of the qualifier, at which point the negation supplied by the qualifier becomes "a superfluous addendum" to the positive information that has already been stored in memory (Wegner, 1984). This explanation echoes the view of Spinoza, who a long time ago proposed that "the acceptance of an idea is part of the automatic comprehension of that idea . . . [whereas] the rejection of an idea occurs subsequent to, and more effortfully than, its acceptance" (Gilbert, 1991, p. 107). According to Spinoza's view, comprehension *automatically* entails acceptance, and only afterward is the mind able to proceed to unaccept the statement. This is an intriguing philosophical contention. Expressed in contemporary terms, negation is second-order affirmation (Horn, 1989), linguistically complex (marked), and cognitively demanding (Gilbert, 1991). For these reasons, the negation supplied by a qualifier will occasionally bypass critical thought and leave the incriminating statement heard but undenied. This tendency will increase when there is an impoverished store of information on the topic (Wegner, 1989).

Evocative Words and Metaphors

Some special words have an extraordinary ability to evoke a particular structuring of beliefs and emotions. These are loaded words. When referring to a collision between two cars, for example, words such as *smash, bump,* and *collide* are loaded words, because they could distort the memories of eyewitnesses as to the speed of cars relative to more neutral words such as *contact* (Loftus & Palmer, 1974). Loaded words can be used to evoke a train of thought and emotions toward a certain desired direction. So, in the example above, an eyewitness may be misled to recall a higher car speed by the use of the word *smash*. Likewise, a couple without children of their own may describe themselves as *childfree*, which would evoke a very different image than would the label *childless*. The labels *rights* and *privileges*, when applied to the treatment of the personal freedom of prison inmates, would have different implications (see Edelman, 1977, for a discussion of loaded linguistic categorization).

As subtle as loaded words are as instruments for evoking particular thoughts and feelings, there is one linguistic phenomenon that is even more subtle (and even more ubiquitous): the metaphor. A frequently articulated position is that all language is metaphoric in that words stand for things (or ideas, actions, etc.). *Running* is a metaphor for the act of moving quickly. (This simple representational view is almost certainly incorrect in some respects, but its details need not concern us here; see Brown, 1958; Rosch, 1973.) As Aristotle put it, metaphor consists in giving the thing a name that belongs to something else. The force of a metaphor varies with the form the metaphor takes. It is relatively weak when the metaphor is expressed in the form of an implicit simile ("X is like Y"), for example, "politicians are like vultures." A stronger force is expressed in the "X is Y" form, as in: "politicians are vultures" (see also Glucksberg & Keysar, 1990).

Metaphors are created when features from one domain are highlighted or made salient for some reason and are seen to reside in or are imposed on another domain. Thus animals such as lions, tigers, and bears possess the following attributes, among others: aggressive behavior toward prey, sexual aggressiveness, impulsiveness, untidiness (by human standards), and occasional churlishness. To say that "men are animals" is to say that human males are similarly aggressive, impulsive, and so on. This example illustrates the selectivity of the metaphoric process; some attributes of some animals intersect with the category "human males." Men are not (like) camels, giraffes, or turtles. Men do not share with snails the attribute of podless locomotion. This metaphor is (and perhaps most other metaphors are) constituted by the intersection of two prototypes—prototypical male humans and prototypical animals. Lions are prototypical, whereas giraffes are not. Male athletes are prototypical whereas male nurses are not. (Of course, knowledge of prototypes is a product of culture, and therefore, for some social groups male athletes and lions will not be prototypical members of superordinate categories or "fuzzy sets.")

The transfer of word meaning from literal to metaphorical use is dynamic and has repercussions on other words that are associated with the word in question. In the case of verbs, for example, Chitoran (1986) made the observation that when a verb in one conceptual field has been transferred to another on the basis of a similar or analogical feature, it will exert pressure on associated words to also undergo metaphorical transfer.

Lakoff and Johnson (1980) have argued that metaphors are not constructions that are simply added on to normal language for purposes of stylistic adornment. Rather, metaphors are essential constituents of both language and thought. Or, in the words of Ortony (1975), metaphors are necessary and not just nice. We can only think of things in terms of other things (or actions, directions, positions, etc.). Thus we have "time is money," "that is beside the point," and "things are looking up." Metaphors reflect the values of a culture or society in many cases (as in the time-money equation), and they may reflect widely spread perceptual experiences (as in the idea that *up* is good). Metaphors are models for thinking about social and physical objects and for communicating a complex set of attributes in a shorthand that can be readily understood. And, very important, models are selectively heuristic; that is, they facilitate the generation of *new thoughts of a particular kind.* Another way of saying this is that models call our attention to some features of experience and blind us to other features, a point similar to one made by Kuhn (1970) in his discussion of scientific paradigms—there is an "essential tension" between the generative potential of a paradigm and the constraints it imposes on innovation.

And therein lies the potential power of a metaphor. Linguistic models can frame the discussion of events, providing boundaries around permissible and impermissible topics and issues. Such models can also point to acceptable solutions while pointing away from solutions that are unacceptable or even unthinkable. The abortion issue provides an interesting and serious case in point, one that is charged with moral and political significance. Prolife groups advocate a particular metaphor of prenatal development that looks something like this: A fetus is like a miniature human adult in that it has the right to life (and presumably also liberty and happiness). Prochoice groups advocate a different metaphor: A fetus is like other forms of tissue, developing dependently in a human host. These competing and incommensurable metaphors suggest radically different possibilities: One can excise tissue, one cannot excise a human adult; one grants autonomy to a human adult, one does not grant autonomy to tissue (which is necessarily nonautonomous); and so on. The capacity of metaphors to generate new thoughts and feelings of a particular kind depends on the particular network of semantic associations in which one word is related to others. In the abortion example above, *adult* and *tissue* have their own networks that generate different thoughts and feelings; these different thoughts and feelings become selectively polarized by the underlying intergroup antagonism. (See Bolinger's, 1980, discussion of other metaphoric clashes in the abortion debate.)

The AIDS epidemic is a frightening phenomenon in modern times. It weakens and usually kills the infected. For society at large, AIDS was and still is a mysterious menace. As with cancer, we in the English-speaking world describe AIDS as an invasion. But in contrast to cancer, which nowadays is understood as a disease incurred by individuals, AIDS is likened to a *plague*. In invoking the ancient plague metaphor, we try to understand—and explain—AIDS as a foreign invasion that originated from the Dark Continent and that is a disease incurred by people both as individuals and as members of a risk group (immigrants with darker skins, gays, and drug addicts) from which the general population should be protected (Sontag, 1988). The plague metaphor—more so than cancer, tuberculosis, or syphilis—generates fear, inculcates guilt, and inflicts stigma. It also leads to the metaphoric inflation of AIDS into a moralistic judgment on the out-group and society at large (see also Norton, 1991).

A subclass of the larger construct of metaphor or model is *social representation* (Moscovici, 1981). We have cognitive representations of social groups that manifest in speech; speech, in turn, creates or reinforces these representations. One study investigated social representations of men and women interacting with each other, using

as a source of data a large number of popular magazines containing articles or stories that included depictions of communication
between the sexes (Kruse, Weimer, & Wagner, 1988). The words
used in such depictions were analyzed closely and used to form
categories that, potentially, would discriminate between men and
women (in terms of frequency of occurrence of various behaviors).

Among other things it was found that males were most likely to
engage in dissociative behaviors, such as hitting and offering
threats; on the other hand, they were relatively likely to be helpful
to their female partners. Men were also much more likely to
evaluate their partners, offering both positive and negative sanc-
tions. Women were much more likely than men to express a
variety of emotions (joy, sympathy, fear, etc.), and they were more
likely to request help. The researchers interpreted their results as
indicating that the social representation of male-female interaction in popular magazines in Germany was highly stereotypical,
and they hypothesized that this representation existed as well in
the subjective culture of the country, that is, in the minds of
individuals. Thus the model is that women are emotional and
dependent, whereas men are aggressive and evaluative. One can
think of a number of specific metaphorical expressions, none very
flattering to either men or women, that would represent the general model. We think that it is very likely that this model is widely
apparent in many countries, going well beyond the confines of
Germany. This is not to say the model has complete hegemony over
thoughts about social communication between men and women, but
it does probably have some significant effect.

Thus metaphors and social representations constitute part of
our thoughts about the world, a world that is largely verbal, that
is, rooted in linguistic knowledge. Needless to say, this is an
important part, one that we draw on when we communicate with
others about our beliefs. He or she who creates a new and influential metaphor gains power over the thoughts of others to some
small or great extent. Of course, the creation of a new and influential metaphor is probably a rare event, if we are talking of
widespread influence. But locally (e.g., within a family), it is no
doubt more common. One of the sources of a metaphor's power
is its transparency at the point at which it becomes a familiar part
of one's mental world. We are typically not aware of our thoughts

as such, nor are we aware of their arbitrary (although sometimes helpful) character. This lack of awareness prevents us from realizing what the metaphor is pointing toward, what it is highlighting, and what it is obscuring. Metaphors come to seem natural and inevitable and, therefore, no more objectionable than one's own field of vision, and unfortunately, one may be misled by one's own selective view of things.

* * *

It appears, then, that speakers (and writers, of course) can mislead hearers (and readers) in a variety of ways: through the use of devious or equivocal messages, lies, slippery words, innuendoes, compelling metaphors, and so on. Hearers are misled when they are denied access to the truth (from the speaker's perspective) or to alternative views of reality and when the fact of that denial is suppressed (as it necessarily is with lies, deviousness, arguments based on true beliefs with unshakeable premises, etc.). Thus, arguably, a speaker who keeps a secret from a hearer with the intention of future revelation (as with a surprise birthday party) is not engaging in misleading communication. On the other hand, a secret keeper who intends never to divulge the secret and never to reveal the fact that information is being withheld is a misleader, even though his or her motives may be benign.

Throughout this chapter we have suggested that much hinges on the speaker's intention regarding communication of beliefs to a hearer—the intention to distort beliefs coupled with the intention to cover up this distortion is essentially misleading. Vague, ambiguous, or indirect language does not necessarily signal the speaker's desire to mislead. There are contexts in which indirection is expected, and this mode can be used to reveal beliefs and feelings with high accuracy. An interesting example is President Bill Clinton's statement made on CBS's *60 Minutes*, amid accusations of marital infidelity that threatened his bid to be the Democratic Party's nominee for president in 1992: "I think that most Americans who are watching this tonight, they'll know what we're saying, they'll get it, and they'll feel that we have been more candid" (Leubsdorf, 1992, p. 1). This was said in the context of also saying: "Are we going to take the position now that if people have problems in their marriage and there are things in their past which they don't want to discuss, which are painful to them, that they can't run?" (Leubsdorf, 1992, p. 1).

So there are marital problems too painful to describe exactly in public discourse, but Americans will know what these problems are when they think about it. They will get the point, and they will recognize that Clinton has been candid in his indirect remarks responding to the question of extramarital relationships. It seems to us that Clinton was rather clear about what happened in the past. The communicative situation was one that demanded indirect and even vague language, but his point was made rather clearly. It seems to us that there was no intention to mislead. (Of course, his statements are open to alternative interpretations.) On the other hand, when asked specifically about the allegation of his long-term involvement with a particular woman, he offered an unambiguous denial, which provides an informative contrast with his response to the more general allegation.

To say that much depends on speaker intentions (whether Clinton's or anybody else's) is to acknowledge the difficulty in detecting misleading communication. An intention is difficult (perhaps impossible in principle) to prove. But there is evidence, which we discussed above, suggesting that deceptive intentions may be leaked to hearers through verbal and nonverbal channels. And we also discussed evidence indicating that hearers have beliefs about behavioral cues that signal deception, even though these beliefs may be inaccurate. Both sorts of evidence suggest that there are behaviors that are noticed by hearers in deception-relevant contexts. On the other hand, speakers engage in various behaviors that typically are not noticed and, to a large extent because they are unnoticed, such behaviors empower speakers: deferential gestures, unspoken promises, tacit threats, and the like. Finally, speakers create metaphors that may or may not be noticed at the time of their creation (probably metaphors that turn out to be important are immediately noticeable), but after these metaphors become familiar tools of thought they become invisible, thereby gaining in potential for misleading hearers, misleading even the speakers themselves, and misleading other parties who perpetuate the metaphors unintentionally and without awareness— all of these persons become pawns of a mindless product of an only dimly remembered thoughtful and creative act.

CHAPTER SEVEN

Masking

Rules and regulations in organizations are directives that *pro*-scribe undesirable and *pre*scribe desirable conduct. They are linguistic representations of social control. By their very nature they impose restrictions on individual freedom, carry threats of punishment for misconduct, and remind organizational members that although they are all equal, some are more equal than others. In short, rules and regulations are potentially aversive speech enactments. When the organizational culture is authoritarian, as it is in the military, rules and regulations may be boldly stated. But such boldness will be at odds with an egalitarian culture in which the power distance among members is small and personal autonomy is valued. Typically, rules and regulations are written from the implicit perspective of the authority and are expressed in specialized linguistic forms that portray the authority's control over ordinary members as a state of affairs rather than an active process that involves commanding and obeying. This can be seen by comparing the following typical example of a library rule (30) with its fuller but rarely used counterpart (31):

30. Silence must be observed during library hours.
31. I, the librarian, require you, a user of the library, to observe silence during library hours.

Sentence 30 is less impolite than sentence 31 in that it is less confrontational and does not explicitly refer to particular individuals. Politeness, however, is not the hallmark of the linguistic representations of rules and regulations; to believe that it is, is to miss the point.

It should also be noted that sentence 30 is indistinguishable from sentence 31 in terms of mitigation—the force of the illocutionary point of the directive is as strong in 30 as in 31. As a depoliticization strategy, mitigation (see Chapter 5) may at first sight appear to be a viable option for expressing rules and regulations. But it is not. In the first place, rules are not meant to be tentative. They are not conditional on the goodwill of the members, nor do they hedge on the warrant or the validity of the authority. Rules are rules. Second, rules must be phrased in such a way that it is possible to pinpoint accurately cases of rule violation in court. This requires that rules be stated with maximal reliance on direct meaning and minimal or no reliance on indirectness. Rules mean what they say. For example, the notice "Silence is golden" found in many libraries is by itself clearly inadequate as a legal statement, even though it may serve as a mitigated request for library users to remain quiet by exalting the desirability of maintaining a quiet atmosphere in the library.

Mitigation, like politeness, cannot *both* reduce the aversive effects and preserve the requirements of rules to be explicit and definite. Neither can misleading words (see Chapter 6), even though many of the principles that underlie misleading words are also exploited by writers of rules and regulations. Instead, it is masking, the final of three depoliticization strategies to be examined in this volume, that best captures the distinct features of the linguistic forms in which rules and regulations are expressed.

This chapter will develop the theme of masking as a depoliticization strategy. The starting point is the role of language in representing reality. From this, an argument will be made that the availability of different linguistic forms for representing reality provides language users with tools for deleting or stressing particular aspects of reality. The various masking devices by means of which this is carried out in single sentences and utterances are then discussed. After this, the discussion will center on masking that uses the richer contextual information contained in multiple sentences and utterances. For the most part in this discussion, rules, regulations, and news headlines are used as prototypical cases of masking. Wherever appropriate, conversations will also be cited for developing the masking theme.

Linguistic Representations of Reality

As a preliminary definition, masking can be thought of as the rendering of reality so as to make it appear different from the "actual" way of the world. Masking does not withhold true information or present false information as if true, rather it presents true information in an incomplete or partial way under the cover of one or more literary masks. The formation of a literary mask consists of, first, the concoction of special phrases and expressions, usually with greater effort and more planning than in the case of the mitigating strategies of tentativeness and indirectness. The act of concoction also involves the removal of cues that may otherwise encourage a more critical reading of the masked reality. This feature further differentiates masking from the mitigation strategies of tentativeness and indirectness, the success of which, as shown in Chapter 5, depends largely on the effort of the speaker to signal tentativeness and to trigger conversational implicatures. A third feature, which may be thought of as a consequence of the second feature, is the reduced level of cognitive activity in comprehending the presented reality. Such mindless message processing reduces the immediate unpleasantness of rules and regulations.

The concoction of special words to form a literary mask that would discourage the critical reading of the masked reality puts masking on a platform similar to that of misleading words. In this sense, the theme of masking is an extension of the principles of misleading words already discussed in Chapter 6. Beyond that, the genres of rules, regulations, and news headlines present both new linguistic devices that have yet to be discussed and new problems that can be best understood as literary masks that cover particular aspects of reality by presenting or foregrounding other aspects of reality.

Reality of Everyday Life

To elaborate the masking process beyond that of misleading words, it will be useful to discuss first the linguistic representation of reality. Reality is meant here not as some ultimate reality in the philosophical or religious sense, but as the everyday, moment-to-moment experience that individuals have when they interact with each other and with the physical environment, together with their interpretation of the interactions. In short, it is the reality of everyday life. To paraphrase Berger and Luckmann (1967):

> My reality of everyday life is organized around the "here" of my body and the "now" of my present. Beyond the immediate here and now, my reality of everyday life also embraces the larger world within my reach and in which I work and interact with others. It is not the only reality I am conscious of, for I have dreams, and even in my wakefulness, I can imagine things and theorize about things. I also know of loved ones whose realities, and their conceptions of them, are not always the same as mine. Even so, my everyday life reality is the reality par excellence among the multiple realities—I use it for making sense of my dreams and my other wakeful realities.
>
> At any one time, I cannot know everything there is to know about this reality, but only some selective aspects of it. At times I even have doubts about it; yet I am often obliged to suspend my doubts—at least temporarily—as I routinely exist in everyday life. As long as the routines of my everyday life continue uninterrupted, so will the order I apprehend in the reality of this life. These routines include what other people do to me, as much as what I do to them, in deeds and in words. In the morning, I would routinely say to my spouse, "Well, it's time for me to go to work," and routinely, I would receive the reply, "Fine, have a good day at work." That the talk exchange can afford to be so casual is evidence to me that I can continue to take for granted the order I apprehend in everyday reality. Yet everyday reality is not just for private experiencing. In my interaction with other human beings, sooner or later I have to construct my private experience verbally into a social reality that is accessible to them.

Reality-Related Functions of Language

From the phenomenological point of view, verbal activity (speaking, listening, writing, and reading) is a source of experience that forms part of the reality of everyday life. Verbal activity is also an account of reality in the sense that when individuals engage in verbal activity, they simultaneously make reference to other, nonverbal aspects of their experience (Halliday, 1985). In addition, there are two other reality-related functions of language that are particularly relevant to the understanding of masking: A person uses language for representing reality mentally to himself or herself and to others as well as for maintaining a sense of reality over time.

As pointed out by Berger and Luckmann (1967) and many other authors, language is the most important sign system of human society. Humans produce signs to stand for, or signify, things that are present or can be recalled from the past. This naming function also covers subjective intentions and experiences. The system of signs may be in the form of gesticulations, dances, gazes, material artifacts, or any number of things. To be functional, signs must be detachable from the immediate expressions of subjectivity, and transportable beyond the here and now. Apart from the quality of transcendence, signs must also be integrated into an objectively available system that is accessible to both users and would-be users as elements of a *common* world. Among all the sign systems, linguistic signification is the most transcendental and objectified (see also Bruner, 1964). Berger and Luckmann (1967) summed up these qualities of language in the following way:

> I can speak about innumerable matters that are not present at all in the face-to-face situation, including matters I never have and will never experience directly. . . . Language provides me with a ready-made possibility for the ongoing objectification of my unfolding experience. Put differently, language is pliantly expansive so as to allow me to objectify a great variety of experiences coming my way in the course of my life. (pp. 52-53)

The transcendental and objectifying qualities of language enable individuals to use language for representing reality both mentally to themselves and outwardly to other persons. These qualities also underline the capacity of language to assist people in maintaining reality as long as the same language is continually used. Recall the routine conversation between spouses given above. If one morning the second spouse does not respond to the time-to-go-to-work conversational move, or that person replies, "Isn't it about time you started your own company and became your own boss?" one can imagine how the ordered reality that the first person has been accustomed to will be brought under scrutiny until the matter has been cleared up. Generally, individuals maintain reality for each other by continuing to use a common language. The common language, Berger and Luckmann (1967) explained, may range

> from the group-idiosyncratic language of primary groups to re-gional or class dialects to the national community that defines itself in terms of language. There are corresponding "returns to reality" for the individual who goes back to the few individuals who under-stand his [sic] ingroup allusions, to the section to which his accent belongs, or to the large collectivity that has identified itself with a particular linguistic tradition. (p. 173)

In a similar vein, but from the more focused perspective of *action* identification, Vallacher and Wegner (1985) described the func-tion of language in compressing actions that are time-consuming and physically complicated (e.g., *robbing a store*) into convenient symbolic summaries (act identities) that people find useful for both talking and thinking. Words can compress enormous periods of time into a single element of thought, and this enables humans to contemplate courses of action that transcend the here and now. Words also compress a chain of specific actions into a single consummated action, which in turn is detachable from the original chain of specific actions. This allows humans the freedom of under-standing that the action can be realizable in more than one way.

The act identities, once compressed into and represented by words, are then implicated in the planning and execution of human action. Vallacher and Wegner (1985) centered their discus-sion of the action implications of language on the maintenance and change (emergence) of actions. The discussion was framed in terms of language, mind, and action control and spanned several disciplines, including linguistic philosophy, symbolic interaction-ism, and psychology. For present purposes, it will be sufficient to highlight the following aspects.

As already noted, individuals are able to, and in fact do, assign verbal identities to their actions and those of others. Among the multiple linguistic identities that are available for representing any given action, some are at a higher and others at a lower identity level. These identity levels correspond to the hierarchical levels in which actions are organized. The action *cleaning the house,* for example, on the one hand subsumes several lower-level actions such as *washing the floors, dusting,* and *doing the dishes,* and, on the other hand, is itself subordinate to a higher-level action such as *preparing for guests.* The latter action also subsumes actions like *getting dressed,* which in turn subsumes *putting on shoes,* and so on. Within this overall action hierarchy, the physical activities involved in dusting may be assigned the lower-level identity *dusting* or the intermediate-level identity *cleaning the house* or the higher-level identity *preparing for guests.* On being asked what he or she is doing while dusting, the person can reply in any one of the three identities. Compared with the higher-level act identity ("I'm expecting guests tonight"), a lower-level identity (e.g., "I'm just dusting") reveals relatively little to the hearer. Conversely, a higher-level identity reveals to the hearer a more comprehensive meaning or account of the action; it also helps the speaker to organize more comprehensively in his or her mind the action plan. Vallacher and Wegner (1985) summed up the latter function in the following principle:

> When an action can be identified at both a higher or a lower level, there will be a tendency for the higher level identity to become prepotent. (p. 25)

This principle may be called the upward principle. Its operation is not unbounded. Higher-level identities provide few specific operational details and will be ineffective for an actor unfamiliar with these details. For example, if one wished to find happiness and thought only "find happiness," then "one is likely to remain frozen at the starting line, buried in thought with no way to get moving" (Vallacher & Wegner, 1985, p. 24). Such considerations lead to another principle, which may be called the downward principle:

> When an action cannot be maintained in terms of its prepotent identity, there will be a tendency for a lower level identity to become prepotent. (p. 26)

The processes depicted in the upward and downward principles set into motion a kind of equilibration that leads to (by our own reckoning) the principle that "an action is maintained in terms of its prepotent identity" (Vallacher & Wegner, 1985, p. 24).

The two reality-related or action-identification functions of language, in general, and the representational function, in particular, are crucial for understanding linguistic masking. The reality that a person (e.g., an accountant, a psychotherapy patient, a politician, or a newspaper reporter) actually represents to self or to others will be called the *presented* reality. Any particular presented reality is only one of many realities that are subjectively experienced. This multiplicity of realities, according to Gestalt and phenomenological analyses (Heider, 1941; Lewin, 1936; Schultz, 1945), is due to the multiplicity of perspectives from which a reality is perceived.

Any presented reality (e.g., a company's financial account, the presented symptoms of a patient, a state-of-the-nation speech, or a news report) can be constructed linguistically in more than one form. For example, a community newspaper reporter who has witnessed a family event is faced with the choice of using any one of a range of possible act identities. These act identities, as noted above, may vary in terms of concreteness or abstractness. They may also vary in their evaluative connotations—the event may be called an agreement, a deal, a bribe, or something else. As the reporter writes up the story, he or she is faced with further selections of linguistic constructions that will convey very different versions of causality and responsibility, as the following examples will make clear: "The father agreed to pay his daughter for doing household chores," "The daughter strikes a chore-for-money deal with her father," and "The father bribes his daughter into doing household chores."

Multiple Representations of Reality

The linguistic bases for *multiple* representations of reality are semantic range, indirect speech acts, and act identities. These linguistic bases will be discussed immediately below. Then the discussion will center on the theme that the availability of multiple representations of reality carries with it the potential for masking, which can be realized to varying degrees. After this, the actual masking devices will be examined.

Words that are comprehended as being somewhat similar are said to be within close semantic range of each other. Synonyms are obvious examples. Words that are normally not synonyms in the dictionary sense may also function as close semantic associates of each other in an appropriate communication context. Thus although *bombed, hit,* and *hurt* are not necessarily dictionary synonyms, they can be used as close semantic associates in the context of military activities:

32. Baghdad was badly bombed by U.S.-led multinational forces.
33. Baghdad was badly hit by U.S.-led multinational forces.
34. Baghdad was badly hurt by U.S.-led multinational forces.

Assuming that sentence 34 is the presented reality (e.g., in the form of a news headline), the other two sentences are reconstructed realities that are compatible with 34 by virtue of their close semantic association. (The associates for action identification are not completely the same but differ, in this case, in terms of abstractness—see "Generalization," below.)

It is not possible to quantify the size of any cluster of close semantic associates. The point here, though, is that it is semantic range, and not synonyms, that sets the limit on the number of reconstructed realities that are compatible with or relevant to the presented reality. For this reason, there is greater scope in the multiple linguistic representations of reality than meets the eye.

Thus far the discussion has been confined to the use of different words for multiple representations within the same sentence form. It is also possible to have multiple representations encoded in differently structured sentences. This can come about, first, in the form of indirect speech acts. Thus as shown in Chapter 5, the directive *Shut the window!* can be represented, and understood by hearers to be represented by differently structured utterances such as *Can you shut the window?* and *It's cold in here.* Second, differently structured sentences can be used to encode act identities at various hierarchical levels, which in turn will give rise to multiple versions of the presented reality. The more competent language users are in enacting indirect speech acts and action identification, the greater will be the scope of encoding multiple representations of reality in differently structured sentences.

Masking is not an all-or-none activity but, rather, occurs in varying degrees. Degrees of masking may be gauged by showing which of the essential dimensions of communication have been omitted from the presented reality. The dimensions in question can be gleaned from research on human communication, most notably from studies carried out by Bavelas et al. (1990) on equivocal communication. As noted in Chapter 6, the dimensions are the sender of a message, the message's content, the receiver, and the context in which the communication occurs. The four-dimensional model has heuristic value for sign posting the areas in which masking may have occurred. Does the presented reality make clear the identity of the sender and that of the receiver? Is the presented reality relevant to the question in hand or, more generally, to the communication context in which it is placed? Is the content of the message clear? Or does it make use of contextual information for not communicating?

Lower-Level Masking Devices

Masking devices will be discussed in two parts. The first part will be concerned with lower-level masking devices that operate on single sentences or utterances. Rules, regulations, and news headlines will be used as prototypical cases for developing this part of the discussion. The second part, to be presented later, will address higher-level masking devices in longer discourses.

Before the discussion of masking devices, it should be noted that even though masking may involve an Orwellian type of manipulation, this is not necessarily or always true. Speakers who suffer from the condition of expressive aphasia (due to a lesion in the cortical-association areas in the brain) are known to exhibit speech patterns that are outwardly heavily masked (Luria, 1966). Other speakers who have been diagnosed as showing thought disorders also produce speeches that often baffle psychiatrists as woolly and vague (Bleuler, 1950) or incongruent (Haley, 1959). To attribute the motive of deliberate duplicity to these speakers would be inaccurate. Writers who concoct special phrases that in effect amount to masking may actually be motivated by the desire to do what is considered to be literally appropriate to the immediate discourse context. Such stylistic demands are intensely strong in the context not only of rules and regulations but also news reporting (van Dijk, 1988). Or writers may, as a result of training (in scientific reporting?) or sheer habit, simply slip into a style of writing that involves one or more of the transformations that will be discussed in the sections below. Kress and Hodge (1979) cited examples of transformation from the writings of highly acclaimed scientists. One such example is the opening of Chomsky's (1957) epoch-making *Syntactic Structures:*

> Syntax is the study of the principles and processes by which sentences are constructed in particular languages. Syntactic investigation of a given language has as its goal the construction of a grammar that can be viewed as a device of some sort for producing the sentences of the language under analysis. (p. 11)

Readers who are familiar with critical linguistics (see below) will easily identify several transformations that Chomsky must have applied in constructing the passage above. An analysis carried out by Kress and Hodge (1979) has shown that by means of these transformations, Chomsky was able to "render his meanings and uncertainties opaque to the normal linguist and perhaps to the revolutionary linguist himself," while at the same time "proceed[ing] without resolving his uncertainty, and without acknowledging it" (p. 33). Chomsky may or may not have done this deliberately; the important point for our purpose is that transformational devices for masking are used widely by writers of science and are not restricted to writers of rules, regulations, and news headlines. Even researchers who deliberately set out to eliminate the confounding influence of language on their interviewees, may nevertheless end up using a form of speech that has actually been systematically transformed in favor of their research hypotheses (see Kress & Hodge, 1979, pp. 50-54). When writing this book, we often despaired at how easily we ourselves had fallen victim to a literary style full of masking devices!

The materials for this section are drawn mainly from critical linguistics and from linguistic intuitions research. Critical linguistics shows the importance of not accepting a presented reality at its face value but, rather, reading it critically. The development of critical linguistics has been most closely associated with Fowler and his associates (Fowler, Hodge, Kress, & Trew, 1979; Kress &

Hodge, 1979) and is based in part on the insights of George Orwell and in part on the work of Halliday (1976) as well as aspects of transformational-generative grammar (e.g., Chomsky, 1957, 1965). The work of Fairclough (1989), appearing under the rubic of *critical language study*, represents a major development in critical linguistics. In German-speaking countries, critical linguistics has been closely associated with Habermas (1979; see also Menz, 1989).

One characteristic of the work of critical linguists, at least insofar as unmasking is concerned, is the speculative interpretations the researchers develop regarding message processing and comprehension. This may not appeal to readers who are more comfortable with empirical research and with the positivist mode of theorizing. Certainly, further research is needed to ascertain the extent to which language users (other than proponents of critical linguistics) would process and comprehend the messages in the same way that the proponents do. That said, we also see sufficient merit in many of the speculative interpretations offered by critical linguists to warrant drawing them to the attention of a wider readership.

Native speakers of a language variety, such as standard English, share certain *intuitions* about their language system. They can sense that some sentence forms, but not others, are correct, complete, or meaningful, although they are not necessarily able to say how they have made the distinctions or explain clearly the relevant rules for doing this. Traditionally, linguistic intuitions of acceptability and appropriateness have been a source of evidence for theories of linguistic competence; more recently, they also have been seen as a potentially important source of evidence for theories of language processing and comprehension (Clark & Haviland, 1977).

Bandler and Grinder (1975) studied linguistic intuitions in the context of language therapy and formulated them from the perspectives of transformational-generative grammar and artificial intelligence. Some of the intuitions that they identified in their research are especially noteworthy, because by exercising these intuitions fully, native speakers can recover, or unmask, bits of reality that may have been distorted in a particular representation of reality. The most important of these intuitions are well formedness, constituent structure, and completeness.

Native speakers know intuitively whether or not groups of words constitute well-formed sequences or sentences. In the following string of words, only sentence 35 is well formed.

35. I, the club president, require you, a member of the club, always to carry your membership card and present it on my request.
36. I, the club president, requires you, a member of the club, always to carries your membership card and presents it on my request.
37. I, the club president, require you, a member of the club, always to carry your club spirit and present it on my request.

Native speakers know intuitively which words in a sentence go together to form a higher-level unit or *constituent structure*. In 35, the word pair *club president* goes together in some way that the word pair *president require* would not. Linguists represent the intuitions of language users about constituent structure by attaching the constituent words to the same node in a "tree structure" (see Bandler & Grinder, 1975, p. 28).

A verb connects two or more persons or things together in a relation defined by the verb. For instance, on encountering the verb *require,* native speakers understand intuitively that there is a person doing the requiring and that another person is being required to behave in a certain way. By exercising critically this intuition about *completeness*, native speakers will sense that the target person is missing in "I, the club president, require that membership cards must be carried at all times and presented on my request."

In the following discussion, masking devices are grouped under four headings: truncation, permutation, generalization, and nominalization. These will be discussed first separately and then in conjunction with each other.

Truncation

Truncated sentences are shortened forms of expression. In truncated expressions from which only redundant information has been deleted, the deleted elements can be recovered instantaneously by readers or hearers. This type of innocuous deletion is shown in the second of the following sentences:

I went to Ellison Hall and Jim went to Ellison Hall too.
I went to Ellison Hall and Jim went too.

The element that is commonly deleted from rules and regulations is the agent, which in the context of rules and regulations refers to the commander who has the authority to administer or enforce the rules. Another commonly deleted element is reference to the commanded. Sentence forms such as 31, in which the commander and the commanded are clearly stated, are almost never found in rules and regulations. One may argue that given the discourse context of rules and regulations, every native speaker should know the identities of the commander and the commanded—to spell out the identities in every clause would be redundant and poor literary style. That may well be so; nevertheless, the potential remains that by omitting the commander and the commanded, rule writers present a reality in which the commander-commanded relationship has been transformed into a relationship between an information giver and an information receiver. It will be shown later how linguistic truncation in tandem with other masking devices can realize this potential.

The use of modal operators (*must, should, ought,* etc.) is often a precursor of the deletion of punishment threats. In "Students must not cheat in examinations," for example, the consequence of cheating has been deleted. This can be shown, and the deleted consequence recovered, by asking, "Or what will happen?"

Permutation

Words inside a sentence, as we have already noted, are strung together in a particular sequence that will satisfy the intuition about constituent structures. Otherwise, the sentence will not make sense. Constituent structures, on the other hand, are relatively free units that can be arranged in two or more different permutations and still convey the same logical proposition, as shown in the following pair of news headlines:

38. Employers always quarrel with unions.
39. Unions always quarrel with employers.

Although the logical proposition is identical in each sentence above, an important difference arises from whether it is *employers* or *unions* that occupies the first position of the sentence. The serial positions within a sentence have unequal prominence. In standard English, the first sentence position is privileged with syntactical prominence: The first word or constituent structure in a sentence grabs the reader's attention and directs the reader's flow of thought from that point (Fowler et al., 1979). First sentence position is also associated with another kind of prominence. In standard English, the basic word order of declarative sentences is the subject → verb → object permutation (Greenberg, 1963). The subject has the status of an active agent: Readers look to the subject as the source of action and hold it responsible for the events entailed in verb → object. This type of prominence, which is associated with first sentence position, may be called *attributional prominence*. By positioning a particular element of reality at the beginning of a sentence, which may be referred to as *initialization* (MacWhinney, 1984), a writer can mobilize the force of attributional prominence in encouraging readers to attribute to the initialized element the responsibility for the stated action or effect.

Returning to headlines 38 and 39, one can see that although they have the same logical proposition, they convey a different sense of syntactical and attributional prominence to employers and unions. In 38, employers acquire syntactical prominence and are portrayed as being responsible for quarreling with the union; this is reversed for unions in 39. The two headlines illustrate how this reversal can be achieved simply by selective initialization.

Reversal can also be achieved by means of initialization coupled with passive transformation, in which the active voice of speech is turned into the passive. Passive transformation is applicable to all declarative sentences of the subject → verb → object type, and this is shown in the second of the following pair of news headlines:

40. Police shot blacks dead as meeting turned into riot.
41. Blacks shot dead by police as meeting turned into riot.

Passive transformation reverses the serial positions of police and blacks, making it possible for the writer to assign blacks to the prominent first position and to embed police in the obscure, middle part of a sentence. Furthermore, the effects of reversal and initialization can be bolstered. For example, the word *rioting* can be placed in front of *blacks* to encourage readers to think of rioting and blacks as a constituent structure (see sentence 42, below). This may be followed by deletion to conceal the instigator (police) completely, as shown in 43:

42. Rioting blacks shot dead by police.
43. Rioting blacks shot dead.

Compared with 43, 40 is a much fuller representation of reality. When reading sentences such as 43, readers "should be sensitive to possible ideologically motivated obfuscation of agency, causality and responsibility" (Fairclough, 1989, p. 124). When the relevant background information about the shooting incident is available, a reader who is sympathetic toward the blacks can reconstruct 43 into 40 by restoring the agent, breaking up the constituent structure *rioting blacks,* and reversing the passive transformation.

Note that in sentence 41, passive transformation makes it possible for transferring blacks to first position. It is possible to achieve first position transference while retaining the active voice of speech (see sentences 38 and 39). The advantage of retaining the active voice, from the point of view of masking, can be shown by the second of the following pair of news headlines:

44. Labor Department barred immigrant workers from subsidized jobs.
45. Immigrants' job applications failed to satisfy criteria.

Insofar as the Labor Department is concerned, the advantage of using the active rather than the passive voice of speech is to assign maximal attributional prominence associated with the active voice to the immigrants. If the ideas about attributional prominence presented above were to be tested in comprehension-oriented empirical research, one working hypothesis would be that a sentence like 45 would have the effect of encouraging readers to think of the immigrants as responsible for failing to obtain jobs more so than would a sentence that employs passivization (e.g., "Immigrants' job applications were turned down for not satisfying job criteria.").

Generalization

Generalizations are nonfocused formulations of reality brought about when writers (and speakers) use nonspecific words without supplying definite referential indices. A male patient who presents himself in a therapy session by saying, "I'm scared of people," probably has in mind some specific persons who scare him but is afraid of naming them or too confused to be able to do so. If that is all this patient has to say, he would be generalizing insofar as the sentence meaning is concerned, even though deep in his mind there is only one particular person who scares him.

In the case of rules and regulations, a generalization that occurs commonly is the use of a broad person category in place of the singular *you*. Instead of "You, a passenger on this plane, are forbidden to enter the cockpit," the rule usually takes the form of "Passengers are forbidden to enter the cockpit." Likewise, *I* may be replaced by *we*, which has an exclusive and an inclusive meaning. The exclusive *we* comprises the speaker and other(s) but excludes the addressee; including the addressee turns it into an inclusive *we*.

The inclusive *we*, like the exclusive *we*, sets up an implicit social categorization of "we" versus "not we." What is unique to the inclusive *we* is that it imposes an in-group membership on the addressee. In-group membership conveys a common social identity (Tajfel & Turner, 1979), a common fate (Sherif, 1966), or a unit relation (Lerner, 1975), all of which can induce in the addressee a sense of affiliation and an obligation of cooperation. A speaker who is in a position to invoke the inclusive *we* is able to use the cognitions and sentiments associated with identification, affiliation, and cooperation in enhancing an influence attempt. Thus a father can exhort his infant daughter to finish her meal by saying, "We're going to eat it all up!" even though she, but not he, will be doing the eating. On the other hand, the potential of the inclusive *we* for masking will diminish when there is already polarization or tension between the speaker and the addressees. The latter will perceive the speaker's use of the inclusive *we* as synthetic and driven by ulterior motive. Imagine how employees at a staff dismissal meeting will react to the employer's use of *we* in, "We will all have to make sacrifices from now on."

Generalizations also occur when verbs are incompletely specified. Bandler and Grinder (1975, p. 90) supply the following type of sentences, which are here arranged in ascending order of generalization. The sentences are claims made by John after he has been kicked in the stomach by his sister.

46. My sister kicked me in the stomach.
47. My sister kicked me.
48. My sister hurt me.

The verb *kicked* conveys the specific use of a foot for kicking. In 46, then, John specifies that he has been kicked in the stomach. If his sister can show that she has not kicked him in the stomach, then she would be able to falsify the claim made in 46. On the other hand, the claim made in 47 would still stand because it does not specify that John has been kicked in the stomach. If John's sister can show that she has punched but not kicked him, then 47 will be falsified, but not 48. The verb *hurt* in 48 is more unfocused and more difficult to contradict than *kicked*. For the same reason, once John has generalized his sister's action from 46 to 48, he will find it that much harder to eliminate his negative stereotype of his sister even if he wants to.

It is interesting to note that the idea of action generalization bears a strong resemblance to Vallacher and Wegner's (1985) action identification theory, already referred to above, as well as Semin and Fiedler's (1988, 1991) linguistic category model. The latter distinguishes four linguistic categories, the first two of which are identical to Bandler and Grinder's (1975): descriptive action verbs (e.g., kick), interpretative action verbs (e.g., hurt), state verbs (e.g., hate), and adjectives (e.g., aggressive). The categories vary in increasing order of abstractness or generalization, such that descriptive action verbs are the most concrete and adjectives the most abstract. Abstract words used for describing an agent (e.g., John in the example above) convey more information about the person and less information about the situation. Abstract words also convey descriptions of the person that are more enduring, more disputable, and consistent with Bandler and Grinder's (1975) thesis, more difficult to falsify.

Nominalization

The process of an action is most fully described by a verb clause comprising a subject, a verb, and an object. The process can be transformed by nominalization into an event that is encoded by a noun or noun phrase. Compare the process-oriented representation in 49 with the nominalized representations in 50 and 51.

49. The club president will expel any member from the club who has been absent from meetings more than three times.
50. Being absent from meetings more than three times means automatic expulsion of the absent member by the club president.
51. Being absent from meetings more than three times means automatic expulsion.

The nominalization of *will expel* into *automatic expulsion* illustrates two important features that are either intrinsic to or otherwise closely associated with nominalization. Readers acquire a feeling of activity from the modality and verb tense in 49. With the replacement of modality and tense by the noun phrase automatic expulsion, the feeling of activity is reduced to that of an event (expulsion) that is timeless and has a fixed uncontrollable outcome.

As a result of nominalization, participants in the sentence are usually deleted. Even when participants are retained in a nominalized sentence, they will normally have been assigned a peripheral syntactic status and for this reason can be deleted much more easily in nominalized than in process sentences, where participants occupy a more central syntactic status.

The combined effect of the replacement of modality and tense by a noun or noun phrase and the deletion of participant is the representation of an unpleasant *activity* carried out by one person to another as an unpleasant *event* that has no named participants. As we have anticipated in Chapter 5, it should be clear by now that the latter representation is not merely a distancing strategy of mitigation (Fraser, 1980) or merely a negative politeness strategy (Brown & Levinson, 1987)—it is also a masking device par excellence.

Joint Use of Masking Devices

The masking devices that have been discussed so far can be used jointly in the representation of reality. Mention has already been made of the joint use of reversal and agent deletion. The use of two or more devices in combination produces a cumulative effect that increases the degree of masking.

Critical linguists (Fairclough, 1989; Fowler et al., 1979; Kress & Hodge, 1979), independently of language therapists and equivocal communication researchers, have called attention to multiple masking. The starting point of reading a text critically in this fashion is the awareness that more than one masking device may have been used either intentionally or unintentionally by writers. Consider the devices responsible for transforming sentence 35 to 53. The latter sentence is the prototypical form in which rules and regulations are written. It is taken from Fowler et al. (1979) together with 35. For purposes of illustration, sentence 52 has been added as an intermediary.

35. I, the club president, require you, a member of the club, always to carry your membership card and present it on my request.
52. Members must always carry membership cards and present them on request.
53. Membership cards must always be carried and presented on request.

In sentence 35, the two participants are related as commander and commanded; the commander is assigned the informationally privileged first position in the sentence, and the active voice of speech is used to direct the flow of activity from the commander to the commanded. The masking devices of truncation, generalization, and permutation have been used jointly to transform 35 into 52. Specifically, the commander has been deleted. The commanded, who was initially stated in second-person singular, has been generalized to third-person plural and transferred from middle to first position. Despite the transformations, in 52, the unpleasant burden of the command is still explicitly placed on the commanded. Masking the burden requires further transformations, and these can be illustrated by comparing 35 with 53. In 53, the commanded (members) are deleted, passive objects (membership cards) are moved from middle to first position, and the active voice of speech is replaced by the passive voice.

The cumulative effect of the transformations is that the direct commander-commanded relationship has been changed into a relationship wherein the commander plays the role of an information giver and the commanded is assigned the role of an information receiver. The two parties are now outside the immediate communication context and exist only invisibly by implication in the realm of the general discourse context of rules and regulations.

Note that in the example above, nominalization has not been involved. To illustrate how nominalization may be used in conjunction with other masking devices, consider the following biblical verse:

54. The wages of sin is death.

Sin implies a religious context and is the nominalized expression of a person sinning against a deity, a god. Both the person and the god have been deleted from sentence 54. *Death* and *wages* are two other nominalized expressions, and these are arranged in a particular permutation with *the wages* occupying a position of syntactical and attributional prominence. By reversing the nominalizations, restoring the participants, and repermutating the constituent structures, one can reconstruct the reality in other ways, such as:

55. If you sin against God, God will pay you back by taking away your life.

The discussion thus far has been concerned with four masking devices that writers often use when constructing particular sentences for the representation of reality. The devices are elementary in the sense that they can be applied to single sentences. When a string of individually masked sentences is turned into an extended discourse, the discourse itself will certainly be masked as well. In this sense, too, the devices are elementary. It is certainly possible to look for incidences of deletion, nominalization, etc. in a discourse. However, as noted by Kress (1987) and others (e.g., Coupland, 1988; Hurtig, 1977), it would be simplistic to view a discourse as the mere

sum of sentences. By examining masking in discourses by applying only the devices in question, one may miss the forest for the
trees. So in the following section we will examine masking in
discourses beyond the single utterance level.

Higher-Level Masking Devices

The opportunity for masking increases from single sentences to
multi-item discourses. Multi-item discourses make available new
opportunities for masking that are otherwise unavailable in single
sentences or utterances—herein lies one source of higher-level
masking devices. Another source of higher-level masking devices,
which is socially more dynamic, arises from the use of a group-
specific language. Spies, for example, can communicate between
themselves in a way that an overhearer will not be able to decipher
easily. So can lovers. More generally, in-group members who have
access to an exclusive way of communication can mask their communication against its leakage to outsiders. This strategic use of a
common language, or more generally, a *common ground*, should be
distinguished from the reality-maintenance function of a common
language referred to above.

The two sources of higher-level masking devices—multi-item
context and in-group-specific language—will be examined with
the aid of the notions of utterance context and common ground.
As both notions are interrelated parts of what is usually known as
contextual information, it is with the latter that we will begin the
discussion.

Using Downes's (1984) classification scheme, one can think of
contextual information as comprising background knowledge,
mutual knowledge, and context of utterance. Background knowledge is the most general sort of contextual information and consists of knowledge of the language, rules for conversational activity,
rules for interpreting social actions, and participants' biographies
and social characteristics. That part of the background knowledge
that is shared, and known to be shared, between the participants
is their mutual knowledge. Background knowledge that is not
mutual plays a relatively minor role in verbal interaction.

The context of utterance consists of, first, the utterance immediately before a given utterance. This is known as the immediate local utterance context. (Bavelas et al.'s, 1990, context, referred to in Chapter 6, is one type of immediate local utterance context in which the immediately prior utterance is a question.) As a passage or a conversation continues, the pool of expired utterances increases, thus building up a global context for subsequent utterances. This global utterance context exists in multi-item discourses but not in single utterances. Another element of the utterance context is the immediate physical setting in which the passage or conversation occurs. Previous readings or conversations between the same participants and the settings in which these occurred form the third element of the utterance context. The utterance context is important both as a direct source of contextual information and also in providing one of the grounds for mutual knowledge. In the following, higher-level masking devices will be discussed in light of the utterance context and then in light of an enlarged conception of mutual knowledge.

Utterance Context

A multi-item discourse has a global utterance context that provides new opportunities for masking that are otherwise unavailable in a single utterance. The global utterance context can be exploited in conversations as well as writings for identity switching, for loosening the coherence (reference) of a discourse, and for embedding a propaganda message. These devices will be discussed in turn.

A speaker can switch from one identity to another more easily in a stretch of utterances than in a single utterance, and more easily in an extended conversation than in one that involves only one speaking turn. A long stretch of utterances, especially when this comprises multiple speaking turns, is likely to introduce new information, new perspectives, new topics, and so forth that will cushion the switching of identities. A speaker may hence identify himself or herself as *I* in one location and as *we* in another. *I* can then be reserved for referring to the agent who can perform pleasant things (e.g., "I'll see what I can do for you."), whereas *we* can be invoked to stand in for unpleasant things (e.g., "We [meaning the speaker plus the speaker's company] can't help you."). Kress and Fowler (1979) reported an interview in which the interviewer, who had the advantage of being free to switch between *I* and *we* during the interview, succeeded in mystifying her role in the mind of the interviewee.

> Mary [interviewee] cannot be sure who addresses her and whom she is addressing. She may feel hostile to Liz [interviewer] only to discover that it is the company which is to blame, or feel that she is with an efficient agency only to find that she owes any help she may be getting to the action of an individual. In this situation the interviewer enjoys all the privileges of power without any of the responsibilities. (Kress & Fowler, 1979, pp. 70-71)

A writer can make clear to readers what he or she is referring to by repeating the word or words, for example, "Nick was so angry with Chris that Nick started to abuse Chris." Repetition, although accurate for referring, is not good literary style, so in its place, writers may use a pronoun. For example, "Nick was so angry with Chris that he started to abuse him." The pronouns *he* and *him* are endophoric referential indices whose identities (Nick and Chris, respectively) can be recovered from the explicit immediate local utterance context. Writers may also use a close semantic associate for referring: "Nick stormed into Chris's house and found a load of rubbish behind the door." Here *door* refers to a door in Chris's house.

By means of these and other referential indices (see Clark, 1974; Halliday & Hasan, 1976; MacWhinney, 1984; Rochester & Martin, 1977), writers and speakers can make clear what they are referring to without repeating the same word or words. The clarity of referential indices, however, depends greatly on the close proximity of the indices to their referents. In the examples above, the referents are located in the immediate local utterance context, and this close proximity contributes to the clarity of the indices. Clarity would be lessened when there are intervening utterances separating the referents from the indices, that is, when the global utterance context becomes wider. In this way, a wide global utterance context creates the potential for masking. To see how the potential can be realized, consider the following items, which have been arranged in increasing order of global utterance context width.

56. Maori youths and white youths looted city shops.
57. Maori youths looted city shops. The incident was particularly rampant in the central part of the city. White youths were also involved in the incident.
58. Maori youths looted city shops. The incident was particularly rampant in the central part of the city, where fighting broke out and several people were injured. As the night grew darker during the power failure, more casualties were reported. White youths were also involved in the incident.

In passage 57, the word *incident* occurs for the first time in the second sentence. Given the immediate local utterance context of *looted city shops* in the preceding sentence, *incident* functions in the second sentence clearly as a nominalized, close semantic associate of *looted city shops;* it is then immediately transferred to the third sentence. So even though the white youths in 57 are not as directly linked with looting behavior as they are in 56, the link in 57 is preserved by the relatively simple global utterance context. For the same reason, in 58 the first *incident* refers clearly to looting. The second *incident* in 58, however, now has *casualties* as the immediate local utterance context and occurs in a heterogeneous global utterance context, consisting of not only *looted city shops* but also *fighting, injured, power failure,* and *casualties.* Consequently, it would seem that the role of white youths in looting is no longer as definite as in 57.

Apart from providing opportunities for identity switching and loose referring, a wide global utterance context may also usher a propaganda message that if left to itself without being embedded in the context would appear obtrusive and unacceptable. Holly (1989) likened the global utterance context to the official passengers of a vehicle and the propaganda message, to a stowaway. To illustrate, he cited President Ronald Reagan's "address to the youth" of Germany given at the Hambach Castle in 1985. The text was a solemn plea for traditional Western values, especially for freedom. After speaking of Germany's postwar success, Reagan continued,

> We remembered Ludwig Erhard's secret; how he blazed Germany's path with freedom by creating opportunity and lowering tax rates, to reward every man and woman who dared to dream and to create

the future—your farmers, labor leaders, carpenters, and engineers—
every German hero who helped to put the pieces of a broken society
together. (p. 124).

The propaganda message, according to the author, is "Reaganom-
ics" (lowering taxes for the rich, who were then supposed to create
opportunities for the middle-class [who had their taxes raised]
and the poor), which is embedded in a passage praising the
glorious 1950s and its personification, Erhard. In this way, Reagan
was trying to convey a positive self-evaluation through praising
the success of somebody else whom the audience of young Ger-
mans could identify with more easily.

In-Group-Specific Common Ground

Mutual knowledge, because of its shared nature and common
accessibility to the participants, facilitates coordination between
participants in their verbal interaction. The coordinating role of
mutual knowledge extends beyond the coordination of verbal
interaction between conversationalists or between writers and
readers—mutual knowledge is generally relevant to the coordination of social interactions that involve even a minimal degree of
language use (see Chapter 4). Without mutual knowledge, coordination is severed and social interaction cannot proceed, however willing the participants may be and however hard they may
have tried. As already noted, the basis of the coordinating role of
mutual knowledge is the mutuality of the information and not the
information per se. By the same token, information other than
knowledge, provided that it is mutual, can also play a coordinating role. Clark (1985) and Clark and Marshall (1981) developed
this point by expanding the concept of mutual knowledge to that
of common ground, which includes mutual beliefs and mutual
suppositions in addition to mutual knowledge (cf. Lewis, 1969;
and "presuppositions" in Levinson, 1983).

Common ground is an important source of contextual information that speakers use to coordinate and to maximize the efficiency
of their talk exchange. A conversation starts on the lowest common denominator of the common ground and gradually builds up
a global utterance context, which in turn enlarges the common

ground (Isaacs & Clark, 1987; see also Fussell & Krauss, 1989). The question arises as to how conversationalists may enlarge the common ground for efficient in-group communication while preventing overhearers from deciphering the content of the communication. The simplest solution is to conduct the conversation in private. In many real-life situations, however, it is not feasible or sufficient to guard secrecy by privacy alone (see Daniel & Herbig, 1982; Tefft, 1980). To get around this problem, conversationalists have to find a piece of common ground specific to themselves, referred to by Clark and Schaefer (1987) as a "private key." Some of the more common varieties of private keys are in-group jargon, cryptograms, and a dialect that is intelligible only to in-group members. Lutz (1989) collected numerous examples of jargon and related special terms (which he called "doublespeak") from publications and speeches made by military, political, business, and advertising personnel. Another common variety of private keys is a spelling ploy that literate adults use when talking about a forbidden topic in front of a preliterate child, as in: "Can you pick up some C-I-G-A-R-E-T-T-E-S on your way?"

When a private key is not readily available, it may be constructed from joint shared experiences that exclude the overhearer. Clark and Schaefer (1987) set up an experiment for observing the collaborative construction of private keys by asking pairs of friends in the experiment to refer to familiar landmarks while concealing the references from an overhearer. In a typical collaboration, the speaker would first throw out a feeler (*preface*) to bring a possible area of common ground into joint focus. The preface may or may not work, though. The following is an example of a preface that is declined by the partner:

Partner:	Okay, Ben, do you remember the place that—
Ben:	Yes?
Partner:	Um, John came and sang. John and Dick and Bill sang "Happy Birthday" to me? A couple of days ago?
Ben:	No.

If the preface is not declined by the partner, the speaker would then use a *try marker* (the pronunciation of a noun phrase with a rising intonation) to check on the partner's understanding of a key.

The speaker would use the preface and the try marker in a controlled manner to reveal the key gradually and to allow the partner to close off the revelation at the earliest possible time so that no more information will be leaked to the overhearer than is necessary. A commonly observed technique for closing off a revelation is the use of a *truncator* to interrupt and cut the speaker off, as shown by the partner in the following example (Clark & Schaefer, 1987, p. 219):

Speaker: My class at the beginning of this quarter
            [was there
 Partner: [Yeah, yeah, yeah, yeah, yeah, yeah.

* * *

In this chapter various masking devices as evidenced in rules, regulations, news headlines, and conversations have been discussed. The devices that are applicable to single utterances and sentences rely heavily on wording and on word order, which in turn can be summarized under the headings of truncation, permutation, generalization, and nominalization. The use of one or more of these devices results in a presented reality that is less complete than the actual reality. In extreme but not uncommon cases, the resulting presented reality is radically different from the actual reality. By disguising the reality of control that is inherent in rules and regulations, masking reduces their unpleasantness while preserving their requirements to be explicit and definite. In this way, rules and regulations are depoliticized.

Opportunities for masking are not confined to wording and word order alone. New opportunities arise when single utterances are multiplied to form a global utterance context that can be exploited for identity switching, for loose referring, and for embedding a propaganda message. Furthermore, two or more individuals may coordinate their conversational activities on the basis of an exclusive common ground to convey meaning among themselves while simultaneously presenting a different reality to overhearers. (This is the only situation in which the masking potential of prosodic devices has been discussed in the present chapter, understandably because of our reliance on rules, regulations, and news headlines as prototypical cases for developing the theme of masking.) These higher-level masking devices become available when the contextual information that is accessible to the speakers contains the requisite global utterance context and exclusive common ground. Even so, they still depend on wording and word order, albeit to a lesser extent than the lower-level masking devices do.

Unlike their lower-level counterparts, higher-level devices are not primarily targeted at rules, regulations, or news headlines. Rather communicators make use of higher-level masking devices for depoliticizing their influence attempts by grounding their attempts in a wider network of contextual information. By comparison, the network of contextual information that is necessary for lower-level masking devices is smaller: Lower-level devices do not require a global utterance context, an exclusive common ground, or an immediately local utterance context. They do require, in the same way that any other communication would also require, the remainder of the contextual information. For example, the physical setting in which a masked sentence occurs, be this a club room, a library reading room, or the front page of a newspaper, provides a powerful cue that the sentence should be read as a club rule, a library regulation, a news headline, and so forth. Apart from physical-setting cues and associated mental framing, time is also a factor that encourages uncritical reading: "For the writer of a *Guardian* editorial the composition of a leading article is a matter of importance. For the commuter it is something to be scanned quickly. Writers tend to create such shadowy worlds of abstract entities, and readers to live in them" (Kress & Hodge, 1979, p. 24). Language users who interpret masked messages uncritically as well as construct masked messages routinely will, as a result of the repeated experience, accept readily a presented reality in which the participants, causality, and accountability are obscured.

CHAPTER EIGHT

Further Issues, Conclusions, and Prospects

Up until now, we have been discussing various ways in which language users can, by exploiting linguistic resources, reveal their power, impress and influence others, and depoliticize their influence attempts. In doing so, we have focused on the microsituation of the interaction and treated language as if it were a freely available slave that serves equally whoever is most skillful in using it. This liberal, individualist analysis ignores the interpenetrations between language and social structure. To redress the balance, we will now outline sociostructural variables that enable one language (or language variety) to dominate over another and discuss how the routine use of the dominant language by members of the dominated group will in turn have important sociostructural and psychological implications.

Sociostructural Bases of Language Dominance

Some languages are "higher," or more dominant, than others because of their stronger sociostructural base rather than any superior intrinsic linguistic qualities they may have. It would be useful to preface the discussion of these sociostructural bases with a brief note on the functional equality of languages. From the beginnings of modern linguistics in the United States, the functional equality of languages has been a tenet of faith. It provided progressive linguists with a new sense of identity that distinguished them from protagonists of the hierarchical view that some languages were more functional than others in evolutionary terms. The controversy lingers on (e.g., Honey, 1983), but under the newfound identity of functional equality, linguists did rally to refute with linguistic evidence the racist ideology of the primitive mind (Sapir, 1929/1963) and language deficit (Labov, 1966). The later part of the 1950s and the early 1960s saw what appeared at first to be an even more liberal idea: All human beings have the same basic intrinsic linguistic competence to generate grammatically acceptable utterances, which implies that all languages should be essentially similar at some deep level (Chomsky, 1965). This idea enhanced greatly the status of linguistics as a science. However, the dominant concern with universal linguistic competence has sidelined the fact of sociostructural inequality both within and between countries and also the interpenetration between social inequality and language:

> It is not that there are writers who deny that multilingualism exists, that standard languages exist, that language minorities exist, that languages sometimes are dominated, sometimes die. It is just that the part of the mind or the faculty which knows these things is isolated from the part that knows what is called "theoretical linguistics." . . . A once progressive critique has come to function as the defense of an academic elite against intellectual change. Radicals champion a liberal idea to conservative effect. (Hymes, 1985, pp. v-vi)

Ethnolinguistic Vitality

A useful starting point for discussing the sociostructural bases of language dominance is the concept of ethnolinguistic vitality. This concept was first proposed in 1977 by Giles, Bourhis, and Taylor, and since then has been widely applied to a range of issues (see Harwood, Giles, & Bourhis, in press). The emergence and subsequent application of the concept of ethnolinguistic vitality reflect the belief of a number of social psychologists that the study of language change, language attitude, ethnolinguistic conflict, and so on can no longer be studied only in terms of the cognitive and affective processes of individuals, but must be situated in a socio-structural context (Johnson, Giles, & Bourhis, 1983; see also Ng, 1980).

According to Giles, Bourhis and their associates, there are three sociostructural variables affecting the strength of an ethnolinguistic community to behave as a distinctive and collective entity vis-à-vis other communities: demography, institutional support, and status. Demographic variables refer to, on the one hand, a community's absolute numeric size and factors affecting their future size (birth rate, immigration, etc.) and, on the other hand, the numeric concentration of group members in various regions. These variables "may constitute the most fundamental asset of ethnolinguistic groups since 'strength in numbers' can sometimes be used as a legitimizing tool to 'empower' groups with the 'institutional control' they need to shape their own collective destiny" (Harwood, et al., in press). Institutional support variables refer to an ethnolinguistic community's representation in the wider society's social institutions, particularly in government, industry, religion, education, and mass media. Representation may be informally undertaken by various pressure groups or formally instituted as incumbents of key positions in the various institutions. Institutional control, derived from informal and formal representation under effective leadership, "is the dimension of vitality *par excellence* available for ethnolinguistic groups to maintain and assert their ascendancy *vis-à-vis* competing ethnolinguistic outgroups" (Harwood, et al., in press). Finally, status variables refer to a community's economic, social, and sociohistorical status as well as the local and international prestige of its language and culture.

Applying the vitality variables to the contemporary language situation in the Canadian province of Quebec, Bourhis (1984; Bourhis & Lepicq, in press) traced the recent ascendancy of French over English to Francophones' demographic strength in the province. Francophones mobilized their demographic strength to elect the Parti-Quebecois in 1976, which in turn raised the status of French as the only official language of Quebec by passing Bill 101. On the basis of its demographic vitality and elevated status, French has increasingly displaced English from institutional control in Quebec. By means of the ethnolinguistic vitality framework, Bourhis analyzed the social identity and speech accommodation processes of ethnic conflict, interethnic communication, and language planning (see Bourhis & Giles, 1977; Giles et al., 1987).

According to the ethnolinguistic vitality taxonomy, then, the power behind language is rooted in demographic, institutional, and status variables. Depending on how broadly the variables are defined, they can accommodate many others not yet discussed by Giles and Bourhis, and this will certainly apply to most of the following discussion in which we extend the taxonomy by highlighting the roles of military invasion, communication technology, and professional specialization.

Military Invasion, Communication Technology, and Professional Specialization

There is a strong correlation historically between a country's military invasion or colonial settlement, on the one hand, and the spread of its language and literature, on the other. Explorers, traders, and religious missionaries are forerunners in linking territorial and cultural expansions that later become more organized, more comprehensive, and more competitive against rival countries and religious faiths.

Following a military conquest or colonial settlement, the foreign occupying power uses its own language to displace the indigenous language from statute books and key institutions such as government administration, education, religion, and the mass media. As a result of the linguistic colonization of institutions by the foreign language, the native language loses its control over institutions and, because it usually follows on from this, also its social status. Over generations, the native language declines demographically as fewer and fewer people are competent in using it. If there are no other users of the language outside the country in question, the language will die. In modern times, English has been a prime example of a killer language, which has endangered or extinguished scores of indigenous languages in former British colonies (Trudgill, 1991). It almost killed the Maori language of New Zealand. With few exceptions (e.g., Malay), the displacement of indigenous languages in the colonies is irreversible even if the indigenous population later regains its sovereignty (see also Breivik & Jahr, 1989; Wolfson & Manes, 1985).

When describing the demographic decline of a language that is brought into contact with a dominant colonial language, we used the word *kill* metaphorically. The metaphor is useful for highlighting the brutal force of military impact and the arrogance of colonial-language policy; yet it ignores the fact that the indigenous population or its leaders may also be responsible for the decline of their own language. In the case of Hawaii, for instance, King Kamehameha III and King Kamehameha IV asked their subjects to become educated in English because of the kings' conviction that unless the Hawaiians did so, there would be no hope of intellectual progress or competing successfully with the foreigners (see Day, 1985). Motivated by a similar strategic consideration, Maori leaders in New Zealand were instrumental in encouraging the Maori population to learn English as their first language (see Bell, 1991). To the extent that indigenous leaders play an active part in the process of language change that contributes to the demographic decline of their own language, the metaphor of kill should be supplemented by the metaphor of suicide (Denison, 1977; see also Dorian, 1989).

Linguistic colonization and ethnolinguistic vitality are causally interrelated. The success or failure of the former depends on, and will in turn affect, the demographic, institutional, and status vitality of the language in question. The Spanish empire has its Spanish-speaking world, and the British empire has its English-speaking world. These X-speaking worlds may survive long after the decline of the empire, depending on how successful X has been in displacing the native languages and becoming the common language in the conquered or colonized parts of the empire. It is this process of language change, in interaction with ethnolinguistic vitality, that preserves the power behind X after the empire has collapsed. More will be said about language change later.

The above discussion shows that military might is also a major component of ethnolinguistic vitality, especially in situations of language contact brought about by colonial or imperial expansion (see also Chomsky, 1987). In addition, the role of communication technology should also be recognized. The printing press, radio and satellite communication, and a worldwide broadcasting network have played a crucial role in the spread of English (Lerner, 1969). Computer technology, like the typewriter, has until recently, been unresponsive to the needs of nonalphabetic languages such as Chinese. For a long time, it was taken for granted that Chinese characters in their present ideographic form could not be typed onto the computer screen via the keyboard. As computers were used more and more widely for communication and information processing, a language like Chinese that did not fit the new technology would inevitably lose part of its vitality. For this reason (and also others), Chinese was at one time dropped as one of the original official languages of the United Nations.

The third basis of language dominance that we will highlight is professional specialization. All professions have developed their own special languages to serve specific professional functions. As the professions become more specialized, their languages are differentiated from everyday language to the extent that laypersons become totally or partly dependent on professionals for interpretation. Legal English is a prime example of a professional language over which lawyers wield considerable power of interpretation. It also illustrates, as will be shown below, how the power of a professional language may be reinforced by wider discoursal practices that are associated with the use of that language.

Insurance policies, commercial contracts, statutes, and other legally binding documents are written in ways that are largely incomprehensible to laypeople. Written legal English has its distinctive lexical and syntactic features (see Danet, 1980; Mellinkoff, 1963). There are also discourse-level features such as uninformative organization (headings and table of contents) and vagueness in communicating what actions citizens or readers are to take (Danet, 1990). Together, these linguistic and discourse-level features render written legal English opaque to the layperson and at the same time preserve its authority.

Because lawyers, and lawyers alone, are trained in authoring and interpreting legal English, they have a monopolistic power over the correct use of a specialized register that defines the substance of a legal document and its legal boundary. In recent years, some of the power has been eroded by the plain English movement and the availability of standard, do-it-yourself contractual forms prepared by various consumer-support groups (Redish,

1985). It is more possible now than before for citizens to understand what is said to them or about them in legal settings without relying totally on lawyers. However, as written legal English cannot be simplified completely into plain English without distorting the substance of legal documents (Bhatia, 1983), for linguistic reasons alone it is unlikely that written legal English will recede to the point at which it will be taken out of the control of the legal profession.

Spoken legal English presents a similar but more complicated picture (Atkinson & Drew, 1979; O'Barr, 1982). When instructing the jury, passing a judgment, or speaking to the record, a judge will use formal legal English that closely parallels written legal English as will lawyers when addressing the court, making motions and requests, and so on. Less formal varieties are used by lawyers and witnesses in court trials. Of these, the most typical one is standard English, which is similar to that taught in classroom situations and is the discoursal context in which most of the studies on powerful and powerless courtroom speech have been set (see Chapter 2). Two other less formal varieties are colloquial English and subcultural dialects such as Black English.

In response to situational demands, or in pursuance of particular goals, lawyers may shift from one language variety to another. For instance, they may address jurors in colloquial English to encourage comradeship but shift to formal English when questioning hostile witnesses in an attempt to discredit or ridicule witnesses. Attorneys habitually use a variety of speech features of formal legal English that restrict witnesses' answers in a predetermined direction and pose difficulty of understanding for witnesses unfamiliar with this linguistic mode (Brennan & Brennan, 1988). Within a particular variety, they may maximize their influence by exercising conversational control (see Chapter 4) as well as making use of linguistic devices such as powerful speech features (Chapters 2 and 3), mitigation (Chapter 5), misleading words (Chapter 6), and various masking devices (Chapter 7). This is not to say that attorneys are necessarily more linguistically competent than witnesses. Rather the power behind spoken legal English lies in certain discoursal procedures that have been developed in the past to govern the conduct of courtroom trials. The procedures cast the trial as an examination *of* witnesses *by* attorneys and not as, for example, a direct debate between the prosecuting and defending counsels or an examination of counsels by jurors. Accordingly, attorneys have the right to call or not call witnesses, interrupt the examination, dictate the topic, and so forth. In short, the procedures empower attorneys to control the courtroom discourse vis-à-vis witnesses.

Routinization of Language Dominance

The process whereby a particular language or variety of language becomes dominant is politically complex and often marked by resistance on the part of the dominated party. It involves, among other things, language change that results in the adoption of the dominant language for regular usage. Becoming dominant also involves becoming natural, that is, moving from a marked to an unmarked status. When this occurs, we can say that language dominance is routinized in everyday life.

From Language Change to Routinization

Language change is most clearly seen in situations of language contact arising from military expansion or colonial settlement. As noted above, language change may be described as beginning with the linguistic colonization of institutions, followed by, under relatively favorable conditions, a stage of additive bilingualism in which the indigenous population successfully acquires the foreign language while maintaining competence in its own language. Where conditions are unfavorable, however, the indigenous population may lose competence in its language without becoming competent in the foreign language. For example, "After three decades of control by various Secretaries of Education from the US" since the United States invaded Spanish-speaking Puerto Rico, "80 percent of the (Puerto Rican) students failed both Spanish and English and had dropped out of school" (Zentella, 1985, p. 43).

In between the above two extremes of language change is the case of subtractive bilingualism. Here competence in the foreign language is acquired, but only at the expense of the native language.

Over time this leads to monolingualism in the foreign language. How worthwhile is subtractive bilingualism? Among those who have mastered the foreign language, some may attain academic, financial, and even political success as individuals, yet the majority would remain at the bottom of a society that no longer speaks the indigenous language (e.g., among Hawaiians). There are also psychological costs associated with becoming monolingual in the dominator's language. To the extent that language is connected to one's self-identity (Edwards, 1979; Halliday, McIntosh, & Strevens, 1968), the dominated party may lose or fail to gain an authentic sense of self through use of the dominator's language. In the extreme case, one may see identification with the oppressor. In such a situation the dominated party lives in a world out of joint, a world that conduces to a schizoid stance toward self in the context of events. This position assumes that language has a causal impact on self or that in a sense language constitutes the self—when one discloses information about self to others, one is also informing oneself about one's own personal values, preferences, and the like (Holtgraves, 1990).

A potentially useful metaphor or analogue might be drawn from research on counterattitudinal advocacy (Nuttin, 1974). Generally, evidence from experiments suggests that speakers who encode public messages that are attitudinally discrepant from their own position may experience an attitudinal shift toward the initially discrepant attitude, especially if their discrepant messages are not coerced. There is some evidence that the linguistic form of messages can affect the outcome of counterattitudinal encoding. Specifically, counterattitudinal encoders who use highly intense language may exhibit larger attitude shifts than their counterparts who use language low in intensity (Burgoon & Miller, 1971). Other studies indicate that communicators who talk to hearers about other people who are liked by the hearers will focus on positive attributes of those others and subsequently will recall more positive than negative characteristics (even though both negative and positive attributes are objectively available) (Higgins, 1981). Thus powerless persons who find themselves using the foreign language may come to have positive feelings about the language, even in situations in which their initial feelings were negative. This might be the case especially when the powerless communicate primarily with those in power (who presumably "like" the

language) and when they perceive themselves as not being coerced into using the language. Gradually, the foreign language
may come to seem natural and a part of the self. As the foreign
language moves from a marked to an unmarked status, the powerless speaker who uses it may become less and less aware of this use.
When this occurs, language dominance is routinized through usage.

Concurrent with linguistic routinization, there is also a subtle
process initiated by the dominant party to protect the now common language from being fully mastered by imitators or passers.
This may be carried out first by setting new standards of profi-
ciency, or changing aspects of the language, that would prevent
imitators from speaking just like the true speakers of the standard
language—or at least to slow the imitators down. "In such circumstances, subordinate groups may find the language or prestige dialect of the dominant group an ever-shifting target to pursue" (Giles
& Johnson, 1981, p. 221). Second, original speakers of the standard
language may use a high status form of the language only among
themselves and thereby limit the possibility of outsiders acquiring
the prestigious form (Ullrich, 1971). These subtle language behaviors
function to preserve an ethnolinguistic group's linguistic supremacy
as well as, from a social identity viewpoint (Bourhis, Giles, Leyens,
& Tajfel, 1979), its ethnolinguistic distinctiveness.

Linguistic Routinization of Male Dominance

The discussion above relates to language dominance that arises
from outside of a country. We now turn to the linguistic routinization of the dominance of males over females within a country.
In the course of its development, standard English has acquired
grammatical prescriptions that treat the female gender unfavor-
ably. These grammatical prescriptions, as distinct from syntax, are
not inherent in the linguistic structure of standard English, and
hence it would be incorrect to say that standard English is intrin-
sically a sexist linguistic system (Black & Coward,1981; also see
Chapter 1 for the distinction between language as a linguistic
system and language in use). In practice, however, the grammatical prescriptions, together with gender-related words and discoursal conventions that relegate females to a secondary position,
have become assimilated into standard English through dictionaries,

handbooks of usage, teaching of grammar at schools, and so forth (see Downes, 1984, and Milroy & Milroy, 1985, for a general discussion of linguistic prescription and standardization).

An example of linguistic sexism and its routinization is masculine generics. In English, in which the sex of the referent is indefinite or both sexes are referred to simultaneously, masculine words (*man*, *he*, and *his*) are the grammatically prescribed generic words to use, for example, "a citizen has the right to vote for the party of his choice," and "all men are equal before the law." Historically, the use of masculine generics is a relatively recent phenomenon (Bodine, 1975). In 1746, John Kirby formulated his 88 grammatical rules and included in them the rule that prescribed the use of masculine generics on the grounds that the male gender was more comprehensive than the female gender. Although this rule found favor with grammarians, who were mainly men, the prescribed usage was rarely adopted by the population at large. Instead, *they* was the common generic word, whether the referent was singular or plural. It was not until the 19th century that masculine generics became more widely used as a result of a staunch Victorian mentality in the teaching of grammar. Then in 1850 a British act of Parliament installed genericism as legal usage. The use of masculine generics has persisted to the present day, although its decline has been taking place (Cooper, 1984). As late as 1980, MacKay (1980) estimated that the average speaker of English will encounter the generic *he* more that 10,000,000 times during his or her lifetime.

The justification of using masculine and not feminine or neuter words had little to do with linguistic features of the words; rather it reflected the social order prevailing at the time and was part of a wider movement toward male linguistic dominance. The movement included, apart from masculine generics, the semantic derogation of females and numerous other aspects of language use (see Henley, 1989; Henley & Kramarae, 1991; Kramarae, 1990; Miller & Swift, 1976; Nilsen, Bosmajian, Gershung, & Stanley, 1977; Smith, 1985; Spender, 1980; Thorne & Henley, 1975; Thorne, Kramarae, & Henley, 1983). The following examples will suffice for the purpose of providing a background to the present discussion of masculine generics.

In manners of speaking, for example, males are supposed to precede females ("yet in speaking, at least let us keep a natural order, and set the man before the woman"; quoted in Bodine, 1975, p. 134). Thus we have, for example, "Adam and Eve" not "Eve and Adam," and "I now pronounce you man and wife" not "woman and husband." The male-before-female word order may seem trivial—if one does not accept it as a natural order, then perhaps one can accept it as a matter of convenience. After all, there is nothing in the syntactical structure of English that would prevent the use of words in the reverse order. Yet as Smith (1985) has suggested, the male-before-female word order may signify to listeners that females are less positive than males, in the same way that the second part of a word pair is commonly reserved for things that are less positive than the first part: good and bad, strong and weak, active and passive, rich and poor, light and dark, life and death.

A second example is the convention of defining the relational identity of females with reference to males as the norm or center. Jill may be referred to as Jack's widow, but it would be unconventional to refer to Jack, should he survive Jill, as Jill's widower, although it is linguistically possible to do so. The possessive *s*, as in "Mrs.," is a linguistic marker of the patriarchal power of owning properties and transferring the ownership of properties (Spender, 1980, 1984).

In an important sense, the biblical story that God created Adam first, and then used one part of Adam's body to create Eve, is the archetype of androcentrism in language use. The story provides a reference point not only for the male-before-female word order and the symbolism of male ownership but also, as will be seen below, for the equally androcentric convention of using masculine words to refer generically to males and females.

Masculine words that serve as generics also have a male-specific meaning (Moulton, Robinson, & Elias, 1978). One might expect that formal teaching on the dual meanings of these words would enable language users to differentiate the generic meaning from the masculine-specific meaning. Yet the usage of masculine generics often shows a male bias even in contexts intended to be gender neutral. This androcentric bias appears in both the encoding and decoding of generics. Martyna (1980) and Ng (1988), among others, have shown that most of their respondents who used masculine generics in a gender-indefinite context meant a male. In his influential *Principles of Psychology,* James (1890/1950) gave the impression that he was using *he, his, and man* to refer to both sexes when in fact he had only males in mind. The following quotation is a clear revelation of James's (1890/1950) androcentric bias:

> The Empirical Self of each of us is all that he is tempted to call by the name *me.* . . . *In its widest possible sense,* however, *a man's Self is the sum total of all that he CAN call his,* not only his body and his psychic powers, but his clothes and his house, his **wife** and children. (p. 291; italic emphasis in the original; bold emphasis added)

The use of masculine generics that are actually androcentric casts doubt on the authenticity and credibility of communicator intent. It also raises the problem of self-deception and the consequences this problem may have on intellectual work. Morgan (1972) depicts the problem in this way:

> If you begin to write a book about man or to conceive a theory about man you cannot avoid using this word (man). You cannot avoid using a pronoun as a substitute for this word, and you will use the pronoun "he" as a simple matter of linguistic convenience. But before you are half-way through the first chapter a mental image of this evolving creature begins to form in your mind. It will be a male image, and he will be the hero of the story: everything in the story will relate to him. (pp. 8-9)

One may wonder if James's *Principles of Psychology* would have been the same had he succeeded in focusing his attention on both sexes and used the appropriate words to maintain a gender-inclusive frame of mind. This is no trivial point for the pursuit of knowledge about *human* behavior and consciousness, unless one assumes that gender differences in behavior and consciousness are superficial or that given an already existing masculine perspective on psychology, a feminine perspective would be redundant.

Androcentric biases also occur in the *decoding* of masculine generics, and these biases have been found at several levels of the decoding process. Thus language users interpret the generics to be male specific (MacKay & Fulkerson, 1979), evaluate them as sexist (Murdock & Forsyth, 1985) and biased against women (Briere & Lanktree, 1983), and form a predominantly masculine impression of them (Cole, Hill, & Dayley, 1983). Given these biases, the question arises as to whether or not the masculine generics would also evoke predominantly male images in the mind of readers. There is some indirect evidence to suggest that this may in fact be the case. For example, Harrison (1975) asked junior high school students to draw pictures of early humans under various instructions. Students receiving the "early man, primitive man, mankind, and he" instruction drew significantly more pictures of males than did students who received other instructions that were written in gender-inclusive forms. Schneider and Hacker (1973) asked junior high school students to select pictures to illustrate the chapter themes of a textbook. The chapter headings were written in masculine generics (e.g., social man, industrial man, and political man) for half of the participants and in a neutral form for the other half (e.g., society, industrial behavior, and political behavior). Relative to the neutral condition, the masculine generic condition resulted in the overselection of male-only photos (see also Martyna, 1980).

In an attempt to obtain a more direct measure of visual images that might be evoked by masculine generics, Wilson and Ng (1988) presented subjects with a masculine generic topic sentence (e.g., "All men are created equal" and "At the university, a student can study whatever he wants") in the upper part of the viewing field of a tachistoscope. With the sentence on constant view, a photograph of either a male or a female face was shown below the sentence. The viewing time of the photograph was carefully predetermined on the basis of a prior test to be slightly shorter than what the respondent would require for correct recognition. This created a situation in which the respondent would see a face but was unable to recognize its gender correctly. In such an ambiguous situation, the image (if any) induced by the sentence would influence the resolution of the ambiguity. If the masculine generic topic sentences were gender-neutral, respondents would report seeing an equal number of female and male faces; if the sentences were androcentric, they would report significantly more male than female faces. The results supported the androcentric hypothesis. The researchers also tested another group of individuals under the feminine generic-topic sentence condition (e.g., "The feminists protested outside the town hall" and "At the university, a student can study whatever she wants"). Respondents reported, as one may expect, more female than male faces. In contrast to the condition in which masculine generic topic sentences were shown, the difference in the feminine condition was not statistically significant.

In light of androcentric biases in the encoding and decoding of masculine generic topic sentences, it is clear that the masculine words in question have failed to function generically for most if not all of English language users. One reason for the failure may lie in the fact that during the course of language acquisition, children acquire the masculine-specific meaning of *man* (and *his*, *he*, etc.) well before they receive grammatical instruction on the word's generic meaning (Hyde, 1984; Nilsen, 1977). The onset of grammatical instruction does not decrease the number of occasions in which the masculine-specific meaning of male words will apply, nor does it cause the speech community to stop giving the usual intermittent reinforcement to those who use the masculine-specific meaning under these occasions. The masculine-specific meaning of the male words remains. In any case, there is evidence showing that male words are coded in the memory primarily in the masculine linguistic category. On the basis of this evidence, Ng (1990b) argued that the androcentric coding of male words in the memory would provide a cognitive base for these words to prime the generic topic sentence for a masculine-specific reading. When a person encounters *man* and/or *his* in a generic topic sentence, the words in question would activate the masculine code through which the person will most instantaneously interpret the sentence. The generic reading of the sentence comes much later, if at all. Readers may try out the following demonstrations: "I am not the man my mother was" and "Man, being a mammal, breast-feeds his babies." Most readers will have experienced an immediate jarring effect that goes away only after a deliberate effort to invoke the generic reading.

The memory results and the androcentric biases cited above cast serious doubt on the efficacy of prescribing male words to serve as generics. For too long these words have been forced to undergo ill-treatment in the service of grammatical prescription, with the result that females are linguistically excluded in the language about them. At the same time, though, when the female category is referred to, it is overmarked in a typically negative way with undesirable sexual connotations. This led Stanley (1977) to propose that there is only negative semantic space for females in standard English (see also Miller & Swift, 1976; Spender, 1980, 1984).

Overcoming routinization

The routinization of language dominance is not an unchangeable terminal state. Decolonization since the end of the World War II has seen the revival of many indigenous languages. Ethnolinguistic nationalism has added to the spread of the indigenous language movement. Multilingualism is now an enshrined policy of language planning in many countries. Androcentric language is giving way to a more gender-inclusive form of language. The plain English movement and changes in court procedures to meet the needs of sexually assaulted victims have eroded lawyers' grip on legal English. All this suggests that routinization can be, and is in fact being, overcome.

What factors bring about the overcoming of routinization? At the sociostructural level, these factors have to do with changes in the relative ethnolinguistic vitality between groups, including, as discussed above, demographic, institutional, status variables as well as a host of related variables such as colonial expansion, communication technology, and professional specialization. At the social psychological level, the literature on language, ethnicity, and women's issues provides some suggestive and, of course, tentative answers. For example, if speakers become strongly identified with their in-group and consider their own language to be high in vitality and an important part of their social identity, the likelihood that they will take collective action to overcome routinization will be higher than if they exhibit weak identification and view their language as unimportant and low in vitality. In addition, if they view the hierarchical boundaries between their group and others as rigid (unpassable by individual efforts), illegitimate (should be changed), and unstable (can be changed by collective effort), tendencies toward overcoming routinization will be comparatively high. These factors, which were first formulated by Tajfel (1974) as part of a general theory of intergroup relations, were offered by Giles (Giles & Johnson, 1987; Bourhis et al., 1979) and more recently discussed by Gudykunst and Ting-Toomey (1990) in the context of intergroup relations for which language is a salient issue.

From the viewpoint of the marked-unmarked continuum of language status, factors that increase the tendency for subordinate group members to contrast their language with that of the dominant group, to focus on language with high consciousness, or in other words, to view language as an opaque (not a transparent) phenomenon will work against linguistic routinization. In a sense, such factors will cause both the dominant and non-dominant languages to become marked forms—language is caught up increasingly in the discussion of domination, oppression, and other highly politicized issues. Examples of factors that increase the likelihood of linguistic awareness are formal linguistic training (Bradac, Martin, Elliot, & Tardy, 1980), initial exposure to the dominant language (as opposed to repeated exposures after the initial exposure, which would increase the likelihood of habituation to the dominant language—see Linz et al., 1984), exposure to an expectancy-violating form of the dominant or the nondominant language (Burgoon, 1990), and processing linguistic input in a context in which the substance of that input is less important than peripheral cues, such as the verbal style of the message (Gibbons et al., 1991; Petty & Cacioppo, 1986).

The overcoming of routinization may involve the revival of a dominated language to displace the currently dominant language. This is typified by ethnolinguistic nationalist movements. In other situations such as linguistic sexism and legal English, overcoming may involve internal changes to a language to make it more gender inclusive, more intelligible, and so on. Multilanguage situations present a more complex and—under multimodal nation conditions such as those described by Fishman (1972)—a quite extraordinary picture altogether. For example, in the Republic of Singapore, the coexistence of several languages before the routinization of English, each with its own literary and cultural tradition (e.g., Malay, Mandarin Chinese, and Tamil), presented a political and psychological dilemma after the nation became independent from British rule. The choice of any one of the languages to replace English would have lead to constant rivalry for greater national prominence among the various ethnolinguistic groups. It would have also handicapped the nation's external trade and undermined the emergence of a supraethnic Singapore identity. Yet to retain English as the dominant, unmarked language would have been an insult to national sovereignty and to ethnic pride. The situation, in short, was "a dilemma between modern progressiveness and traditional values, between supra-ethnic identity and ethnic-cultural rooting, between instrumental association and sentimental commitment—all entangled with the language issue" (Kuo, 1985, p. 350). Singapore's response to the dilemma was to make English and the ethnic languages co-official languages and to promote English for its utilitarian functions and the ethnic languages for their traditional cultural values.

Epilogue

Earlier in this chapter, we indicated that many (probably all) of the molecular features of language associated with power in both the monologues and dialogues discussed throughout this volume are surrounded by a broader sociostructural context. Languages, dialects, styles, and grammatical forms wax and wane in vitality and prestige as a function of a variety of social forces and events, for example, military invasions, political coups, and religious crusades. It is no doubt also the case that particular modes of linguistic depoliticization will change as changes occur in society —that is particular ways of being devious or equivocal or polite or obfuscating. We have also suggested that linguistic forms that reinforce (or, probably rarely, create) group dominance may come to seem natural and inevitable with increasing use. A clear case in point is that of the ubiquitous masculine (ostensibly generic) pronoun *he*. But this tendency toward linguistic routinization can be overcome as vigilance and awareness increase. (We hope that our book will make some small contribution to this increasing vigilance and awareness.)

This would seem to be a good place to summarize additional points and issues that have been raised throughout this volume (it is now or never). Four different positions on the connection between language and power have been represented. Each position has merit, presenting one part of a larger and more complete picture. Essentially, each position reflects a particular metaphor or model for the power-language relationship. (In the spirit of what we said in Chapter 6, we will note here that it is no doubt the case that our four models or metaphors do not exhaust the conceptual possibilities.)

First, *language reveals power:* A linguistic sign may be taken by a hearer as an indication of a speaker's powerful or powerless condition. The hearer's inference regarding speaker power may accurately or inaccurately reflect the speaker's true condition, say, in a socioeconomic sense or in terms of the speaker's beliefs about this condition. Power-revealing signs may be detectable by naive persons, on the one hand, or by specialists with arcane knowledge (e.g., linguists or communication analysts), on the other. Only the former type of sign has direct consequences for everyday communication, which is why we focused on this type in Chapters 2 and 3. Some power-revealing signs may be used by communicators to appear powerful or powerless, that is, these signs may be consciously controlled. Other such signs may be less controllable. The controllable signs present an interesting problem: If hearers come to realize that these signs can be manipulated by speakers to produce an impression of high or low power, the hearers may come to distrust these signs as true indicators of a speaker's powerful or powerless condition. As a result, these signs may lose their validity and their effectiveness (from the communicator's standpoint).

The second position, *language creates power,* is a model offered in Chapters 2, 3, and 4. The idea here is that power is an achievement accomplished through a speaker's use of specific linguistic and paralinguistic features. Thus a rapid rate of speech or a high level of language intensity (when used by a male) may increase the likelihood that a speaker will be persuasive or will gain a message recipient's compliance. Or, to give another example, a speaker who gains a turn at talk through interruption also gains control, at least for the moment. An issue here is, What is the relationship between power achieved at a local level (say, in a given conversation) and generalized or global power? It seems to us that local and global power have a weak positive correlation in that the achievement of one will make the other more probable. For example, someone who is locally persuasive on a number of occasions may come to be seen as a generally persuasive person. Contrarily, to illustrate the indeterminacy here, a speaker who interrupts frequently in a variety of contexts and who constantly changes the topic of conversation may come to be perceived as communicatively incompetent. And there are globally powerful people who are typically inept in controlling conversations, winning arguments, and so on. But, more generally, we have no difficulty in accepting the claim that language is the primary instrument of power (in human affairs) at both the local and global levels. Language is a strong force in society, although it competes with other forces (physical attractiveness, guns, fists, and so forth).

The third position is that *language reflects power*. This notion is broached in Chapter 5 and again in Chapter 8. Here, power is taken as a given, an accomplished fact. People who are in power have their language, and those who are disenfranchised also have theirs. Power comes first and language follows. A language becomes more prestigious as the prestige of its users increases. Language is a conditioned stimulus contingent on the unconditioned stimulus of speaker power. Related to this is the idea that language can be interpreted in more than one way, depending on the interpreter's beliefs regarding a message sender's powerful or powerless condition. For example, a threat is threatening only if a message sender is believed to have punishment power over the message recipient; a promise is promising only if a message sender has reward power. Beliefs about power may bias message recipients' reactions to the language in which a message is encoded. Such beliefs carry more weight than does language form or style on this view. Virtually any statement may be taken as powerful or powerless, depending on the nature and strength of the message recipients' beliefs regarding a message sender's power. In line with this we have heard people say things like: "She [or he] can get away with talking like that because of who she [or he] is."

The fourth and last position (model, metaphor) to be mentioned here is that *language obscures or depoliticizes power*. In this case, language is used to attain some goal or fulfill some intention (as with our second model) and at the same time it is used to cover up or minimize the fact of the attempt at goal attainment or intention fulfillment. In some ways, this is the most subtle and complex of the four models because of the twofold function of language here. There are many ways in which language can be used to conceal attempts at gaining power, some of which we discussed in Chapters 5 to 7. The possibilities are almost infinitely intricate in this case: We can use a powerful style in the belief that our hearer will perceive this as a bluff and will infer accordingly that we really are not powerful when, in fact, we really are, and so forth and so forth.

As suggested in the preceding paragraph, the models can be combined—they are not as discrete as one might initially infer. At some level, the models are mutually causal. Perhaps most basically (although we do not really want to give priority to any one model), a group achieves power and their language accordingly comes to seem powerful; this achievement in turn causes some linguistic forms to reveal a speaker's powerful or powerless condition, which allows speakers to use these forms to enhance or reinforce their ability to achieve goals and to control hearers. After power is secured, various devices will be invented to obscure its existence. But, on the other hand, as language enhances or creates power, it allows for the possibility of revolution and the creation of new, powerful groups whose language will reflect and then reveal this power. Again, following the revolution, depoliticizing devices will be invented. No doubt this picture of causation oversimplifies the truth in many circumstances. It is likely that the influences are often simultaneously interactive. But, as we think more about it, the events suggested by the second and third models have empirical priority over the events suggested by the first and fourth models; the achievement of power through language or other instruments typically comes before the linguistic revelation or depoliticization of power. Regardless of the particular order of priority, the four models collectively summarize the power in language that arises from language's ability to reveal, create, reflect, and depoliticize power.

Apart from the four models, we conclude by emphasizing the importance of both communicator knowledge and communicator intentions to all of the topics discussed throughout this volume. In regard to communicator knowledge, there are two important forms that have been discussed or implied in various places in this book: implicit or tacit knowledge and explicit or conscious knowledge. The learning of grammatical or stylistic forms that are powerful or powerless is typically a process that occurs outside of awareness; for example, a child's acquisition of his or her parents' dialect, which happens to be a prestigious variety, occurs without (or with little) direct parental intervention and with low effort and low consciousness on the child's part. The child's dialectal knowledge is tacit; he or she almost certainly could not describe the phonological or syntactic rules underlying the dialect if asked to do so. Similarly, we speculate (there is no evidence here) that a person learning to use powerful and powerless styles in particular contexts does not typically set out to learn the styles, does not analyze their components, and does not consciously imitate users of the styles. But there are exceptions: Liza in Shaw's *Pygmalion* consciously and systematically attempted to learn RP English and Professor Higgins had explicit knowledge of this variety of language, which allowed him to teach it to her. No doubt after reading this book, some of our readers will possess explicit knowledge of powerful forms of language and will consciously draw from this knowledge to achieve personal goals and to dominate friends and rivals.

Regarding communicator intentionality, we have indicated or implied in various places in this volume that some of the most interesting questions about language and power revolve around the interrelated concepts of awareness, consciousness, and intent. Clearly, these questions are related to the notions discussed in the preceding paragraph—tacit versus explicit knowledge. But in the paragraphs that follow, we will focus more specifically on the intentions that may undergrid powerful or powerless communicative acts.

As a baseline case, it seems to us that a speaker cannot unintentionally mislead a hearer, despite the fact that some people say, "I didn't mean to mislead you." Lying and deviousness, for example, are constituted by specific sets of intentions and beliefs—one cannot accidentally tell a lie, although one can accidentally convey erroneous information. Or one cannot accidentally keep a secret and accidentally cover up the act of secret keeping, although one can accidentally forget to reveal something, even something important. As we move to other types of acts that serve to obscure or depoliticize a part of reality, the role of communicator intentions sometimes becomes more variable. For example, sometimes polite forms are used manipulatively with a clear communicative purpose; at other times these same forms are produced reflexively with low awareness (as when we say, "excuse me," after bumping into someone.) And, apart from depoliticizing acts although in the same vein as the preceding example, a speaker can use the high power style consciously with a specific purpose or unconsciously, habitually, and with low awareness.

From the standpoint of the hearer or message recipient, intentions attributed to communicators are crucially important. A speaker may have intended to lie (only the speaker himself or herself knows this for sure), but a hearer may construe the speaker's message as one that accidentally conveyed erroneous information. In this case the hearer may think that the speaker is low in competence, but the hearer probably would not infer that the speaker is evil, malevolent, or low in trustworthiness. The effect of a message hinges to some extent on the message recipient's attribution regarding communicator intentions. The communicator who can control this type of attribution gains considerable power. If a speaker using the high power style can lead his or her hearer to infer that this use is spontaneous, unplanned, natural, and normal, the effect of the style may be more positive (from the communicator's standpoint) than if the hearer perceives the speaker's use of a high power style to be contrived, planned, and so forth. The ways in which communicators affect or control hearer attributions regarding intentionality have not been studied (to our knowledge), so this would seem to be an important new area for investigation as we continue to learn more about the complex and intriguing connections between language and power in the intricate affairs of *Homo humanis.*

References

Ackerman, B. P., Szymanski, J., & Silver, D. (1990). Children's use of the common ground in interpreting ambiguous referential utterances. *Developmental Psychology, 26,* 234-245.

Antaki, C. (1988). *Analysing everyday explanation: A casebook of methods.* London: Sage.

Aristotle. (1909). *The rhetoric of Aristotle* (R. C. Jebb, Trans.; J. E. Sandys, Ed.). Cambridge, UK: Cambridge University Press.

Atkinson, J. M., & Drew, P. (1979). *Order in court: The organization of verbal interaction in judicial settings.* London: Macmillan.

Atkinson, J. M., & Heritage, J. C. (Eds.). (1984). *Structures of social action: Studies in conversation analysis.* Cambridge, UK: Cambridge University Press.

Austin, J. (1962). *How to do things with words.* Oxford, UK: Oxford University Press.

Austin, P. (1990). Politeness revisited: The dark side. In A. Bell & J. Holmes (Eds.), *New Zealand ways of speaking English* (pp. 277-293). Clevedon: Multilingual Matters.

Bach, K., & Harnish, R. M. (1979). *Linguistic communication and speech acts.* Cambridge: MIT Press.

Bachrach, P., & Baratz, M. S. (1962). Two faces of power. *American Political Science Review, 56,* 947-952.

Bakeman, R., & Gottman, J. M. (1986). *Observing interaction: An introduction to sequential analysis.* Cambridge, UK: Cambridge University Press.

Bales, R. F. (1950). *Interaction process analysis: A method for the study of small groups.* Reading, MA: Addison-Wesley.

Ball, P., Giles, H., Byrne, J., & Berechree, P. (1984). Situational constraints on the evaluative significance of speech accommodation: Some Austrailian data. *International Journal of the Sociology of Language, 46,* 115-129.

Bandler, R., & Grinder, J. (1975). *The structure of magic I: A book about language and therapy.* Palo Alto, CA: Science and Behavior Books.

Bavelas, J. B., Black, A., Chovil, N., & Mullett, J. (1990). *Equivocal communication.* Newbury Park, CA: Sage.

Baxter, L. A. (1984). An investigation of compliance-gaining as politeness. *Human Communication Research, 10,* 427-456.

Beal, C. R., & Flavell, J. H. (1984). Development of the ability to distinguish communicative intention and literal meaning. *Child Development, 55,* 920-928.

Beattie, G. (1982). Turn-taking and interruption in political interviews: Margaret Thatcher and Jim Callaghan compared and contrasted. *Semiotica, 39,* 35-45.

Bell, A. (1984). Language style as audience design. *Language in Society, 13,* 145-204.

Bell, A. (1991). The politics of English in New Zealand. In G. McGregor, M. Williams, & R. Harlow (Eds.), *Dirty silence: Aspects of language and literature in New Zealand* (pp. 63-75). Auckland: Oxford University Press.

Bem, D. J. (1972). Self-perception theory. In L. Berkowitz (Ed.), *Advances in experimental social psychology* (Vol. 6, pp. 2-62). New York: Academic Press.

Bennett, M. (1990). Children's understanding of the mitigating function of disclaimers. *Journal of Social Psychology, 130,* 29-37.

Berger, C. R. (1979). Beyond initial interaction: Uncertainty, understanding, and the development of interpersonal relationships. In H. Giles & R. N. St. Clair (Eds.), *Language and social psychology* (pp. 122-144). Oxford, UK: Basil Blackwell.

Berger, C. R. (1985). Social power and interpersonal communication. In M. L. Knapp & G. R. Miller (Eds.), *Handbook of interpersonal communication* (pp. 439-499). Beverly Hills, CA: Sage.

Berger, C. R., & Bradac, J. (1982). *Language and social knowledge: Uncertainty in interpersonal relations.* London: Arnold.

Berger, C. R., & Calabrese, R. J. (1975). Some explorations in initial interaction and beyond: Toward a developmental theory of interpersonal communication. *Human Communication Research, 1,* 99-112.

Berger, C. R., & Chaffee, S. H. (Eds.). (1987). *Handbook of communication science.* Newbury Park, CA: Sage.

Berger, C. R., Karol, S. H., & Jordan, J. M. (1989). When a lot of knowledge is a dangerous thing: The debilitating effects of plan complexity on verbal fluency. *Human Communication Research, 16,* 91-119.

Berger, C. R., & Roloff, M. (1980). Social cognition, self-awareness, and interpersonal communication. In B. Dervin & M. Voigt (Eds.), *Progress in communication sciences* (Vol. 2, pp. 1-50). Norwood, NJ: Ablex.

Berger, P. L., & Luckmann, T. (1967). *The social construction of reality.* Hammondsworth, UK: Penguin.

Bernstein, B. (1971). *Class, codes, and control* (Vols. 1 & 2). London: Routledge & Kegan Paul.

Bettinghaus, E. P., & Cody, M. J. (1987). *Persuasive communication* (4th ed.). New York: Holt, Rinehart, & Winston.

Bhatia, V. K. (1983). Simplification is falsification: The case of legal texts. *Applied Linguistics, 4,* 42-43.

Black, M., & Coward, R. (1981). Linguistic, social, and sexual relations: A review of Dale Spender's *Man-made Language. Screen Education, 39,* 69-85.

Bleuler, E. (1950). *Dementia praecox; or the group of schizophrenias.* New York: International University Press.

Blum-Kulka, S. (1983). The dynamics of political interviews. *Text, 3,* 131-153.

Blum-Kulka, S., Danet, D., & Gherson, R. (1985). The language of requesting in Israeli society. In J. P. Forgas (Ed.), *Language and social situation* (pp. 113-139). New York: Springer-Verlag.

Bodine, A. (1975). Androcentrism in prescriptive grammar: Singular 'they', sex-indefinate 'he', and 'he or she'. *Language in Society, 4,* 129-146.

Bolinger, D. (1980). *Language—The Loaded Weapon*. London: Longman.

Bonitatibus, G. (1988a). Comprehension monitoring and the apprehension of literal meaning. *Child Development, 59,* 60-70.

Bonitatibus, G. (1988b). What is said and what is meant in referential communications. In J. W. Astington, P. L. Harris & D. R. Olson (Eds.), *Developing theories of mind* (pp. 326-338). Cambridge, UK: Cambridge University Press.

Bourhis, R. Y. (1984). Introduction: Language policies in multilingual settings. In R. Y. Bourhis (Ed.), *Conflict and language planning in Quebec* (pp. 1-28). Clevedon: Multilingual Matters.

Bourhis, R. Y., & Giles, H. (1977). The language of intergroup distinctiveness. In H. Giles (Ed.), *Language, ethnicity and intergroup relations* (pp. 119-133). London: Academic Press.

Bourhis, R. Y., Giles. H., Leyens, J. P., & Tajfel. H. (1979). Psycholinguistic distinctiveness: Language divergence in Belgium. In H. Giles & R. St. Clair (Eds.), *Language and social psychology* (pp. 158-185). Oxford, UK: Blackwell.

Bourhis, R. Y., & Lepicq, D. (in press). Quebec French and language issues in Quebec. In R. Posner & J. N. Green (Eds.), *Trends in romance linguistics and philology. Vol. 5: Bilingualism and linguistic conflict in Romance.* The Hague: Moulton de Gruyter.

Bowers, J. W. (1963). Language intensity, social introversion and attitude change. *Speech Monographs, 30,* 345-352.

Bowers, J. W. (1964). Some correlates of language intensity. *Quarterly Journal of Speech, 50,* 415-420.

Bowers, J. W., Elliott, N. D., & Desmond, R. J. (1977). Exploiting pragmatic rules: Devious messages. *Human Communication Research, 3,* 235-242.

Bradac, J. J. (Ed.). (1989). *Message effects in communication science.* Newbury Park, CA: Sage.

Bradac, J. J. (1990). Language attitudes and impression formation. In H. Giles & W. P. Robinson (Eds.), *Handbook of language and social psychology* (pp. 387-412). Chichester, UK: Wiley.

Bradac, J. J., Bowers, J. W., & Courtright, J. A. (1979). Three language variables in communication research: Intensity, immediacy, and diversity. *Human Communication Research, 5,* 257-269.

Bradac, J. J., Courtright, J. A., & Bowers, J. W. (1980). Effects of intensity, immediacy, and diversity upon receiver attitudes towards a belief-discrepant message and its source. In H. Giles, W. P. Robinson & P. Smith (Eds.), *Language: Social psychological perspectives* (pp. 217-221). Oxford, UK: Pergamon Press.

Bradac, J. J., Davies, R. A., & Courtright, J. A. (1977). The role of prior message context in judgments of high- and low-diversity messages. *Language and Speech, 20,* 295-307.

Bradac, J. J., Desmond, R. J., & Murdock, J. I. (1977). Diversity and density: Lexically determined evaluative and informational consequences of linguistic complexity. *Communication Monographs, 44,* 273-283.

Bradac, J. J., Friedman, E., & Giles, H. (1986). A social approach to propositional communication: Speakers lie to hearers. In G. McGregor (Ed.), *Language for hearers* (pp. 127-151). Oxford, UK: Pergamon.

Bradac, J. J., Hemphill, M. R., & Tardy, C. H. (1981). Language style on trial: Effects of 'powerful' and 'powerless' speech upon judgments of victims and villains. *Western Journal of Speech Communication, 45,* 327-341.

Bradac, J. J., Konsky, C. W., & Davies, R. A. (1976). Two studies of the effects of lexical diversity upon judgments of communicator attributes and message effectiveness. *Communication Monographs, 43,* 70-79.

Bradac, J. J., Martin, L. W., Elliot, N. D., & Tardy, C. H. (1980). On the neglected side of linguistic science: Multivariate studies of sentence judgment. *Linguistics, 18,* 967-995.

Bradac, J. J., & Mulac, A. (1984a). A molecular view of powerful and powerless speech styles: Attributional consequences of specific language features and communicator intentions. *Communication Monographs, 51,* 307-319.

Bradac, J. J., & Mulac, A. (1984b). Attributional consequences of powerful and powerless speech styles in a crisis-intervention context. *Journal of Language and Social Psychology, 3,* 1-19.

Bradac, J. J., Mulac, A., & House, A. (1988). Lexical diversity level and magnitude of convergent versus divergent style shifting: Perceptual and evaluative consequences. *Language and Communication, 8,* 213-228.

Bradac, J. J., Mulac, A., & Thompson, S. (n.d.). Hedges and intensifiers in same-sex and mixed-sex interaction. Unpublished manuscript.

Bradac, J. J., Sandell, K. I., & Wenner, L. A. (1979). The phenomenology of evidence: Information-source utility in decision making. *Communication Quarterly, 27,* 35-46.

Bradac, J. J., & Street, R. S., Jr. (1989/1990). Powerful and powerless styles of talk: A theoretical analysis of language and impression formation. *Research on Language and Social Interaction, 23,* 195-242.

Bradac, J. J., & Wisegarver, R. (1984). Ascribed status lexical diversity, and accent: Determinants of perceived status, solidarity, and control of speech style. *Journal of Language and Social Psychology, 3,* 239-255.

Brazil, D., Coulthard, M., & Johns, C. (1980). *Discourse intonation and language teaching.* London: Longman.

Brehm, J. W. (1966). *A theory of psychological reactance.* New York: Academic Press.

Breivik, L. E., & Jahr, E. H. (Eds.). (1989). *Language change: contributions to the study of its causes.* Berlin: Mouton de Gruyter.

Brennan, M., & Brennan, R. E. (1988). *Strange language: Child victims under cross examination.* Wagga Wagga: Riverina Institute of Higher Education.

Briere, J., & Lanktree, C. (1983). Sex-role related effects of the sex bias in language. *Sex Roles, 9,* 625-633.

Britain, D. (1992). Linguistic change in interaction: The use of high rising terminals in New Zealand English. *Language Variation and Change, 4,* 77-104.

Brooke, M. E., & Ng, S. H. (1986). Language and social influence in small conversational groups. *Journal of Language and Social Psychology, 5,* 201-210.

Brown, B. (1980). Effects of speech rate on personality attributions and competency evaluations. In H. Giles, W. P. Robinson, & P. Smith (Eds.), *Language: Social psychological perspectives* (pp. 294-300). Oxford, UK: Pergamon.

Brown, B. L., Giles, H., & Thackerar, J. N. (1985). Speaker evaluations as a function of speech rate, accent, and context. *Language & Communication, 5,* 207-220.

Brown, P., & Levinson, S. C. (1987). *Politeness: Some universals in language usage.* Cambridge, UK: Cambridge University Press.

Brown, R. (1958). *Words and things.* New York: The Free Press.

Brown, R. (1965). *Social psychology.* New York: The Free Press.

Brown, R., & Gilman, A. (1989). Politeness theory and Shakespeare's four major tragedies. *Language in Society, 18,* 159-212.

Bruner, J. (1964). The course of cognitive growth. *American Psychologist, 19,* 1-15.

Buck, J. (1968). The effects of Negro and white dialectal variations upon attitudes of college students. *Speech Monographs, 35,* 181-186.

Bull, P., & Mayer, K. (1988). Interruptions in political interviews: A study of Margaret Thatcher and Neil Kinnock. *Journal of Language and Social Psychology, 7,* 35-45.

Burgoon, J. K., Birk, T., & Pfau, M. (1990). Nonverbal behaviors, persuasion, and credibility. *Human Communication Research, 17,* 140-169.

Burgoon, M. (1989). Messages and persuasive effects. In J. J. Bradac (Ed.), *Message effects in communication science* (pp. 129-164). Newbury Park, CA: Sage.

Burgoon, M. (1990). Language and social influence. In H. Giles & W. P. Robinson (Eds.), *Handbook of language and social psychology* (pp. 51-72). Chichester, UK: Wiley.

Burgoon, M., Birk, T. S., & Hall, J. R. (1991). Compliance and satisfaction with physician-patient communication: An expectancy theory interpretation of gender differences. *Human Communication Research, 18,* 177-208.

Burgoon, M., Jones, S. B., & Stewart, D. (1975). Toward a message-centered theory of persuasion: Three empirical investigations of language intensity. *Human Communication Research, 1,* 240-256.

Burgoon, M., & Miller, G. R. (1971). Prior attitude and language intensity as predictors of message style and attitude change following counterattitudinal advocacy. *Journal of Personality and Social Psychology, 20,* 240-253.

Burgoon, M., & Miller, G. R. (1985). An expectancy interpretation of language and persuasion. In H. Giles & R. N. St. Clair (Eds.), *Recent advances in language, communication, and social psychology* (pp. 199-229). London: Erlbaum.

Burke, K. (1941). *The philosophy of literary form.* Baton Rouge, LA: Louisiana State University.

Burke, K. (1966). *Language as symbolic action.* Berkeley: University of California Press.

Burling, R. (1986). The selective advantage of complex language. *Ethology and Sociobiology, 7,* 1-16.

Button, G., & Lee, J. R. E. (1987). *Talk and social organisation.* Clevedon: Multilingual Matters.

Cameron, D., McAlinden, F., & O'Leary, K. (1988). Lakoff in context: The social and linguistic functions of tag questions. In J. Coates & D. Cameron (Eds.), *Women in their speech communities: New perspectives on language and sex* (pp. 74-93). London: Longman.

Cappella, J. N., & Street, R. L. (1989). Message effects: Theory and research on mental models of messages. In J. J. Bradac (Ed.), *Message effects in communication science* (pp. 24-51). Newbury Park, CA: Sage.

Carli, L. L. (1990). Gender, language, and influence. *Journal of Personality and Social Psychology, 59*, 941-951.

Carranza, M. A. (1982). Attitudinal research on Hispanic language varieties. In E. B. Ryan & H. Giles (Eds.), *Attitudes towards language variation: Social and applied contexts* (pp. 63-83). London: Edward Arnold.

Carrell, P. L. (1981). Children's understanding of indirect requests: Comparing child and adult comprehension. *Journal of Child Language, 8*, 329-345.

Chitoran, D. (1986). Metaphor in the English lexicon: the verb. In D. Kastovsky & A. Szwedek (Eds.), *Linguistics across historical and geographical boundaries. Vol. 2: Descriptive, contrastive and applied linguistics* (pp. 837-849). Berlin: Mouton de Gruyter.

Chomsky, N. (1957). *Syntactic structures.* Cambridge: MIT Press.

Chomsky, N. (1965). *Aspects of a theory of syntax.* Cambridge: MIT Press.

Chomsky, N. (1987). *On power and ideology: The Managua lectures.* Boston: South End Press.

Cialdini, R. B. (1984). *Influence: How and why people agree to things.* New York: Morrow.

Clark, H. H. (1974). Semantics and comprehension. In T. A. Sebeok (Ed.), *Current trends in linguistics. Vol. 12: Linguistics and adjacent arts and sciences* (pp. 1291-1428). The Hague: Mouton.

Clark, H. H. (1985). Language use and language users. In G. Lindzey & E. Aronson (Eds.), *The handbook of social psychology* (3rd ed; pp. 179-231). New York: Harper & Row.

Clark, H. H., & Carlson, T. B. (1982). Hearers and speech acts. *Language, 58*, 332-373.

Clark, H. H., & Haviland, S. E. (1977). Comprehension and the given-new contract. In R. O. Freedle (Ed.), *Discourse production and comprehension* (pp. 1-40). Norwood, NJ: Ablex.

Clark, H. H., & Lucy, P. (1975). Understanding what is meant from what is said: A study in conversationally conveyed requests. *Journal of Verbal Learning and Verbal Behavior, 14*, 56-72.

Clark, H. H., & Marshall, C. R. (1981). Definite reference and mutual knowledge. In A. K. Joshi, B. L. Webber, & I. A. Sag, (Eds.), *Elements of discourse understanding* (pp. 10-63). Cambridge, UK: Cambridge University Press.

Clark, H. H., & Schaefer, E. F. (1987). Concealing one's meaning from overhearers. *Journal of Memory and Language, 26*, 209-225.

Clarke, D. (1983). *Language and action: A structural model of behavior.* Oxford, UK: Pergamon Press.

Clayman, S. E. (1988). Displaying neutrality in television news interviews. *Social Problems, 35*, 474-492.

Coates, J. (1988). Gossip revisited: Language in all-female groups. In J. Coates & D. Cameron (Eds.), *Women in their speech communities: New perspectives on language and sex* (pp. 94-122). London: Longman.

Cody, M. J., & McLaughlin, M. L. (1985). Models for the sequential construction of accounting episodes: Situational and interactional constraints on message selection and evaluation. In R. L. Street, Jr., & J. N. Cappella (Eds.), *Sequence and pattern in communicative behavior* (pp. 50-69). London: Edward Arnold.

Cohen, R. (1987). Problems of intercultural communication in Egyptian-American diplomatic relations. *International Journal of Intercultural Relations, 11*, 29-47.

Cole, C. M., Hill, F. A., & Dayley, L. J. (1983). Do masculine pronouns used generically lead to thoughts of men? *Sex Roles, 9,* 737-749.

Cook, T. D., & Campbell, D. T. (1979). *Quasi-experimentation: Design and analysis issues for field settings.* Chicago, IL: Rand McNally.

Cooper, R. L. (1984). The avoidance of androcentric generics. *International Journal of the Sociology of Language, 50,* 5-20.

Coulmas, F. (1981). *Conversational routine: Explorations in standardised communications situations and prepatterned speech.* The Hauge: Mouton.

Coulthard, M. (1977). *An introduction to discourse analysis.* London: Longman.

Coupland, N. (1988). Introduction: Towards a stylistics of discourse. In N. Coupland (Ed.), *Styles of discourse* (pp. 1-19). London: Croom Helm.

Coupland, N., & Giles, H. (1988). Introduction: The communicative contexts of accommodation. *Language and Communication, 8,* 175-182.

Coupland, N., Grainger, K., & Coupland, J. (1988). Politeness in context: Intergenerational issues. Review of P. Brown and S. Levinson (1987) *Politeness: Some universals in language usage.* Cambridge: Cambridge University Press. *Language in Society, 17,* 253-262.

Coupland, N., Henwood, K., Coupland, J., & Giles, H. (in press). Accommodating troubles-talk: The young's management of elderly self-disclosure. In G. McGregor & R. White (Eds.), *Reception and response: Hearer creativity and the analysis of spoken and written tests.* London: Croom Helm.

Craig, R. T., Tracy, K., & Spisak, F. (1986). The discourse of requests: Assessment of a politeness approach. *Human Communication Research, 12,* 437-468.

Crosby, F., & Nyquist, L. (1977). The female register: An empirical study of Lakoff's hypotheses. *Language in Society, 6,* 313-322.

Crow, B. K. (1983). Topic shifts in couples' conversations. In R. T. Craig & K. Tracy (Eds.), *Conversational coherence: Form, structure and strategy* (pp. 136-156). Beverly Hills, CA: Sage.

Danet, B. (1980). Language in the legal process. *Law & Society Review, 14,* 445-564.

Danet, B. (1990). Language and law: An overview of 15 years of research. In H. Giles & P. Robinson (Eds.), *Handbook of language and social psychology* (pp. 537-559). Chichester, UK: Wiley.

Daniel, D. C., & Herbig, K. L. (Eds.). (1982). *Strategic military deception.* New York: Pergamon.

Dascal, M. (1989). On the roles of context and literal meaning in understanding. *Cognitive Science, 13,* 253-257.

Day, R. R. (1985). The ultimate in equality: Linguistic genocide. In N. Wolfson & J. Manes (Eds.), *Language of inequality* (pp. 162-181). Berlin: Mouton.

Denison, N. (1977). Language death or language suicide. *International Journal of the Sociology of Language, 12,* 13-22.

DePaulo, B. M., Stone, J. I., & Lassiter, G. D. (1985). Telling ingratiating lies: Effects of target sex and target attractiveness on verbal and nonverbal deceptive success. *Journal of Personality and Social Psychology, 48,* 1191-1203.

de Turk, M. A., & Miller, G. R. (1985). Deception and arousal: Isolating the behavioral correlates of deception. *Human Communication Research, 12,* 181-201.

de Turk, M. A., & Miller, G. R. (1990). Training observers to detect deception: Effects of self-monitoring and rehearsal. *Human Communication Research, 16,* 603-620.

de Villiers, J. G. (1984). Form and force interactions: The development of negative and questions. In R. L. Schiefelbusch & J. Pickar (Eds.), *The acquisition of communicative competence* (pp. 193-236). Baltimore: University Park Press.

Dindia, K. (1987). The effects of sex of subject and sex of partner on interruptions. *Human Communication Research, 13,* 345-371.

Donohue, W. A., Diez, M. E., & Hamilton, M. (1984). Coding naturalistic negotiation interaction. *Human Communication Research, 10,* 403-425.

Dore, J. (1977). Children's illocutionary acts. In R. O. Freedle (Ed.), *Discourse production and comprehension* (pp. 227-244). Norwood, NJ: Ablex.

Dorian, N. (Ed.). (1989). *Investigating obsolescence.* Cambridge, UK: Cambridge University Press.

Downes, W. (1984). *Language and society.* London: Fontana.

Duncan, H. D. (1962). *Communication and social order.* London: Oxford University Press.

Duncan, S. Jr., & Fiske, D. W. (1977). *Face-to-face interaction: Research, methods, and theory.* Hillsdale, NJ: Lawrence Erlbaum.

Duval, S., & Wicklund, R. A. (1973). *A theory of objective self-awareness.* New York: Academic Press.

Edelman, M. (1977). *Political language: Words that succeed and policies that fail.* New York: Academic Press.

Edelsky, C., & Adams, K. (1990). Creating inequality: Breaking the rules in debates. *Journal of Language and Social Psychology, 9,* 171-190.

Eder, D. (1990). Serious and playful disputes: Variation in conflict talk among female adolescents. In A. D. Grimshaw (Ed.), *Conflict talk: Sociolinguistic investigations of arguments in conversations* (pp. 67-84). Cambridge, UK: Cambridge University Press.

Edmondson, W. (1981). *Spoken discourse: A model for analysis.* New York: Longman.

Edwards, J. (1979). *Language and disadvantage.* London: Edward Arnold.

Ekman, P. (1985). *Telling lies: Clues to deceit in the marketplace, politics, and marriage.* New York: Norton.

Ekman, P., & Friesen, W. V. (1974). Detecting deception from the body or face. *Journal of Personality and Social Psychology, 29,* 288-298.

Erickson, B., Lind, A. E., Johnson, B. C., & O'Barr, W. M. (1978). Speech style and impression formation in a court setting: The effects of 'powerful' and 'powerless' speech. *Journal of Experimental Social Psychology, 14,* 266-279.

Ervin-Tripp, S. (1976). Is Sybil there? The structure of some American English directives. *Language and Society, 5,* 25-66.

Ervin-Tripp, S., & Gordon, D. (1986). The development of requests. In R. L. Schiefelbusch (Ed.), *Language competence: Acquisition and intervention* (pp. 61-95). London: Taylor & Francis.

Fairclough, N. (1989). *Language and power.* London: Longman.

Fasold, R. (1984). *The sociolinguistics of society.* Oxford, UK: Basil Blackwell.

Fasold, R. (1990). *The sociolinguistics of language.* Oxford, UK: Basil Blackwell.

Festinger, L. (1957). *A theory of cognitive dissonance.* Stanford, CA: Stanford University Press.

Fishman, J. A. (1972). *The sociology of language.* Cambridge, MA: Newbury Press.

Folkes, V. S. (1985). Mindlessness and mindfulness: A partial replication and extension of Langer, Blank, & Chanowitz. *Journal of Personality and Social Psychology, 48,* 600-604.

Fowler, R., Hodge, B., Kress, G., & Trew, T. (1979). *Language and control.* London: Routledge & Kegan Paul.

Fraser, B. (1980). Conversational mitigation. *Journal of Pragmatics, 4,* 341-350.

French, P., & Local, J. (1983). Turn-competitive incomings. *Journal of Pragmatics, 7,* 17-38.

Friedman, H. S., & Tucker, J. S. (1990). Language and deception. In H. Giles & W. P. Robinson (Ed.), *Handbook of language and social psychology* (pp. 257-270). Chichester, UK: Wiley.

Fussell, S. R., & Krauss, R. M. (1989). The effects of intended audience on message production and comprehension: Reference in a common ground framework. *Journal of Experimental Social Psychology, 25,* 203-219.

Gibbons, P., Bradac, J. J., & Busch, J. D. (1992). The role of language in negotiations: Threats and promises. In L. L. Putnam & M. E. Roloff (Eds.), *Communication and negotiation* (pp. 156-175). Newbury Park, CA: Sage.

Gibbons, P., Busch, J., & Bradac, J. J. (1991). Powerful versus powerless language: Consequences for persuasion, impression formation, and cognitive response. *Journal of Language and Social Psychology, 10,* 115-133.

Gibbs, R. (1979). Contextual effects in understanding indirect requests. *Discourse Processes, 2,* 1-10.

Gibbs, R. (1982). A critical examination of the contribution of literal meaning to understanding nonliteral discourse. *Text, 2,* 9-27.

Gibbs, R. (1983). Do people always process the literal meaning of indirect requests? *Journal of Experimental Psychology: Learning, Memory, and Cognition, 9,* 524-533.

Gibbs, R. (1984). Literal meaning and psychological theory. *Cognitive Science, 8,* 275-304.

Gibbs, R. (1989). Understanding and literal meaning. *Cognitive Science, 13,* 243-251.

Gilbert, D. T. (1991). How mental systems believe. *American Psychologist, 46,* 107-119.

Giles, H. (1973). Accent mobility: A model and some data. *Anthropological Linguistics, 15,* 87-105.

Giles, H., Bourhis, R. Y., & Taylor, D. M. (1977). Towards a theory of language in ethnic group relations. In H. Giles (Ed.), *Language, ethnicity and intergroup relations* (pp. 307-348). London: Academic Press.

Giles, H., & Coupland, N. (1991). *Language: Contexts and consequences.* Buckingham: Open University Press.

Giles, H., Henwood, K., Coupland, N., Harriman, J., & Coupland, J. (1992). Language attitudes and cognitive mediation. *Human Communication Research, 18,* 500-527.

Giles, H., & Hewstone, M. (1982). Cognitive structures, speech, and social situations: Two integrative models. *Language Sciences, 4,* 187-219.

Giles, H., & Johnson, P. (1981a). The role of language in ethnic group relations. In J. C. Turner & H. Giles (Eds.), *Intergroup behavior* (pp. 199-243). Oxford, UK: Blackwell.

Giles, H., & Johnson, P. (1987). Ethnolinguistic identity theory: A social psychological approach to language maintenance. *International Journal of the Sociology of
Language, 68,* 69-99.

Giles, H., Mulac, A., Bradac, J. J., & Johnson, p. (1987). Speech accommodation
theory: The first decade and beyond. *Communication Yearbook, 10,* 37-56.

Giles, H., & Powesland, P. F. (1975). *Speech style and social evaluation.* London:
Academic Press.

Giles, H., & Robinson, W. P. (Eds.). (1990). *Handbook of language and social psychology.*
Chichester, UK: Wiley.

Giles, H., & Sassoon, C. (1983). The effect of speaker's accent, social class background and message style on British listeners' social judgements. *Language &
Communication, 3,* 305-313.

Giles, H., & Street, R. L., Jr. (1985). Communicator characteristics and behavior. In
M. L. Knapp & G. R. Miller (Eds.), *Handbook of interpersonal communication*
(pp. 205-262). Newbury Park, CA: Sage.

Giles, H., & Wiemann, J. M. (1987). Language, social comparison, and power. In C.
R. Berger & S. H. Chaffee (Eds.), *Handbook of Communication Science* (pp. 350-
384). Newbury Park, CA: Sage.

Gilligan, C. (1982). *In a different voice.* Cambridge, MA: Harvard University Press.

Glucksberg, S., & Keysar, B. (1990). Understanding metaphorical comparisons:
Beyond similarity. *Psychological Review, 97,* 3-18.

Goffman, E. (1959). *The presentation of self in everyday life.* Garden City, NY: Doubleday.

Goffman, E. (1974). *Frame analysis.* New York: Harper & Row.

Goffman, E. (1981). *Forms of talk.* Philadelphia: University of Pennsylvania Press.

Goodwin, M. H. (1980a). He-said-she said: Formal cultural procedures for the
construction of a gossip dispute activity. *American Ethnologist, 7,* 674-695.

Goodwin, M. H. (1980b). Directive-response speech sequences in girls' and boys'
task activities. In S. McConnell-Ginet, R. Borker & N. Furman (Eds.), *Women and
language in literature and society* (pp. 157-173). New York: Praeger.

Gordon, D., & Lakoff, G. (1971). Conversational postulates. In *Papers from the
seventh regional meeting of the Chicago Linguistic Society* (pp. 63-84). Chicago:
Chicago Linguistic Society.

Greatbatch, D. (1988). A turn-taking system for British news interviews. *Language
in Society, 17,* 401-430.

Greene, J. O., O'Hair, H. D., Cody, M. J., & Yen, C. (1985). Planning and control of
behavior during deception. *Human Communication Research, 11,* 335-364.

Greenberg, J. H. (1963). Some universals of grammar with particular reference to
order of meaningful elements. In J. H. Greenberg (Ed.), *Universals of language*
(pp. 58-90). Cambridge, MA: MIT Press.

Grice, H. P. (1975). Logic and conversation. In P. Cole & I. L. Morgan (Eds.), *Syntax
and semantics. Vol. 3: Speech acts* (pp. 41-58). New York: Academic Press.

Gudykunst, W. B., & Ting-Toomey, S. (1990). Ethnic identity, language and communication breakdowns. In H. Giles & W. P. Robinson (Eds.), *Handbook of
language and social psychology* (pp. 309-327). Chichester, UK: Wiley.

Gumperz, J. J., & Hymes, D. (Eds.). (1972). *Directions in sociolinguistics: The ethnography of communication.* New York: Holt.

Gunderson, D. F., & Perrill, N. P. (1989). Extending the 'speech evaluation instrument' to public speaking settings. *Journal of Language and Social Psychology, 8,* 59-62.

Gurr, T. R. (1970). *Why men rebel.* Princeton, NJ: Princeton University Press.

Guy, G., & Vonwiller, J. (1984). The meaning of an intonation in Australian English. *Australian Journal of Linguistics, 4,* 1-17.

Habermas, J. (1979). *Communication and the evolution of society* (T. McCarthy, Trans.). Boston: Beacon.

Haley, J. (1959). An interactional description of schizophrenia. *Psychiatry, 22,* 321-332.

Halliday, M. A. K. (1976). *System and function in language* (G. Kress, Ed.). London: Oxford University Press.

Halliday, M. A. K., & Hasan, R. (1976). *Cohesion in English.* London: Longman.

Halliday, M. A. K., McIntosh, A., & Strevens, P. (1968). The users and uses of language. In J. Fishman (Ed.), *Readings in the sociology of language* (pp. 139-169). The Hague: Mouton.

Hamilton, D. L., & Zanna, M. P. (1972). Differential weighting of favorable and unfavorable attributes in impression formation. *Journal of Experimental Research in Personality, 6,* 204-212.

Harris, R. (1983). Language and speech. In R. Harris (Ed.), *Approaches to language* (pp. 1-15). Oxford, UK: Pergamon.

Harrison, L. (1975). Cro-magnon woman-in eclipse. *The Science Teacher, 42,* 8-11.

Harwood, J., Giles, H., & Bourhis, R. Y. (in press). The genesis of vitality theory: Historical patterns and discoursal dimensions. *International Journal of the Sociology of Language.*

Haslett, B. (1984). Communication development in children. In R. Bostrom (Ed.), *Communication yearbook 8* (pp. 198-266). Newbury Park, CA: Sage.

Haslett, B. (1990). Social class, social status and communicative behavior. In H. Giles & W. P. Robinson (Eds.), *Handbook of language and social psychology* (pp. 329-344). Chichester, UK: Wiley.

Hawkins, R. P., Pingree, S., Fitzpatrick, M. A., Thompson, M., & Bauman, I. (1991). Implications of concurrent measures of viewer behavior. *Human Communication Research, 17,* 485-504.

Heider, F. (1941). The description of the psychological environment in the work of Marcel Proust. *Character and Personality, 9,* 295-314.

Henley, N. M. (1989). Molehill or mountain? What we know and don't know about sex bias in language. In M. Crawford & M. Gentry (Eds.), *Gender and thought* (pp. 59-78). New York: Springer-Verlag.

Henley, N. M., & Kramarae, C. (1991). Gender, power, and miscommunication. In N. Coupland, H. Giles, & J. Wiemann (Eds.), *Problem talk and problem contexts* (pp. 18-43). Newbury Park, CA: Sage.

Heritage, J. (1985). Analyzing news interviews: Aspects of the production of talk for an overhearing audience. In T. van Dijk (Ed.), *Handbook of discourse analysis* (Vol. 3, pp. 95-117). London: Academic Press.

Heritage, J. (1988). Explanations as accounts: A conversation analytic perspective. In C. Antaki (Ed.), *Analysing everyday explanation* (pp. 127-144). London: Sage.

Hewes, D., & Graham, M. L. (1989). Second-guessing theory: Review and extension. In J. A. Anderson (Ed.), *Communication yearbook 12* (pp. 213-248). Newbury Park, CA: Sage.

Hewitt, J. P., & Stokes, R. (1975). Disclaimers. *American Sociological Review, 40,* 1-11.

Higgins, E. T. (1981). The 'communication-game': Implications for social cognition and persuasion. In E. T. Higgins, C. P. Herman & M. P. Zanna (Eds.), *Social cognition: The Ontario symposium* (Vol. 1, pp. 343-392). Hillsdale, NJ: Lawrence Erlbaum.

Hilbert, R. (1981). Toward an improved understanding of 'role.' *Theory and Society, 10,* 207-226.

Hogg, M. A. (1985). Masculine and feminine speech in dyads and groups: A study of speech style and gender salience. *Journal of Language and Social Psychology, 4,* 99-112

Hollander, E. P. (1985). Leadership and power. In G. Lindzey & E. Aronson (Eds.), *Handbook of social psychology* (3rd ed., pp. 485-537). New York: Random House.

Holly, W. (1989). Credibility and political language. In R. Wodak (Ed.), *Language, power and ideology: Studies in political discourse* (pp. 115-131). Philadelphia: John Benjamins.

Holmes, J. (1983). The structure of teachers' directives. In J. C. Richards & R. W. Schmidt (Eds.), *Language and communication* (pp. 89-115). London: Longman.

Holmes, J. (1984a). Modifying illocutionary force. *Journal of Pragmatics, 8,* 345-365.

Holmes, J. (1984b). Hedging your bets and sitting on the fence: Some evidence for hedges as support structures. *Te Reo, 27,* 47-62.

Holmes, J. (1986). Functions of *you know* in women's and men's speech. *Language in Society, 15,* 1-22.

Holtgraves, T. (1986). Language structure in social interaction: Perceptions of direct and indirect speech acts and interactants who use them. *Journal of Personality and Social Psychology, 51,* 305-314.

Holtgraves, T. (1990). The language of self-disclosure. In H. Giles & W. P. Robinson (Eds.), *Handbook of language and social psychology* (pp. 191-207). Chichester, UK: Wiley.

Honey, J. (1983). *The language trap: Race, class and the 'standard English' issue in British schools.* Kenton, UK: National Council for Educational Standards.

Hopper, R., & Bell, R. A. (1984). Broadening the deception construct. *Quarterly Journal of Speech, 70,* 287-302.

Horn, L. R. (1989). *A natural history of negation.* Chicago: University of Chicago Press.

Horvath, B. (1985). *Variation in Australian English: The sociolects of Sydney.* Cambridge, UK: Cambridge University Press.

Hosman, L. A. (1989). The evaluative consequences of hedges, hesitations, and intensifiers: Powerful and powerless speech styles. *Human Communication Research, 15,* 383-406.

Hosman, L. A., & Siltanen, S. A. (1991, November). *The attributional and evaluative consequences of powerful and powerless speech styles: An examination of the 'control of others' and 'control of self' explanations.* Paper presented at the meeting of the Speech Communication Association, Atlanta.

Hosman, L. A., & Wright, J. W. II, (1987). The effects of hedges and hesitations on impression formation in a simulated courtroom context. *Western Journal of Speech Communication, 51,* 173-188.

Houck, C. L., & Bowers, J. W. (1969). Dialect and identification in persuasive messages. *Language and Speech, 12*, 180-186.

House, J., & Kasper, G. (1981). Politeness markers in English and German. In F. Coulmas (Ed.), *Conversational routine* (pp. 157-185). The Hague: Mouton.

Hovland, C. I., Janis, I. L., & Kelley, H. H. (1953). *Communication and persuasion.* New Haven, CT: Yale University Press.

Howeler, M. (1972). Diversity of word usage as a stress indicator in an interview situation. *Journal of Psycholinguistic Research, 1*, 243-248.

Hurtig, R. (1977). Toward a functional theory of discourse. In R. O. Freedle (Ed.), *Discourse production and comprehension* (pp. 89-106). Norwood, NJ: Ablex.

Hyde, J. S. (1984). Children's understanding of sexist language. *Developmental Psychology, 20*, 697-706.

Hyman, R. (1989). The psychology of deception. *Annual Review of Psychology, 40*, 133-154.

Hymes, D. (1967). Models of the interaction of language and social setting. *Journal of Social Issues, 23*, 8-28.

Hymes, D. (1985). Preface. In N. Wolfson & J. Manes (Eds.), *Language of inequality* (pp. v-viii). Berlin: Mouton.

Isaacs, E. A., & Clark, H. H. (1987). References in conversation between experts and novices. *Journal of Experimental Psychology: General, 116*, 26-37.

James. W. (1890/1950). *The principles of psychology* (authorized edition, Vol. 1). New York: Dover.

Jaworski, A. (1993). *The power of silence: Social and pragmatic perspectives.* Newbury Park, CA: Sage.

Jefferson. G. (1972). Side sequences. In D. Sudnow (Ed.), *Studies in social interaction* (pp. 294-338). New York: Free Press.

Jefferson, G., & Lee, J. R. E. (1981). The rejection of advice: Managing the problematic convergence of a 'troubles-telling' and a 'service encounter.' *Journal of Pragmatics, 5*, 399-422.

Johnson, P., Giles, H., & Bourhis, R. Y. (1983). The viability of ethnolinguistic vitality: A reply. *Journal of Multilingual and Multicultural Development, 4*, 255-269.

Jourard, S. (1971). *The transparent self.* New York: Van Nostrand Reinhold.

Kahneman, D. (1973). *Attention and effort.* Englewood Cliffs, NJ: Prentice-Hall.

Kahneman, D., Slovic, P., & Tversky, A. (Eds.). (1982). *Judgment under uncertainty: Heuristics and biases.* New York: Cambridge University Press.

Kahneman, D., & Tversky, A. (1979). Prospect theory. *Econometrica, 47*, 263-292.

Kanouse, D. E., & Hanson, L. R., Jr. (1972). Negativity in evaluations. In E. E. Jones, D. E. Kanouse, H. H. Kelley, R. E. Nosbett, S. Valins, & B. Weiner (Eds.), *Attribution: Perceiving the causes of behavior* (pp. 47-62). Morristown, NJ: General Learning Press.

Kassin, S. M., Williams, L. N., & Saunders, C. L. (1990). Dirty tricks of cross-examinations: The influence of conjectural evidence on the jury. *Law and Human Behavior, 14*, 373-384.

Kellermann, K. (1984). The negativity effect and its implication for initial interaction. *Communication Monographs, 51*, 37-55.

Kellermann, K. (1989). The negativity effect in interaction: It's all in your point of view. *Human Communication Research, 16*, 147-183.

Kellermann, K., & Lim, T. S. (1989). Inference-generating knowledge structures in message processing. In J. J. Bradac (Ed.), *Message effects in communication science* (pp. 102-128). Newbury Park, CA: Sage.

Kellermann, K., & Sleight, C. (1989). Coherence: A meaningful adhesive of discourse. In J. Anderson (Ed.), *Communication yearbook 12* (pp. 95-129). Newbury Park, CA: Sage.

Kelley, H. H. (1984). The theoretical description of interdependence by means of transition lists. *Journal of Personality and Social Psychology, 47,* 956-982.

Kelley, H. H. (1991, September 8-12). *The sequential-temporal structure of interpersonal relations.* Keynote address at the Third International Conference on Social Value Orientations in Interpersonal and Intergroup Relations: An International Conference in Honour of Harold Kelley, Leuven.

Kempton, W. (1986). Two theories of home heat control. *Cognitive Science, 10,* 75-90.

Kennedy, G. (1963). *The art of persuasion in Greece.* London: Routledge.

Keysar, B. (1989). On the functional equivalence of literal and metaphorical interpretations in discourse. *Journal of Memory and Language, 28,* 375-385.

Kintsch, W. (1988). The role of knowledge in discourse comprehension: A construction-integration model. *Psychological Review, 95,* 163-182.

Knapp, M. L., & Comadena, M. E. (1979). Telling it like it isn't: A review of theory and research on deceptive communication. *Human Communications Research, 5,* 270-285.

Knapp, M. L., & Miller, G. R. (Eds.). (1985). *Handbook of interpersonal communication.* Beverly Hills, CA: Sage.

Kramarae, C. (1982). Gender: How she speaks. In E. B. Ryan & H. Giles (Eds.), *Attitudes toward language variation: Social and applied contexts* (pp. 84-89). London: Edward Arnold.

Kramarae, C. (1990). Changing the complexion of gender in language research. In H. Giles & W. P. Robinson (Eds.), *Handbook of language and social psychology* (pp. 345-361). Chichester, UK: Wiley.

Kramarae, C., Schultz, M., & O'Barr, W. M. (Eds.). (1984). *Language and power.* Beverly Hills, CA: Sage.

Kress, G. (1987). *Linguistic process in sociocultural practice.* Geelong: Deakin University Press.

Kress, G., & Fowler, R. (1979). Interviews. In R. Fowler, B. Hodge, G. Kress & T. Trew (1979), *Language and control* (pp. 63-80). London: Routledge & Kegan Paul.

Kress, G., & Hodge, R. (1979). *Language as ideology.* London: Routledge & Kegan Paul.

Krosnick, J. A., Li, F., & Lehman, D. R. (1990). Conversational conventions, order of information acquisition, and the effect of base rates and individuating information on social judgments. *Journal of Personality and Social Psychology, 59,* 1140-1152.

Kruglanski, A. W., & Freund, T. (1983). The freezing and unfreezing of lay inference: Effects on impressional primacy, ethnic stereotyping, and numerical anchoring. *Journal of Experimental Social Psychology, 19,* 448-468.

Kruse, L., Weimer, E., & Wagner, F. (1988). What men and women are said to be: Social representation and language. *Journal of Language and Social Psychology, 7,* 243-262.

Kuhn, T. S. (1970). *The structure of scientific revolutions.* Chicago: University of Chicago Press.

Kuiken, D. (1981). Nonimmediate language style and inconsistency between private and expressed evaluations. *Journal of Experimental Social Psychology, 17,* 183-196.

Kuo, E. C. Y. (1985). Language and social mobility in Singapore. In N. Wolfson & J. Manes (Eds.), *Language of inequality* (pp. 337-354). Berlin: Mouton.

Labov, W. (1966). *The social stratification of speech in New York City.* Washington, DC: Center for Applied Linguistics.

Labov, W. (1970). The study of language in its social context. *Studium Generale, 23,* 30-87.

Labov, W. (1972). *Language in the inner city: Studies in the black English vernacular.* Philadelphia: University of Pennsylvania Press.

Labov, W., & Fanshel, D. (1977). *Therapeutic discourse: Psychotherapy as conversation.* New York: Academic Press.

Lakoff, G., & Johnson, M. (1980). *Metaphors we live by.* Chicago: University of Chicago Press.

Lakoff, R. (1973). Language and woman's place. *Language in Society, 2,* 45-80.

Lakoff, R. (1974). What you can do with words: Politeness, pragmatics and performatives. *Berkeley Studies in Syntax and Semantics, 1,* 1-55.

Lakoff, R. (1975). *Language and woman's place.* New York: Harper & Row.

Langer, E. J., Blank, A., & Chanowitz, B. (1978). The mindlessness of ostensibley thoughtful action: The role of 'placebic' information in interpersonal interaction. *Journal of Personality and Social Psychology, 36,* 635-642.

Langer, E. J., Chanowitz, B., & Blank, A. (1985). Mindlessness and mindfulness in perspective: A reply to Valerie Folkes. *Journal of Personality and Social Psychology, 48,* 605-607.

Leech, G. N. (1983). *Principles of pragmatics.* London: Longman.

Leichty, G., & Applegate, J. L. (1991). Social-cognitive and situational influences on the use of face-saving persuasive strategies. *Human Communication Research, 17,* 451-484.

Lerner, D. (1969). Managing communication for modernization: A developmental construct. In A. A. Rogow (Ed.), *Politics, personality, and social science in the twentieth century: Essays in honor of Harold D. Lasswell* (pp. 171-196). Chicago: University of Chicago Press.

Lerner, M. J. (1975). The justice motive in social behavior. *Journal of Social Issues, 31,* 1-19.

Leubsdorf, C. P. (1992, January 27). Clinton: Infidelity question irrelevant. *Santa Barbara News Press,* pp. 1, 8.

Levinson, S. C. (1983). *Pragmatics.* Cambridge, UK: Cambridge University Press.

Lewin, K. (1936). *Principles of topological psychology.* New York: McGraw-Hill.

Lewis, D. (1969). *Convention: A philosophical study.* Cambridge, MA: Harvard University Press.

Lim, T. S., & Bowers, J. W. (1991). Facework: Solidarity, approbation, and tact. *Human Communication Research, 17,* 415-450.

Linz, D., Donnerstein, E., & Penrod, S. (1984). The effects of multiple exposures to filmed violence against women. *Journal of Communication, 34,* 130-147.

Loftus, E., & Palmer, J. (1974). Reconstruction of automobile destruction. *Journal of Verbal Learning and Verbal Behavior, 13,* 585-589.

Luria, A. R. (1966). *Higher cortical functions in man*. New York: Basic Books.

Lutz, W. (1989). *Doublespeak*. New York: Harper & Row.

MacKay , D. G. (1980). Language, thought and social attitudes. In H. Giles, P. Robinson & P. M. Smith (Eds.), *Language: Social psychological perspectives* (pp. 89-96). Oxford, UK: Pergamon.

MacKay, D. G., & Fulkerson, D. C. (1979). On the comprehension and production of pronouns. *Journal of Verbal Learning and Verbal Behaviour, 18*, 661-673.

MacWhinney, B. (1984). Grammatical devices for sharing points. In R. L. Schiefelbusch & J. Pickar (Eds.), *The acquisition of communicative competence* (pp. 323-374). Baltimore: University Park Press.

Maltz, D. N., & Borker, R. A. (1982). A cultural approach to male-female mis-communication. In J. J. Gumperz (Ed.), *Language and social identity* (pp. 195-216). Cambridge, UK: Cambridge University Press.

Martyna, W. (1980). The psychology of the generic masculine. In S. McConnell-Ginet, R. Borker & N. Fulman (Eds.), *Women and language in literature and society* (pp. 69-78). New York: Praeger.

Mazur, A., & Cataldo, M. (1989). Dominance and deference in conversation. *Journal of Social Biological Structure, 12*, 87-99.

McClure, J. (1991). *Explanations, accounts, and illusions*. Cambridge, UK: Cambridge University Press.

McDermott, R., & Tylbor, H. (1983). On the necessity of collusion in conversation. *Text, 3*, 277-297.

McEwen, W. J., & Greenberg, B. S. (1970). Effects of message intensity on receiver evaluations of source, message, and topic. *Journal of Communication, 20*, 340-350.

Mehrley R. S., & McCroskey, J. C. (1970). Opinionated statements and attitude intensity as predictors of change and source credibility. *Speech Monographs, 37*, 47-52.

Mellinkoff, D. (1963). *The language of the law*. Boston: Little, Brown.

Menz, F. (1989). Manipulation strategies in newspaper: A program for critical linguistics. In R. Wodak (Ed.), *Language, power and ideology: Studies in political discourse* (pp. 227-247). Philadelphia: John Benjamins.

Metts, S. (1989). An exploratory investigation of deception in close relationships. *Journal of Social and Personal Relationships, 6*, 159-179.

Milgram, S. (1974). *Obedience to authority: An experimental view*. London: Tavistock.

Miller, C., & Swift, K. (1976). *Words and women: New language in new times*. New York: Anchor Press.

Miller, G. R. (1987). Persuasion. In C. R. Berger & S. H. Chaffee (Eds.), *Handbook of communication science* (pp. 446-483). Newbury Park, CA: Sage.

Miller, G. R., & Basehart, J. (1969). Source trustworthiness, opinionated statements, and responses to persuasive communication. *Speech Monographs, 36*, 1-7.

Miller, N., Maruyama, G., Beaber, R. J., & Valone, K. (1976). Speed of speech and persuasion. *Journal of Personality and Social Psychology, 34*, 615-624.

Mills, C. W. (1959). *The sociological imagination*. Hammondsworth, UK: Penguin.

Milroy, J., & Milroy, L. (1985). *Authority in language: Investigating language prescription and standardisation*. London: Routledge & Kegan Paul.

Moerman, M. (1988). *Talking culture: Ethnography and conversation analysis*. Philadelphia: University of Pennsylvania Press.

Mondry, H., & Taylor, J. R. (1992). On lying in Russian. *Language & Communication, 12*, 133-143.

Morgan, E. (1972). *The ascent of woman*. London: Corgi.

Morley, I. E., & Stephenson, G. M. (1977). *The social psychology of bargaining*. London: Allen & Unwin.

Moscovici, S. (1981). On social representations. In J. Forgas (Ed.), *Social cognition* (pp. 181-209). London: Academic Press.

Moscovici, S., & Doise, W. (1974). Decision making in groups. In C. Nemeth (Ed.), *Social psychology: Classic and contemporary integrations* (pp. 250-287). Chicago: Rand McNally.

Motley, M. T. (1991, November). *When the predominant meaning in interpersonal communication is not nonverbal: Facial expressions of emotion as ambiguous interjections*. Paper presented at the meeting of the Speech Communication Association, Atlanta.

Motley, M. T., & Camden, C. T. (1988). Facial expression of emotion: A comparison of posed expressions versus spontaneous expressions in an interpersonal communication setting. *Western Journal of Speech Communication, 54*, 1-20.

Moulton, J., Robinson, G. M., & Elias, C. (1978). Sex bias in language use: Neutral pronouns that aren't. *American Psychologist, 33*, 1032-1036.

Mueller, C. (1973). *The politics of communication: A study in the political sociology of language, socialization, and legitimation*. New York: Oxford University Press.

Mugny, G. (1982). *The power of minorities*. London: Academic Press.

Mulac, A. (1975). Evaluation of the speech dialect attitudinal scale. *Speech Monographs, 42*, 182-189.

Mulac, A. (1976). Assessment and application of the revised speech dialect attitudinal scale. *Communication Monographs, 43*, 238-245.

Mulac, A., & Gibbons, P. (1992, November). *Male/female language differences viewed from an intercultural perspective: A test of the 'gender as culture' hypothesis*. Paper presented at the meeting of the Speech Communication Association, Chicago.

Mulac, A., Incontro, C. R., & James, M. R. (1985). A comparison of the gender-linked language effect and sex-role stereotypes. *Journal of Personality and Social Psychology, 49*, 1099-1110.

Mulac, A., & Lundell, T. L. (1982). An empirical test of the gender-linked language effect in a public speaking setting. *Language and Speech, 25*, 243-256.

Mulac, A., & Lundell, T. L. (1986). Linguistic contributors to the gender-linked language effect. *Journal of Language and Social Psychology, 5*, 81-101.

Mulac, A., Lundell, T. L., & Bradac, J. J. (1986). Male/female language differences and attributional consequences in a public speaking situation: Toward an explanation of the gender-linked language effect. *Communication Monographs, 53*, 115-129.

Mullen, B., Salas, E., & Driskell, J. E. (1989). Salience, motivation, and artifact as contributions to the relation between participation rate and leadership. *Journal of Experimental Social Psychology, 25*, 545-559.

Murdock, J. I., Bradac, J. J., & Bowers, J. W. (1984). Effects of power on the perception of explicit threats, promises, and thromises: A rule-governed perspective. *Western Journal of Speech Communication, 48*, 344-361.

Murdock, N. L., & Forsyth, D. R. (1985). Is gender-biased language sexist? A perceptual approach. *Psychology of Women Quarterly, 9,* 39-49.

Nemeth, C. (1981). Jury trials: Psychology and law. In L. Berkowitz (Ed.), *Advances in experimental social psychology* (Vol. 14, pp. 309-367). New York: Academic Press.

Ng, S. H. (1980). *The social psychology of power.* London: Academic Press.

Ng, S. H. (1988). *Masculine generics and sexism in language.* A final report prepared for the Social Sciences Research Fund Committee, Wellington. Unpublished manuscript.

Ng, S. H. (1990a). Language and control. In H. Giles & P. Robinson (Eds.), *Handbook of language and social psychology* (pp. 271-286). Chichester, UK: Wiley.

Ng, S. H. (1990b). Androcentric coding of man and his in memory by language users. *Journal of Experimental Social Psychology, 26,* 455-464.

Ng, S. H. (in press). Power. In T. Manstead & M. Hewstone (Eds.), *Blackwell dictionary of social psychology.* Oxford: Blackwell.

Ng, S. H., Bell, D., & Brooke, M. (in press). Gaining turns and achieving high influence in small conversational groups. *British Journal of Social Psychology.*

Nilsen, A. P. (1977). Sexism in children's books and elementary teaching materials. In A. P. Nilsen, H. Bosmajia, H. L. Gershung, & J. P. Stanley (Eds.), *Sexism and language.* Urbana, IL: National Council of Teachers of English.

Nilsen, A. P., Bosmajian, H., Gershung, H. L., & Stanley, J. P. (Eds.). (1977). *Sexism and language.* Urbana, IL: National Council of Teachers of English.

Nofsinger, R. E. (1991). *Everyday conversation.* Newbury Park, CA: Sage.

Norton, R. (1991, August). *The battle of "politically correct" language in the AIDS crisis.* Paper presented at the Fourth International Conference on Language and Social Psychology, Santa Barbara, CA.

Nuttin, J. H., Jr. (1974). *The illusion of attitude change.* London: Academic Press.

O'Barr, W. M. (1982). *Linguistic evidence: Language, power, and strategy in the courtroom.* New York: Academic Press.

O'Barr, W., & Atkins, B. (1980). 'Women's language' or 'powerless language'? In S. McConnell-Ginet, R. Borker & N. Fulman (Eds.), *Women and Language in Literature and Society* (pp. 93-110). New York: Praeger.

Olson, D. R., & Hildyard, A. (1981). Assent and compliance in children's language. In W. P. Dickson (Ed.), *Children's oral communication skills* (pp. 313-335). New York: Academic Press.

Ortony, A. (1975). Why metaphors are necessary and not just nice. *Educational Theory, 26,* 395-398.

Orwell, G. (1954). *Nineteen eighty-four.* Harmondsworth, UK: Penguin.

Osgood, C. E. (1953). *Method and theory in experimental psychology.* New York: Oxford University Press.

Owsley, H. H., & Scotton, C. M. (1984). The conversational expression of power by television interviewers. *Journal of Social Psychology, 123,* 261-271.

Palmer, M. T. (1989). Controlling conversations. *Communication Monographs, 56,* 1-18.

Parker, K. C. H. (1988). Speaking turns in small group interaction: A context-sensitive event sequence model. *Journal of Personality and Social Psychology, 54,* 965-971.

Parsons, T. (1951). *The social system.* New York: Free Press.

Pearce, W. B. (1976). The coordinated management of meaning: A rule-based theory of interpersonal communication. In G. R. Miller (Ed.), *Explorations in interpersonal communication* (pp. 17-35). Beverly Hills, CA: Sage.

Peeters, G. (1971). The positive-negative asymmetry: On cognitive consistency and positivity bias. *European Journal of Social Psychology, 1,* 455-474.

Peeters, G., & Czapinski, J. (1990). Positive-negative asymmetry in evaluations: The distinction of affective and informational effects. In W. Stroebe & M. Hewstone (Eds.), *European Review of Social Psychology* (Vol. 1, pp. 33-60). Chichester, UK: Wiley.

Petty, R. E., & Cacioppo, J. T. (1986). *Communication and persuasion: Central and peripheral routes to attitude change.* New York: Springer-Verlag.

Potter, J., & Wetherell, M. (1987). *Discourse and social psychology: beyond attitudes and behaviour.* London: Sage.

Preisler, B. (1986). *Linguistic sex roles in conversation: Social variation in the expression of tentativeness in English.* Berlin: Mouton de Gruyter.

Preston, D. R. (1989). *Sociolinguistics and second language acquisition.* Oxford, UK: Blackwell.

Reddy, M. (1979). The conduit metaphor: A case of frame conflict in our language about language. In A. Ortony (Ed.), *Metaphor and thought* (pp. 284-324). Cambridge, UK: Cambridge University Press.

Redish, J. C. (1985). The plain English movement. In S. Greenbaum (Ed.), *The English language today* (pp. 125-128). New York: Pergamon.

Rice, M. (1984). Cognitive aspects of communicative development. In R. L. Schiefelbusch & J. Pickar (Eds.), *The acquisition of communicative competence* (pp. 141-189). Baltimore: University Park Press.

Richmond, V. P. (1984). Implications of quietness: Some facts and speculations. In J. A. Daly & J. C. McCroskey (Eds.), *Avoiding communication: Shyness, reticence, and communication apprehension* (pp. 145-155). Beverly Hills, CA: Sage.

Robinson, W. P. (1979). Speech markers and social class. In K. R. Scherer & H. Giles (Eds.), *Social markers in speech* (pp. 211-249). Cambridge, UK: Cambridge University Press.

Rochester, S. R., & Martin, J. R. (1977). The art of referring: The speaker's use of noun phrases to instruct the listener. In R. O. Freedle (Ed.), *Discourse production and comprehension* (pp. 245-269). Norwood, NJ: Ablex.

Roger, D. (1989). Experimental studies of turn-taking behavior. In D. Roger & P. Bull (Eds.), *Conversation: An interdisciplinary perspective* (pp. 75-97). Clevedon: Multilingual Matters.

Roger, D., & Bull, P. (Eds.). (1989). *Conversation: An interdisciplinary perspective.* Clevedon: Multilingual Matters.

Roger, D., Bull, P., & Smith, S. (1988). The development of a comprehensive system for classifying interruptions. *Journal of Language and Social Psychology, 7,* 27-34.

Rommetveit, R. (1983). Prospective social psychological contributions to a truly interdisciplinary understanding of ordinary language. *Journal of Language and Social Psychology, 2,* 89-104.

Rosch, E. (1973). Natural categories. *Cognitive Psychology, 4,* 328-350.

Russell, B. (1938). *Power: A new social analysis.* London: George Allen & Unwin.

Ryan, E. B., & Bulik, C. M. (1982). Evaluations of middle class speakers of standard American and German-accented English. *Journal of Language and Social Psychology, 1,* 51-62.

Ryan, E. B., & Giles, H. (Eds.). (1982). *Attitudes towards language variation: Social and applied contexts.* London: Edward Arnold.

Sachs, J. (1987). Preschool boys' and girls' language use in pretend play. In Philips, S., Steele, S., & Tanz, C. (Eds.), *Language, gender and sex in comparative perspective* (pp. 178-188). Cambridge, UK: Cambridge University Press.

Sacks, H., Schegloff, E. A., & Jefferson, G. (1974). A simplest systematics for the organization of turn-taking for conversation. *Language, 50,* 696-735.

Sanders, R. E. (1989). Message effects via induced changes in the social meaning of a response. In J. J. Bradac (Ed.), *Message effects in communication science* (pp. 165-194). Newbury Park, CA: Sage.

Sankoff, D., & Lassard, R. (1975). Vocabulary richness: A sociolinguistic analysis. *Science, 190,* 689-690.

Sapir, E. (1963). The status of linguistics as a science. In D. G. Mandelbaum (Ed.), *Selected writings of Edward Sapir in language, culture and personality* (pp. 160-166). Berkeley: University of California Press. (Original work published 1929)

Schegloff, E., & Sacks, H. (1974). Opening up closings. In R. Turner (Ed.), *Ethnomethodology: Selected readings* (pp. 233-264). Baltimore: Penguin.

Scherer, K. (1979). Voice and speech correlates of perceived social influence in simulated juries. In H. Giles & R. St. Clair (Eds.), *Language and social psychology* (pp. 88-120). Baltimore: University Park Press.

Schneider, J. W., & Hacker, S. L. (1973). Sex role imagery and use of the generic "man" in introductory texts: A case in the sociology of sociology. *American Sociologist, 8,* 12-18.

Schutz, A. (1945). On multiple realities. *Philosophical and Phenomenological Research, 5,* 533-576.

Scotton, C. M. (1988). Self-enhancing codeswitching as interactional power. *Language & Communication, 8,* 199-211.

Searle, J. (1969). *Speech acts.* Cambridge, UK: Cambridge University Press.

Searle, J. (1975). Indirect speech acts. In P. Cole & I. L. Morgan (Eds.), *Syntax and semantics. Vol. 3: Speech acts* (pp. 59-82). New York: Academic Press.

Searle, J. (1976). A classification of illocutionary acts. *Language in Society, 5,* 1-23.

Searle, J. (1986). Introductory essay: Notes on conversation. In D. G. Ellis & W. A. Donohue (Eds.), *Contemporary issues in language and discourse processes* (pp. 7-19). Hillsdale, NJ: Lawrence Erlbaum.

Semin, G., & Fiedler, K. (1988). The cognitive functions of linguistic categories in describing persons: Social cognition and language. *Journal of Personality and Social Psychology, 54,* 558-568.

Semin, G. R. & Fiedler, K. (1991). The linguistic category model, its bases, applications and range. In W. Stroebe & M. Hewstone (Eds.), *European review of social psychology* (vol. 2, pp. 1-30). Chichester: John Wiley.

Shaw, M. E. (1971). *Group dynamics: The psychology of small group behavior.* New Delhi: McGraw-Hill.

Sherblom, J., & Van Rheenen, D. D. (1984). Spoken language indices of uncertainty. *Human Communication Research, 11,* 221-230.

Sherif, M. (1936). *The psychology of social norms.* New York: Harper & Row.

Sherif, M. (1966). *In common predicament: Social psychology of intergroup conflict and cooperation.* Boston: Houghton-Mufflin.

Siegal, M. (1990). *Knowing children: Experiments in conversation and cognition.* Hillsdale, NJ: Lawrence Erlbaum.

Sigman, S. J. (1983). Some multiple constraints placed on conversational topics. In R. T. Craig & K. Tracy (Eds.), *Conversational coherence: Form, structure and strategy* (pp. 174-195). Beverly Hills, CA: Sage.

Simons, H. W. (1986). *Persuasion: Understanding, practice, and analysis.* New York: Random House.

Sinclair, J. M., & Coulthard, R. M. (1975). *Towards an analysis of discourse: The English used by teachers and pupils.* Oxford, UK: Oxford University Press.

Smith, P. M. (1985). *Language, the sexes and society.* Oxford, UK: Blackwell.

Snow, C. E., & Ferguson, C. A. (Eds.). (1977). *Talking to children.* Cambridge, UK: Cambridge University Press.

Sontag, S. (1988). *AIDS and its metaphors.* New York: Farrar, Straus & Giroux.

Spender, D. (1980). *Man made language* (2nd ed.). London: Routledge & Kegan Paul.

Spender, D. (1984). Defining reality: A powerful tool. In C. Kramarae, M. Schulz, & W. M. O'Barr (Eds.), *Language and power* (pp. 194-205). Beverly Hills, CA: Sage.

Sperber, D., & Wilson, D. (1982). Mutual knowledge and relevance in theories of comprehension. In N. Smith (Ed.), *Mutual knowledge* (pp. 61-87). London: Academic Press.

Stanley, J. (1977). Gender marking in American English. In A. P. Nilsen, H. Bosmajian, H. L. Gershung, & J. Stanley (Eds.), *Sexism and language.* Urbana, IL: National Council of Teachers.

Stasser, G., & Taylor, L. A. (1991). Speaking turns in face-to-face discussions. *Journal of Personality and Social Psychology, 60,* 675-684.

Stern, G. S., & Manifold, B. (1977). Internal locus of control as a value. *Journal of Research in Personality, 11,* 237-242.

Stewart, M. A., & Ryan, E. B. (1982). Attitudes toward younger and older adult speakers: Effects of varying speech rates. *Journal of Language and Social Psychology, 1,* 91-109.

Stiles, W. B. (1978). Verbal response models and dimensions of interpersonal roles: A method of discourse analysis. *Journal of Personality and Social Psychology, 36,* 693-703.

Street, R. L., Jr. (1985). Participant-observer differences in speech evaluation. *Journal of Language and Social Psychology, 4,* 125-130.

Street, R. L., Jr., & Brady, R. M. (1982). Speech rate acceptance ranges as a function of evaluative domain, listener speech rate, and communication context. *Communication Monographs, 49,* 290-308.

Street, R. L., Jr., Brady, R. M., & Putman, W. B. (1983). The influence of speech rate stereotypes and rate similarity on listeners' evaluations of speakers. *Journal of Language and Social Psychology, 2,* 37-56.

Street, R. L., Jr., & Hopper, R. (1982). A model of speech style evaluation. In E. B. Ryan & H. Giles (Eds.), *Attitudes towards language variation: Social and applied contexts* (pp. 175-188). London: Edward Arnold.

Sunnafrank, M. (1986). Predicted outcome value during initial interactions: A reformulation of uncertainty reduction theory. *Human Communication Research, 13*, 3-33.

Swann, J. (1988). Talk control: An illustration from the classroom of problems in analysing male dominance of conversation. In J. Coates & D. Cameron (Eds.), *Women in their speech communities: New perspectives on language and sex* (pp. 123-140). London: Longman.

Tajfel, H. (1974). *Intergroup behavior, social comparison and social change.* Katz-Newcomb Lectures, University of Michigan, Ann Arbor.

Tajfel, H. (1981). *Human groups and social categories: Studies in social psychology.* Cambridge, UK: Cambridge University Press.

Tajfel, H., & Turner, J. C. (1979). An integrative theory of intergroup conflict. In W. G. Austin & S. Worchel (Eds.), *The social psychology of intergroup relations* (pp. 33-47). Wadsworth: Belmont.

Tannen, D. (1979). What's in a frame? Surface evidence for underlying expectations. In R. O. Freedle (Ed.), *New directions in discourse processing* (pp. 137-181). Norwood, NJ: Ablex.

Tannen, D. (1984). *Conversational style: Analyzing talk among friends.* Norwood, NJ: Ablex.

Tannen, D. (1986). *That's not what I meant!: How conversational style makes or breaks your relations with others.* New York: Ballantine.

Tefft, S. K. (Ed.). (1980). *Secrecy: A cross-cultural perspective.* New York: Human Science Press.

Thorne, B., & Henley, N. (1975). Difference and dominance: an overview of language, gender, and society. In B. Thorne & N. Henley (Eds.), *Language and sex: Difference and dominance* (pp. 5-42). Rowley, MA: Newbury House.

Thorne, B. Kramarae, C. & Henley, N. (Eds.). (1983). *Language, gender and society.* Rowley, MA: Newbury House.

Ting-Toomey, S. (1985). Toward a theory of conflict and culture. In W. Gudykunst, L. Stewart, & S. Ting-Toomey (Eds.), *Communication, culture, and organizational processes* (pp. 71-86). Beverly Hills, CA: Sage.

Tracy, K. (1985). Conversational coherence: A cognitively grounded rules approach. In R. L. Street, Jr. & J. N. Cappella (Eds.), *Sequence and pattern in communicative behavior* (pp. 30-49). London: Edward Arnold.

Tracy, K. (1990). The many faces of facework. In H. Giles & W. P. Robinson (Eds.), *Handbook of language and social psychology* (pp. 209-226). Chichester, UK: Wiley.

Tracy, K., & Coupland, N. (Eds.). (1990). Multiple goals in discourse. *Journal of Language and Social Psychology, 9*, 1-170.

Trudgill, P. (1974). *Sociolinguistics.* Harmondsworth, UK: Penguin.

Trudgill, P. (1991). Language maintenance and language shift: preservation versus extinction. *International Journal of Applied Linguistic, 1*, 61-69.

Ullrich, H. E. (1971). Linguistic aspects of antiquity: A dialect study. *Anthropological Linguistics, 13*, 106-113.

van Dijk, T. A. (Ed.). (1985). *Handbook of discourse analysis* (4 vols.). London: Academic Press.

van Dijk, T. A. (1987). *Communicating racism.* Newbury Park, CA: Sage.

van Dijk, T. A. (1988). *News analysis.* Hillsdale, NJ: Lawrence Erlbaum.

Vallacher, R. R., & Wegner, D. M. (1985). *A theory of action identification.* Hillsdale, NJ: Lawrence Erlbaum.

Vinokur, A., & Burnstein, E. (1978). Novel augmentation and attitude change: The case of polarisation following group discussion. *European Journal of Social Psychology, 8,* 335-348.

Vinson, L., & Johnson, C. (1989). The use of written transcripts in powerful and powerless language research. *Communication Reports, 2,* 16-21.

Weber, M. (1947). *The theory of social and economic organization* (T. Parsons, Trans.). London: Allen & Unwin.

Wegner, D. M. (1984). Innuendo and damage to reputations. *Advances in Consumer Research, 11,* 694-696.

Wegner, D. M. (1989). *White bears and other unwanted thoughts.* New York: Viking Penguin.

Wegner, D. M., Coulton, G. F., & Wenzlaff, R. (1985). The transparency of denial: Briefing in the debriefing paradigm. *Journal of Personality and Social Psychology, 49,* 338-346.

Wegner, D. M., Wenzlaff, R., Kerker, R. M., & Beattie, A. E. (1981). Incrimination through innuendo: Can media questions become public answers? *Journal of Personality and Social Psychology, 40,* 822-832.

Wells, F., & Bayard, D. (1992). *Age, gender, and the high rising contour in New Zealand English.* Paper presented at the Language Use and Social Interaction Club, University of Otago.

Wiemann, J. M. (1985). Interpersonal control and regulation in conversation. In R. L. Street, Jr. & J. N. Cappella (Eds.), *Sequence and pattern in communicative behavior* (pp. 85-102). London: Edward Arnold.

Wiley, M. G., & Eskilson, A. (1985). Speech style, gender stereotypes, and corporate success: What if women talk more like men? *Sex Roles, 12,* 993-1007.

Williams, F., Whitehead, J. L., & Miller, L. A. (1972). Relations between attitudes and teacher expectancy. *American Educational Research Journal, 9,* 263-277.

Wilson, E., & Ng, S. H. (1988). Sex bias in visual images evoked by generics: A New Zealand study. *Sex Roles, 18,* 159-168.

Wilson, T. P., Wiemann, J. M., & Zimmerman, D. H. (1984). Models of turn taking in conversational interaction. *Journal of Language and Social Psychology, 3,* 159-183.

Winefield, H. R., Chandler, M. A., & Bassett, D. L. (1989). Tag questions and powerfulness: Quantitative and qualitative analyses of a course of psychotherapy. *Language in Society, 18,* 77-86.

Wolfson, N., & Manes, J. (Eds.). (1985). *Language of inequality.* Berlin: Mouton.

Wood, L. S., & Kroger, R. O. (1991). Politeness and forms of address. *Journal of Language and Social Psychology, 10,* 145-168.

Wright, J. W., & Hosman, L. A. (1983). Language style and sex bias in the courtroom: The effects of male and female use of hedges and intensifiers on impression formation. *Southern Speech Communication Journal, 48,* 137-152.

Zahn, C. J., & Hopper, R. (1985). Measuring language attitudes: The speech evaluation instrument. *Journal of Language and Social Psychology, 4,* 113-123.

Zimmerman, D. H. (1988). On conversation: The conversation analytic perspective. In J. A. Anderson (Ed.). *Communication yearbook* (Vol. 11). Newbury Park, CA: Sage.

Zimmerman, D. H., & West, C. (1975). Sex roles, interruptions and silences in conversation. In B. Thorne & N. Henley (Eds.), *Language and sex: Difference and dominance* (pp. 105-129). Rowley, MA: Newbury House.

Zentella, A. C. (1985). The fate of Spanish in the United States: The Puerto Rican experience. In N. Wolfson & J. Manes (Eds.), *Language of inequality* (pp. 41-60). Berlin: Mouton.

Zuckerman, M., DePaulo, B. M., & Rosenthal, R. (1981). Verbal and nonverbal communication of deception. In L. Berkowitz (Ed.), *Advances in experimental social psychology* (Vol. 14, pp. 1-59). New York: Academic Press.

Index

About the Authors

James J. Bradac obtained his Ph.D. from Northwestern University in 1970. He taught at the University of Iowa from 1970 to 1980, and since 1980 he has been Professor of Communication at the University of California, Santa Barbara. His research on language and social evaluation has been published in a wide variety of scholarly journals. He co-authored *Language and Social Knowledge* and edited *Message Effects in Communication Science*. Currently, he is co-editor of the *Journal of Language and Social Psychology;* he is a past editor of *Human Communication Research*. In 1991, he was elected Fellow of the International Communication Association.

Sik Hung Ng received his Ph.D. in Social Psychology from Bristol University in 1978. He has a strong research interest in power as a sociostructural variable in interpersonal and intergroup relations and in the power processes of social and communicative behavior. A recipient of the 1986 Hunter Award for distinction in research, he was later elected Fellow of the New Zealand Psychological Society and Fellow of the British Psychological Society. His publications include *The Social Psychology of Power* and *Nurses and Their Work* (co-author), and various journal articles. He has taught at the Chinese University of Hong Kong and Otago University, New Zealand. Currently, he is Professor of Psychology at Victoria University of Wellington, New Zealand, and an Executive Member of the International Association of Applied Psychology.